The Viceroy's Fall

The Viceroy's Fall

How Kitchener destroyed Curzon

PETER KING

SIDGWICK & JACKSON
LONDON

First published in Great Britain in May 1986
by Sidgwick & Jackson Limited

Copyright © 1986 by Peter King

ISBN 0–283–99313–8

Typeset by Falcon Graphic Art Limited
Wallington, Surrey
Printed in Great Britain by
Garden City Press Limited
Letchworth, Hertfordshire
for Sidgwick & Jackson Limited
1 Tavistock Chambers, Bloomsbury Way
London WC1A 2SG

Contents

Preface

The various biographies of Lord Curzon as Viceroy all relate how he brought Lord Kitchener to India to be Commander-in-Chief of the Indian Army, only to find that Kitchener disagreed with the way in which control of the Army was organized. Curzon would not submit to Kitchener's plan to make himself the supreme military commander, and Kitchener therefore set out to break Curzon. He succeeded in 1905. Kitchener's biographies present the same story but, as might be expected, from a different point of view.

None of these biographies seems to explain the motivation of the main characters satisfactorily. Why did Curzon stubbornly engineer his own downfall? How did Kitchener wield enough influence at home to bring about Curzon's fall? Why did the Cecils and Curzon's friends amongst 'the Souls' turn against him? Did he really resign on a personal issue?

This is the first book devoted to the subject. The secret correspondence between Kitchener and his 'spy' in Whitehall, Major Marker, is here published for the first time in detail. It reveals that Marker was originally on Curzon's own staff, and explains what happened when Marker fell in love with Curzon's sister-in-law. It explains why Curzon's old friend, St John Brodrick, working in Whitehall while Curzon was in India, turned against him and then betrayed him. It also describes how Brodrick falsified the facts thirty years later, and how Kitchener ordered the official history to be re-written to wipe out Curzon's contribution to India's defense.

It discusses the relevance to the story of Kitchener's homosexual nature; and how he contrived to win Lady Salisbury and even

Preface

Curzon's wife Mary to his aid. Finally, it discloses the naked ambition of the man who wished to displace Curzon so that he could be Viceroy himself.

Every student of the circumstances surrounding Curzon's resignation owes a debt of gratitude to Professor Dilks whose book is a mine of information and whose judgements command respect. By concentrating on the episode alone, I have tried to add something to our understanding and, like Dilks, I admit, as he does in the Foreword to his second volume, that I have not concealed my admiration for Curzon's gifts, or my conviction that he was ill-used; to this I must add that I have gone further in throwing into stronger emphasis the unpleasant side of his opponent, Kitchener.

Many other writers have been helpful, and in particular I should like to mention the two Nicolsons, the father for his book on the last phase of Curzon's career which contains such a perceptive analysis of his character; and Nigel Nicolson for his imaginative book on Mary Curzon from which I have quoted extensively.

My special thanks to Lord Curzon's daughter, Lady Alexandra Metcalfe, for her encouragement and help, and I also thank Lord and Lady Scarsdale, the Earl of Suffolk, Mr Arnold-Forster and Lord and Lady Salisbury for allowing me to quote from the letters in their possession and for the assistance of their librarian Robin Harcourt Williams. Amongs other librarians who have been most helpful are those of the India Office Library, the National Army Museum, the Royal Geographical Society and the Bodleian. I am also grateful for advice from Professor Bradley, Angela Lambert, and Roy MacLaren. I wish to thank Sandra den Hertog for deciphering my handwriting and Cherry Carroll for her encouragement. Finally my thanks to my publishers, particularly my editor Susan Hill, for her help and patience.

List of Illustrations

Two Superior Persons

My name is George Nathaniel Curzon
I am a most superior person

The Masque of Balliol

'One of the FEW VERY SUPERIOR British Officers'

Sir Samuel Baker on Kitchener

The wit has said that time wounds all heels and there are many, even today, who believe that is exactly what befell George Nathaniel Curzon, Marquis Curzon of Kedleston, popularly known as the superior person. But the disaster that struck Lord Curzon, as he then was, in 1905 had nothing to do with the retribution of Time, but with Tragedy, whose laws apply to this superior person who through fatal flaws in his nature was brought to a fall.

And what a tragic fall it was; the loss of India, then of his dearly-loved wife, then of the coveted Viscountcy, then the loss of further preferment in government and politics. It brought him to a life in the wilderness, where he was doomed to continue for another decade. That was not the end of the story, because he was to harbour, during all those years, the ambition that he would one day be chosen to lead his country, as Prime Minister, only to have that honour, too, snatched from his grasp. But it was the loss of India that was the key. As his biographer says, 'It was the tragedy of Lord Curzon's life that India, the scene of his greatest achievements, should have been the scene of his greatest disaster. The series of events which culminated in his resignation of the Vice-

royalty shook him to the foundations of his being and left a scar on
him which he carried to the grave.'[1]

The story has been told before of how that other superior person,
Horatio Herbert Kitchener, 1st Viscount Kitchener of Khartoum,
of Vaal in the Colony of the Transvaal, and of Aspall in the county
of Suffolk, took it upon himself to destroy Lord Curzon, and used
every weapon to hand to ensure success. What has not been
explained is the motivation of both men, the tangled web of their
ambitions, and those of the others with whom they were engaged,
politicians such as William St John Freemantle Brodrick, later
Lord Midleton; and Raymond Marker, an obscure army major,
who served the Secretary of State for War at the crucial period.

It is only by studying the motivation of these people in England,
as well as those of the two principal actors in India, that it can be
clearly seen that Curzon was an honourable and high-minded man,
who rose by his own fine qualities, and was brought low by his own
nature, aided and abetted by the devious Kitchener and those
confederates he drew into his web including, incredibly, Curzon's
own wife. During his lifetime there were some who thought Curzon,
from his earliest days, suffered from a surplus of pride. There is the
verse about the Superior Person written by 'friends' at Oxford, of
which Curzon himself said, 'Never has more harm been done to one
single individual than that accursed doggerel has done to me.'[2] The
reason the verse was so often quoted was that many of his friends,
as well as his enemies, knew the glove fitted. There was something
about Curzon which was too 'pushy', too ambitious. For example,
there was the time, a little later, when he was staying with
acquaintances at a country house, and the German governess they
employed asked him innocently, 'Please tell me, Mr Curzon, what
is the meaning of the word 'bounder' that I sometimes hear you
called?' Without hesitation, Curzon replied, 'It is one who succeeds
by leaps and bounds.'[3] Certainly, he made enemies, and what great
man does not? Certainly he did not relish having his friends point
out to him his faults of character, and tell him that if he would only
amend them, he would be a more popular fellow. Are faults of
character so easily amended? There is no need to catalogue here all
the flaws which characterized Curzon, because they will be an
essential thread in the story which follows.

Kitchener, too, has suffered from the stereotyped image of the moustachioed Field Marshall, staring out of the poster, pointing out to the recruit that 'Your Country Needs You'. He, too, was a complex and subtle man; artistic, acquisitive, homosexual with an almost extraordinary belief in his own abilities. He was also, it appears, an inveterate liar if lies helped achieve his ends. It was by failing to understand this highly-charged character that Curzon brought about his own downfall.

The foregoing assertion about Kitchener's homosexuality is not an essential element in the story although without doubt it is a pointer to his character and helps to explain his behaviour towards Curzon, who was aggressively heterosexual. There is no new or conclusive evidence to present on the subject. In his book *Mars Without Venus*, Major-General Franklin Richardson, late of the Royal Army Medical Corps, makes it clear that he believes Kitchener to have been an active homosexual and not, like Gordon, a suppressed one. The evidence is all very circumstantial; the widespread belief that there was a homosexual element in the circle of Kitchener's 'Boys' including 'Brat' Maxwell and Oswald Fitzgerald who died with him. Richardson quotes generalized critical views, like those of Churchill, who said, 'My father was War Minister before he was thirty-seven. Before I am thirty-seven I will be War Minister. There is time enough for me to get my knife into Kitchener.'[4] Yet the behaviour of Kitchener towards the young Churchill in the Sudan gives adequate cause for the latter's dislike and there is therefore no need to suppose that Churchill suspected homosexuality. Queen Victoria, too, may have said, 'They say he dislikes women, but I can only say he was very nice to me.'[5] but what does that prove? His biographer Lord Esher made a comment which is also vague – a mention of a 'flaw in his character'. A journalist* working in Egypt (quoted by Pearl) said, 'He drinks, and has the other failing acquired by most of the Egyptian officers, a taste for buggery.'[6] Egypt is also quoted in a strange sentence in Brodrick's memoirs, written in 1939, which might be explained as a

---

*Sydney Mosely wrote a book *With Kitchener in Cairo* which was suppressed by Kitchener and published after his death, which makes the vague but curious comment that he had 'weaknesses without which he could not have held claim to his sex'. Philip Warner, author of *The Man Behind the Legend*, 1985, clearly believes this refers to homosexuality, although he does not say so explicitly.

reference to homosexuality: 'Egypt, though he made his name there, must be admitted to have left some indelible and perhaps unenviable marks on his character.'[7] But if Kitchener's major biographer Magnus knew something, he did not reveal it; and the latest books on Kitchener have nothing to say on the subject. The only direct comment I have been given regarding Kitchener's homosexual nature came from a lady who moved in the same social circles as he before the 1914-1918 war. She was told by a young man of whom she was very fond that he could not marry her because he was a homosexual. When pressed, he admitted that 'he had been initiated into the practice by Lord Kitchener.' She was convinced he was telling the truth.

Why, then, discuss it? It is too widely believed a characteristic to be ignored, and it does in part explain Kitchener's particular fascination for women, including Mary Curzon, and also his behaviour to Curzon himself. It is clear from his reference to Curzon's masochism that Kitchener had an understanding of aspects of Curzon's sexual nature which he used when he came to defeat him. Such personal characteristics as homosexuality are only of significance if they affect the course of major events, and it must be made clear that this struggle between the two men was not a mere quarrel, over a minor administrative matter, which both men got out of proportion.

First, this was a major constitutional battle by those who wished to put the Army above the civilians, initially in India, and later at home in London. They believed war with Russia was inevitable and that the Empire was ill-prepared for it, and they wanted to be sure the Empire could fight such a war and win. Second, the defeat of Curzon had extraordinary repercussions for the future of the Conservative party, which he might well have led. Thirdly, Kitchener's victory ensured that his steady climb to a position of military preeminence continued unchecked, despite fatal flaws of character. Had these been exposed ten years earlier, the deaths of tens of thousands of soldiers in Mesopotamia would not have resulted. His eminence was only brought to an end by the unexpected and curious appearance of a German mine in British waters in the summer of 1916, which sent him to his death.

Curzon's defeat was thus a considerable historical event, not merely a personal catastrophe. Beaverbrook's quip, often quoted, to the effect that for the remainder of his mortal existence Curzon was influenced by his sudden journey to heaven at the age of thirty-nine and then by his return to earth seven years later, tells less than half the story. India was often hell, or at any rate, purgatory for Curzon, but he returned there, and pursued his struggle with Kitchener when he could have abandoned it, largely because he saw it as a major constitutional matter; indeed, he believed Kitchener's desire 'to set up. . .as an absolute military autocrat. . .would revolutionize our constitution.'[8] Furthermore, he thought 'the scheme, if accepted, would collapse within a year of Kitchener's leaving India'.[9]

Alas, as Winston Churchill pointed out in *Great Contemporaries*, 'One of Curzon's characteristic weaknesses was that he thought too much about stating his case, and too little about getting things done. When he had written his cogent dispatch, or brought a question before the Cabinet in full and careful form with all his force and knowledge, he was inclined to feel that his function was fulfilled. He had done his best. Events must take their course.'

This book describes how events took their course, aided and abetted by a man who believed, unlike Curzon, that if you planned for every eventuality, then events would probably take the course you desired. Kitchener and his army friends fought without giving quarter because they knew 'how very difficult it is to. . .render an Empire reasonably secure under Parliamentary institutions such as ours'.[10]

Some of those who have studied these events cannot understand how two men of such eminence can have quarrelled in such a self-destructive way; they develop an intense dislike of both men's characteristics, judging one or the other of them to be the more despicable. But what was unusual about the quarrel was that it was so public, and was conducted almost entirely in writing, so that, unlike many political disputes which remain private, it broke out into the general arena, embroiling every politician of the time and two great nations in the distasteful necessity of having to take sides. In the end, very few holds were barred, almost nothing that could be said remained unsaid – indeed unwritten. No wound to the public man is so deep as that which is written, and reputations, honour, friendships and, in Curzon's case, the future of a considerable statesman, suffered irreparable injury.

Part One

The Background

Chapter One

Up the Ladder of Power

Curzon's fall has been described as Shakespearean in nature, not only because of the part he himself played in bringing it about, but also because his protagonist was a close member of his own courtly circle, and a protagonist who, if Curzon had not been blinded by pride, he would have seen as dangerous from the moment they met. It would be wrong to think of Curzon as a patrician intellectual and Kitchener as a proletarian lout. This does justice to neither of these complex beings who fought out their tragic duel, as clever men who had reached the top of their respective professions through their own efforts, propelled by an excess of ambition.

It is interesting to begin an examination of their characters by drawing attention to the likenesses of their respective upbringings and family backgrounds. Both their mothers died young, both were watched over by stern disciplinarians, and both had a difficult time at school. Curzon could trace his family back to the Norman Conquest, but his father was a simple and somewhat indolent country parson, who just happened to become Lord Scarsdale when his elder brother was thrown from his horse in Rotten Row and killed. The eldest child, George Nathaniel, born on 11th January 1859 at the stately home, Kedleston, near Derby, grew up to love his mother dearly, but saw comparatively little of her because in his first sixteen years she was bearing eleven children, most of whom died in childbirth. Kitchener, born nine years earlier, on 24th June 1850 the son of an Army officer, whose family had risen to gentility (his grandfather was a London tea merchant), also lost touch with his mother from an early age. She developed an illness in India which was prolonged and eventually fatal. Kitchener's father had resigned his commission to bring her home from India, first to Ireland, where Kitchener was born, and later to Switzerland, where the family lived for some years. Kitchener 'lavished' love on his frail, pretty mother but his family noticed that 'he began to hate baring even the slightest emotion'.[1]

Curzon's father did his best for George, but his childhood was unhappy, and he later complained, 'I suppose no children, well-born and well-placed, every cried so much, or so justly as we.'[2] These lamentations were made because Lord Scarsdale placed the education of his children in the hands of the strangely-named Miss Paraman. Curzon later said, 'She persecuted and beat us in the most cruel way and established over us a system of terrorism so complete that not one of us ever mustered the courage to walk upstairs and tell our father or mother. She spanked us with brushes, tied us up for long hours in uncomfortable positions . . . wounded our pride by dressing us (me in particular) in red shining calico petticoats (I was obliged to make my own) with an immense conical cap upon our heads, round which, as well as our own breast and backs, there were several strips of paper bearing in enormous characters, written by ourselves, the words LIAR, SNEAK, COWARD and the like. In this guise she compelled us to go out in the pleasure ground and show ourselves to the gardeners. She made me write a letter to the butler asking him to make a birch for me with which I was to be punished for lying – and requested him to read it out, in the Servants' Hall . . . For weeks we were not allowed to speak to each other or to a human soul.'[3]

Kitchener's sadomasochistic experiences came at the hands of his father, whom he described as 'a rigid disciplinarian'.[4] He explained how the father encouraged the small family (of which Kitchener was the natural leader) to inflict punishments upon one another when the family code was broken. 'The justice of the punishments was never questioned,' he wrote. 'We endured them all with resignation . . . I submitted to being spreadeagled on the lawn in the attitude of a crucified man – on my back, in the hot sun, pinioned down by the arms and legs which were roped securely to croquet hoops.'[5] As his father detested schools, the Kitchener children were taught at home by tutors and a governess who described him as 'a very pretty fair boy, with golden hair, small pearly teeth, blue penetrating eyes, and an angelic smile'.[6] Kitchener's knowledge was tested from time to time by his cousin Francis, a Fellow of Trinity College, Cambridge, and later a master at Rugby School. The latter said he had 'never known a boy more totally devoid of any groundwork of education'.[7]

Like the rest of his family, the boy was also arrogant. Kitchener's father was publicly humiliated by a local Irish aristocrat and neighbour, the Knight of Glin, who horsewhipped him at the races, yet his children were brought up 'to look upon themselves as belonging to a superior race, benighted among an alien people, and from an early age his sons, noticeably Herbert, behaved in an imperious and arrogant way towards the Irish'.[8]

In due course Curzon escaped the attentions of Miss Paraman, yet curiously he remained in touch with her, writing frequently. He recorded that 'in her ordinary and sensible moments she was devoutly attached to us and continued to be until 1892, when she died'.[9] One of the mourners at her graveside was Curzon. When he was ten his father sent the boy to a private school in Hampshire where he was put under the attention of a Mr Dunbar, the headmaster's assistant. Said Curzon: 'I became his great favourite, though this did not cause him to spare one jot or tittle of his displeasure or punishment if we had provoked either.'[10] Dunbar's administration was sterner, if possible, than Miss Paraman's. Years later, Curzon is very explicit. 'He executed all or nearly all the punishments whether by spanking on the bare buttocks or by caning on the palm of the hand or by swishing on the posterior. I remember well all three experiences. He was a master of spanking, although he used to say that it hurt him nearly as much as it did us. I remember that it was at about the fifteenth blow that it really began to hurt, and from thence the pain increased in geometrical proportion. At about the 28th blow, one began to howl. The largest number of smacks I ever received was, I think, 42. But comic to relate, I still remember the feeling of warmth that ensued about five to ten minutes later when the circulation was thoroughly restored, and the surface pain had subsided. With the birch I think he never gave beyond ten or twelve strokes, and that for some particularly grave offence, in his bedroom at night.'[11]

Kitchener, who understood the effect of similar childhood experiences only too well, later gave his opinion: 'There is only one thing that Curzon likes more than hurting another, and that is to persuade others to humiliate him.' Mosely, who quotes this, adds that 'It could almost be said that he spent his life looking for stronger, more ruthless characters upon whom he could bruise himself.'[12] That is revealing of an insight by Kitchener which seems surprisingly modern. It was through such understanding, perhaps, that he was able to dominate others, when necessary.

But Curzon developed a determination to overcome resistance – physical or mental – that stood him in good stead when he reached Eton. He affirmed that he was determined to succeed and 'bent on being first in what I undertook . . . in my own way not theirs'.[13] For a start, the other boys called him 'Moonface' and he was convinced that his head was abnormal in breadth from side to side, and claimed that he could never get hats to fit him. His intellectual advantages over fellow pupils were considerable, and he wrote to his mother 'I am alright here'.[14] Years later he tried to analyze why the masters misunderstood him, or was it that he misunderstood them? 'The misunderstanding was partly due to three features or faults in my character, which, years afterwards, seem to stand out quite clear. The first was the tendency, common with public schoolboys, to conceal my virtues, such as they were, and to represent myself as worse than I was. The second was a sort of innate rebelliousness which has been with me all my life. The third was a passionate desire to WIN, to be first in whatever I undertook, and to defeat competition.'[15] It is clear that he was ambivalent as to whether these were faults at all.

Here are two examples of his 'innate rebelliousness': 'I made it a point of honour to attend Ascot races every year, not because I cared in the least for racing, but because it was forbidden and therefore dangerous. I also had a zinc lining made for the bottom drawer of the oak bureau in which I kept an illicit cellar. It was not that I cared for drinking, but I enjoyed the supreme cheek as an Eton boy of giving wine parties in my room. I used to make excellent champagne and claret cup, procuring the ice, soda and herbs in the Eton shop.'[16]

Kitchener, at the parallel period in his life, had moved to Switzerland, where his mother could attend a sanatorium; while she lay dying, the boys were sent to boarding school near Geneva. Her death, when Kitchener was fourteen, left a void in his background which no one was ever able to fill. After she died, the family moved to Brittany, although the boys continued to study in Switzerland. It was in 1867, while at school there, that Kitchener suffered the first of a number of minor breakdowns, mental and physical, which would come on him during his life when faced with difficulties. Kitchener was forced to acquire fluent French as well as some German, and had to work hard to catch up after the relatively unacademic early years in Ireland. Kitchener later confessed he 'hated the written word'.[17] But he became a good linguist.

By contrast, Curzon, whose mother died when he was sixteen, had by this age quite fallen in love with words and was to become one of the best stylists in the language. On his mother's death he wrote a poem which contains the following verses, under the title 'Kedleston':

> *Still as ever, proud thou standest,*
> *Green thy meadows as of yore*
> *But a chill of desolation*
> *Mid the sunbeams clouds thee o'er.*
>
> *Merry voices that but lately*
> *Laughing echoed through thy halls*
> *Sound no longer there, and silence*
> *Reigns instead within thy walls.*

Hackneyed, maybe, but not bad for a boy of sixteen lamenting his lost mother.

Both young men early appreciated the advantages to be gained by bringing their existence to the attention of the famous. The following fragment is preserved amongst the papers referring to Curzon's period at Eton (he seems to have thrown nothing away): 'An Ascension Day, May 30th 1878, being in London for the day, called on the Rt Hon W. E. Gladstone with reference to the possibility of his coming to lecture at Eton on Homer. Sent in my card. He was at breakfast with a large party of ladies and gentlemen, but came out at once, shook hands most kindly, and took me into a small side room, where he said he looked upon the visit as a bargain which was certainly to be kept.'

Later he notes, 'I called again on June 20th: introduced me to Mrs G., young G., Albert Grey and others. Everything's arranged.'

We shall see later how Kitchener's same determination to hobnob with the great was a crucial element in the drama.

While Curzon was to go to Oxford, Kitchener joined the Royal Military College, Woolwich, being determined to enter the Royal Engineers; his father, who had been a cavalry colonel, gave him every encouragement and sent him to a crammer in Kensington Square, the Rev. George Frost. But Kitchener did not cut much of a figure at Woolwich and his report said that he was ill-dressed, untidy and not overcareful of his person. Nevertheless he was successful in passing his examinations, and was duly commissioned in 1873.

Curzon, in contrast, cut a brilliant dash at Oxford, although he then believed that his time there ended in disaster. Alfred Lyttleton wrote to him, 'You have earned the name of the most famous Oxonian that in my knowledge of Oxford I can remember.' How this was achieved, Curzon described as follows: 'I rarely attended lectures, but never missed the Union.'[18] Yet he worked ten hours a day before his final exams, and was horrified when notified that he had been placed in the second class. He could not believe that he had not gained a first, so he sent a reply-paid telegram requesting a correction. When told that it was indeed so, he burst into uncontrollable sobbing. His friends did their best to console him. Edward Lyttelton wrote: 'Well old boy, this is of course a mouldy bore.'[19] But Curzon saw it as a matter of much greater moment. He exclaimed, 'I cannot believe it. I suspect skullduggery. A second! It was a deep disappointment. In the public eye, I was forever stamped with the brand of mediocrity! All I can do is to spend the rest of my life showing the examiners how wrong they have been.'[20] Alfred Lyttleton was probably more objective when he wrote, 'Of course you would have got the first class for certain had you denied yourself the Union, the gaming club, and those other literary, political and social enterprises.'[21]

Curzon, with an almost daemonic energy, now set out to win some of the most prestigious university prizes, and as a result was offered and accepted a Fellowship of All Souls.

He left Oxford when he was twenty-three years old; Kitchener had left the Royal Military Academy at the same age (but of course nine years earlier). Curzon was to move faster than Kitchener did in his early career, but by 1892 when Kitchener was forty-two and

Curzon only thirty-three, both men had the potential for great fame, and both had their feet firmly on the ladder they would then climb to positions of great eminence. Their formative years, after their education was concluded, had a number of interesting parallels, and it could be argued that Kitchener, though he moved more slowly, achieved as much, or more – for one who began as an army engineer, unnoticed by his contemporaries. Both spent substantial periods of time out of England, and both made their reputations abroad. Neither of them formed a permanent emotional attachment to a member of the opposite sex until they were in their thirties, and both exhibited considerable signs of extraordinary bravery. Their respective passions for personal exhibitionism, particularly in dress, were well-developed in this period of their lives and both showed the first indications of a taste for great houses which was to characterize them in their later years.

Curzon travelled almost continuously from December 1882 until February 1895, and with the sole exception of the year 1886 (when he succeeded in winning a seat in the House of Commons) he spent a great part of each year abroad. One reason was his passion for travel; another, almost as important, was the need to supplement his finances by writing and journalism. In 1882, on leaving Oxford, he went to Rome and Greece with three university friends and then continued on alone to Egypt and Palestine, returning home via Vienna, Dresden, Prague and Berlin. Less than a year later he was in Spain and Tangier, and in the spring of 1885 in Italy, Sicily, Tunis, Carthage and Kairwan. In August 1887 he went to Canada and the United States, and on via Japan and China to India. By the autumn of the following year he was on the Continent, and then in Persia for several months collecting material for his classic book *Persia and the Persian Question*. During 1891 and 1892 he was on the Continent again for lengthy periods, then in Greece and Turkey, and in August 1892 he set off on his second journey round the world, obtaining material for another book, *Problems of the Far East*.

Kitchener's travels were less extensive, and whereas it was the Far East which beckoned to Curzon ('Asia . . . vast, magnificent, inspiring'[22] he wrote) Kitchener was drawn to the Middle East. He had left England in November 1874, and was abroad almost continuously from then on. One of his reasons for being abroad so much was that his father, who had married again, was engaged in arranging a separation from his second wife, and there was no family home to which Kitchener could return. Kitchener himself said that he had never spent a winter in England.

Curzon's itinerary was thus much more demanding, and when considering his travels, there are two special factors to be borne in mind. The first is that he was not a rich man (until he married) and he had to augment the small allowance his father gave him with income from journalism and authorship, writing regularly for such periodicals as *Fortnightly Review*. The other factor was that he was by no means fit; when about to go to Oxford he had developed particularly severe back pains. These had long troubled him and restricted the games he could play at school. The cause was diagnosed as incurable curvature of the spine. He described it thus: 'Since I came back from France, I have felt out-shooting [sic] pains in my side, in the region of my hip, and noticed an unusual prominence of that member. I went up to London about it and saw the best men. They said it was weakness of the spine resulting from natural weakness and overwork, and that I must give up Oxford for the present and lie down on my back.'[23] Another doctor gave a different opinion and 'saw no harm in my going to Oxford if I obey strict injunctions – wear an appliance, lie down a good deal, and take no violent, or indeed, very active exercise'.[24] Curzon was, therefore, condemned to wear a steel corset for the remainder of his life.

Bravery may be a curious word to apply to a man who walks and rides across the Pamirs wearing a corset. But the physical pain must have been appalling, although he spoke little of it. Indeed, in the books he wrote about his travels, the anguish of his back is never mentioned. Only after his death on a sheet of notepaper in a drawer in his house at Hackwood, his executors found the following *crie de coeur*: 'Who knows what an effort and often a pain to me is public appearance of any kind? I am supposed to seek the footlights. Little do they know what a business it is to get me on the stage! How many of them, I wonder, have any idea of the long hours spent in bed, of the aching back, of the incessant nerve pain in the legs, of the fearful steel cage in which I have to be incased when I undergo any strain in which standing up is involved? They think me strong and arrogant and self-sufficient . . . It is an invalid addressing them . . . who probably goes back to his bed to writhe in agony as an expiation of his foolishness.'

Kitchener also suffered from regular pain, and his bravery in surmounting it was no less marked than Curzon's. Before leaving Woolwich, he had taken leave and gone back to France, without official permission, to see action in the Franco-Prussian War. He seems to have been motivated by knowledge that his father's army career had been blighted because he had never seen active service, and Kitchener, physically brave, was determined that this should not happen to him. He did not in fact see active service but was employed as an ambulanceman after the battle of Le Mans, and also ascended in an artillery balloon commanded by a French Army officer. Since he did not bother to put on warm clothing, he became ill as a result and developed pleurisy. When he returned to Britain, he was called to the Horse Guards to be reprimanded by the Commander-in-Chief the old Duke of Cambridge, who, after listening to his story, and calling him 'every name he could lay his tongue to' added 'with a funny sort of twinkle, "Well, anyhow, boy, go away and don't do it again." '[25]

On leaving the Royal Military Academy with his commission, Kitchener was posted to the School of Military Engineering at Chatham, where he was rewarded by an appointment as ADC to a General Greaves during the Austrian manoeuvres, and his good looks and spirited bearing so captivated the Emperor Franz Josef that he made the young lieutenant sit next to him at meals. He was described as 'handsome to the point of being almost feminine in his features'[26] although he apparently had a cast in his left eye. He spent his summer leave in Hanover, perfecting his German. On returning to England he applied for special service in Palestine, along with a young friend, and together they became experts in map-making, surveys and archaeological studies. He seems to have travelled over every square yard of the country examining and describing in detail 816 ruins. The story of his service reads somewhat like the exploits of T. E. Lawrence, and while Kitchener did not leave behind him quite such a highly coloured account, there is little doubting his personal bravery, for example, in 1875 when he saved his friend's life during an Arab attack, armed only with a cane.[27]

Two years later he was off to Constantinople where the Turks were engaged in a fierce struggle with the Bulgarians, and here Kitchener formed another of his attachments to the influential which was to help his career. His mentor was Valentine Baker Pasha, who was fighting with the Turkish Army, having recently been dismissed from the British Army for assaulting a young lady in a train. He was, luckily, a friend of the Prince of Wales, who took up his case and, as we shall see, he later turned up, reinstated in the Egyptian Army, in Cairo.

In 1878 Kitchener succeeded in gaining a posting to Cyprus, reporting to the Foreign Office and making written reports direct to Lord Salisbury on conditions there. Again he attached himself to the influential, sharing a house in Nicosia with Lord John Kennedy. The two men were both rather wild and Kitchener introduced into the household a tame bear which he had acquired in Bulgaria. In Cyprus he also met Sir Samuel Baker, the famous explorer, and brother of Valentine, and Pandeli Ralli, the financier, who was to be a lifelong friend. Kitchener now spoke fluent Arabic, and was a first-class horseman racing on both flat and over the sticks, and whipper-in for the local hunt. All this was heady stuff, and Kitchener, whose ambition was never far below the surface, applied to be appointed consul at Mosul, an honour which was refused him. It was while in Cyprus that he grew the distinctive moustache, later to be so famous on the posters in World War I. It can be presumed that it also added to the appearance of masculinity which he was keen to cultivate.

His ambition, and his yearning for active service, caused him to act in a way which did not endear him to the authorities. He once took leave, and went to Egypt with a friend where, both disguised as Arabs, they embarked on a 24-hour spying mission well away from the coast and reconnoitred Egyptian army positions. Told to return to Cyprus, Kitchener adopted a Nelson-like attitude by embarking on the wrong ship 'by mistake' but his youth, his good looks, and his enthusiasm enabled him to escape reprimand.

Indeed, by the time he had completed five years in Cyprus, he was chosen, along with twenty-five other officers, to go to Egypt to train its army on European lines. His ruthless and unconcealed ambition made him unpopular with his other army comrades, but he rode roughshod over the critics and even designed his own uniform of light blue for the Egyptian cavalry over whom he had charge. In 1884 he was heading towards the Sudan asking, 'Can I do anything for you, General Gordon?' Gordon was so taken with Kitchener's efficiency that he wrote, 'I like Baker's description of Kitchener, "The man I have always placed my hopes on. One of the FEW VERY SUPERIOR British officers, with a cool head and a hard constitution, combined with untiring energy".' Gordon added, 'Whoever comes up here had better appoint him Governor General.'[28]

We know little about Kitchener's attitude to women at this time, or whether during these years in the Middle East he had discovered the homosexual tendency which may have become prominent later in his life. Certainly he formed no permanent relationship with any one woman, although he was attractive to women in general. His biographer George Cassar says, 'His sexual instincts were wholly sublimated like those of a Roman Catholic priest', and, 'He lived a life of inviolable purity and self-control,'[29] but we do not know what facts this assessment are based upon.

In Cairo, Kitchener had again taken up with Valentine Baker, now back in fashion. Baker had two daughters, the elder of whom, Hermione, fell passionately in love with Kitchener, although she was only eighteen. It seems that there was a clear arrangement that they would marry, but two years later she died, in Cairo, of typhoid fever. We do not know how Kitchener took the news although a letter from a lady who was staying at Shepheard's Hotel in Cairo in 1884 says she heard her mother talking to Kitchener as Hermione Baker lay dying. We are told that for many years he wore a locket under his shirt which contained a miniature portrait of her given him by Valentine Baker.

Years later, Kitchener's sister Millie told a journalist that her brother was bored by women. Marriage was out of the question, as he would soon tire of seeing the same face at breakfast each day. 'It is the funniest thing to see him paying attention one day to a pretty girl and the next day to hear him wonder what her name is, and when he met her. She imagines that she has the lion of London in her silken fetters while he has forgotten her existence.'[30]

In contrast, Curzon had always been attracted to women. After he was widowed, his mistress for many years until 1916, Eleanor Glynn, described him as a passionate lover. In his twenties he formed no permanent attachment, although he had a reputation

for waylaying society girls in corridors, woods and trains. A story
by a Miss Balfour illustrates this. She was staying with Lord and
Lady Elcho at Stanway for a large shooting party. George Curzon
was another of the guests. 'I wish I could reproduce George's
swelling eighteenth century manner and phraseology,' she wrote.
' "I had heard of you," he told me, "as a great addition to your
circle; clever, brilliant, a good talker, and I had imagined to myself
a woman of a certain age without any other charms but those of
intellect. But what do I find? A young, buxom creature, charming."
He and I were alone at the breakfast table, for a few moments. I got
up to go, but before I reached the door, George got there in front of
me, shut it, and kissed me with fervour. I was not displeased.'

And the following extract from one of his poems, composed in
under half an hour for the Souls, a parody of Edgar Allen Poe, is a
clear marker to his tastes:

> *I sing of the attractions of the Belles,*
> *London Belles*
> *Society Belles*
> *Of the manifold allurements of the Belles:*
> *Oh what rhapsodies their charm deserves;*
> *How delicious and delirious are the curves*
> *With which their figure swells –*
> *Voluptuously and voluminously swells . . .*

It also appears that Curzon established a liaison with a woman
who lived in Westbourne Terrace, then a suitably discreet area, like
St John's Wood, in which to house a mistress. She was sent to
Switzerland, presumably to have an abortion. She then threatened
to send telegrams to Lord Salisbury and other ministers denounc-
ing him – but these were stopped and destroyed. Curzon was aided
in his negotiations with her and her 'protector' by George Wyndham, also a young MP. 'No horror that I have gone through
equalled that,' wrote Curzon. 'All I can say is God have mercy on
me and save me from such a fate again.'[31]

The fact is, whatever his amorous tastes, Curzon was strongly
motivated to marry money, and the first attempt at a serious
attachment, so far as is known, was when Lord Grosvenor died and
Curzon pressed his widow to marry him, proposing altogether on
three separate occasions. Their correspondence has not survived,

but it is believed her refusal was due to her passion for Curzon's friend George Wyndham whom she married in 1887. Curzon needed money to provide for the style which he hoped to attain. He was already making plans to launch on a political career – after two years as Lord Salisbury's Assistant Private Secretary he sought a seat in Parliament, and was selected for Southport in 1886. When he made his maiden speech, one journalist remarked that it would have done credit to a Cabinet Minister.[32] And his first step up the ladder of political success was taken in 1891 when he accepted Lord Salisbury's invitation to join his government as Undersecretary of State for India.

This was the year, too, in which Kitchener also ascended the lower rungs of the ladder to fame. He had been in Egypt for nearly ten years and had earned the reputation of a 'very gallant officer' who had often 'risked and, at least on one occasion, nearly lost his life in the performance of his military duties'.[33] This was at Suakin where he was shot in the jaw during an attack. News of his success in this 'skirmish' was received with much jubilation in England and encouraged Kitchener's ambition and taste for glory. He was at this time only a colonel, but was also Governor-General of Eastern Sudan and the Red Sea Littoral, and as such enjoyed being addressed as 'Your Excellency'. He acquired his first ADC, 'Monkey' Gordon, nephew of the General, and had a fine residence and a personal yacht.

On his return to England on leave in 1888, Lord Salisbury, who had noted the Suakin victory, invited him to Hatfield, the home of the Cecils, who were to be so useful to Kitchener in later years. Salisbury told him that he would return to Egypt as Adjutant-General to Sir Francis Grenfell who had been appointed Sirdar (Commander-in-Chief of the Egyptian Army) in 1885. For a thirty-nine-year-old colonel it was an extraordinary appointment, and as a result he was unpopular with his fellow officers and lived a lonely but, for his rank, a rather lavish existence. His brother described his fine house in Cairo like this: 'Simply perfection in the way of taste . . . There seem to be rooms in all directions, and armour, carving, tiles, and draperies from floor to ceiling. The furniture is all most handsome . . . How he could have got all these things together seems extraordinary.'[34] He used this house to advantage, feeling secure enough to invite influential friends in

England to come out and visit him, and he told Cranborne, the Prime Minister's son, 'The Egyptian question requires to be studied on the spot.'[35] Kitchener relished visiting such families, too, on his annual leave in England. His social life had blossomed after 1895, when his friend of Cyprus days, Pandeli Ralli, a man of great wealth and an avid socialite, asked Kitchener to consider his house at 17 Belgravia Square as his home whenever he was in London. As his reputation increased, hostesses vied with each other for the privilege of welcoming this good-looking bachelor who made great efforts with the ladies. It could well have been the homosexual side of his nature which, subconsciously, appealed to such women. Some of the letters from women which Kitchener retained in his correspondence (most of his private letters he destroyed in December 1902 on the way to India) are revealing of the effect he had on the opposite sex. For example, Winifred, wife of the Duke of Portland: 'It was so sad saying goodbye yesterday . . . It seems like some sort of lovely dream now and one longs to have some means of fixing it as a reality . . . I can't yet realise that it must be such *years* till I see you again. I felt it at the station those last minutes, didn't you?'

On another occasion she scrawled a letter to Kitchener in pencil after he had been to dinner at her house: 'I just had to write to tell you!! My house looked so nice with your glorious flowers . . . I felt like a child out for a holiday. I shall be in London next Tuesday till Thursday and do hope I may see you again perhaps.'

And Mary Minto, wife of Curzon's successor as Viceroy, writing in 1909, as she leaves India: 'It makes me so sad to think that this line is my last farewell to you in this country. . .We shall miss you very much indeed. . .I shall always look back to the four years spent in India together as the most interesting of our lives. . . We are letting you go with the greatest regret. Always yours, sincerely. . .'

At home he was soon intimate with the Grenfells and Cecils and families of the Portlands, Londonderrys, Dufferins, Waterfords and Powis. W. H. Grenfell (later Lord Desborough) had introduced him to country house life during his leave in 1885. But it must be emphasised that this popularity did not extend either to the hostesses in Cairo or to the Egyptian army, and amongst the latter Kitchener was regarded as 'a toady who gained power by cultivat-

ing friendships with people in high places'[36] Sir Evelyn Baring
(later Lord Cromer) tried to explain the animosity Kitchener
aroused when writing to Lord Salisbury. 'This is partly due to the
fact that he is a severe taskmaster, with a harsh and unsympathetic
manner; and partly to his mania for economy which, although
generally laudible, he sometimes pushes too far.' Kitchener had
already confided to Baring that when Sir Francis Grenfell relin-
quished the post of Sirdar (Commander-in-Chief of the Egyptian
army) he wished to be considered for it. In addition to his military
duties Baring made him Inspector-General of Police and early in
1892 it became possible to recommend him as Sirdar. The Duke of
Cambridge readily agreed, promoting him from Colonel to Major-
General and saying that 'he had always considered him a very good
man for the place.'

It is said that the Egyptian army received the news with surprise
and disgust, not only because Kitchener was disliked but because it
was known that he had used his political influence with the Barings
and Cecils to obtain the appointment. Kitchener was only forty-one
and he was unable to cope with the jealousy his rapid promotion
aroused in the other officers. He adopted a very reserved attitude
and has been described as more like a machine than a man: the
only people in Cairo with whom he was popular were the group of
young men with whom he surrounded himself. His confidant ten
years later, 'Brat' Maxwell explained this as follows: 'He really
feels nice things, but to put tongue to them, except in very intimate
society, he would rather die.'[37]

On leave in England, Kitchener used personally to interview
candidates for service in his army, meeting each of them at the
Junior United Services Club. 'He made marriage, or even an
engagement to marry, an absolute bar. He told candidates that
marriage interfered with work because it involved a divided
loyalty. . . . He succeeded presently in surrounding himself with an
impressive band of extraordinarily youthful colonels who were
completely imbued with their chief's methods and ideals.'[38]

Curzon, in contrast, made what was by any standards an
exceptional marriage. He had met Mary Leiter, daughter of a
Chicago meat baron (and founder of Marshal Fields emporium) in
1890 and they conducted a protracted but deeply-felt courtship,
interspersed on Curzon's side by long periods of neglect when there

seemed a clear tendency to put his career first. Mary was the one who took the first steps to ensure that the courtship came to an end. In 1893 she visited Cairo for a ball organized for Kitchener, at the end of a holiday with her mother in Egypt. She heard that Curzon had just passed through the Suez Canal, returning from one of his Eastern tours. She and her mother embarked on a boat and followed him to France, calling on him in the lounge of his hotel in Paris. Curzon agreed to the engagement, but insisted that it should remain secret until he had completed his travels, and she respected this. The marriage took place in April 1895. She was all he could want in a wife – rich, beautiful, dedicated to him, and charming to other men, including, curiously enough, Kitchener. After her death, Curzon was to write a note which he placed amongst her papers between the letters from Kitchener. 'This was the man who was half in love with Mary.'

Kitchener had met Mary Curzon in Egypt, before her marriage, and there was instant affection between them. At the time of her marriage, he was of course advancing his career in Cairo, but he did not neglect his female friends in London of whom without doubt the most intense and the most influential was Lady Cranborne, later to be Lady Salisbury.

Lady Salisbury religiously kept all Kitchener's letters (and most of the envelopes and enclosures) but he destroyed all hers to him, and there were many more of the latter. His first letter is at the end of 1889 when he says, 'I write to remind you of your half-promise that you would come out to Cairo this winter and stay with me.' There is little more over the next decade, but the correspondence escalates very rapidly when he goes out to the Boer War. She must have written every week, although at first he does not answer so regularly. Not only does she write letters which he calls 'amusing' and 'lively' but she sends books and small presents such as silver cigarette cases and inkstands. For his part, as their friendship warms up, he sends photographs, and then skins of animals to which he no doubt helped himself when on tour.

But in the early period of the Boer War, his letters are almost all routine comments on his Army work, invariably four pages only, about 200 words. The tone is pessimistic throughout, as if he found his life under Lord Roberts, his Commander-in-Chief, far from glamorous. For example he wrote in March 1900: 'I hope the authorities at home will keep their hair on and if they want a victim to sacrifice I am always at their disposal. War means risks and you cannot play the game and always win.' And in November 1900: 'I am getting quite frightened at these rumours that I shall go to the War Office. I could do no good there, and would far sooner sweep a crossing.' Things are no better next year, and he whines, 'I hope if they have anyone [who] can do the work better, they will send him out. It is not fair on the Army if anyone else could bring matters to a nearer end.'[39] Kitchener's attitude to her is curious – as if he is asking for sympathy by bearing his breast to reveal the inner – quivering – man beneath the iron exterior.

He knows, however, that he can count on her being on his side, and does not hesitate to show his rougher nature. For example on the matter of concentration camps, he comments, 'I see Miss Hobhouse [who went out to investigate conditions in the camps] has taken an action against me. I shall probably be put in prison on arrival in England . . . We were quite right in getting rid of her.' And, respecting the deaths of children in the camps, which he blamed on the Boer mothers, 'I am thinking of having some of the worst cases tried for manslaughter.'[40]

Eventually when he returned to England and to Hatfield, we find him writing to Lady Salisbury at her London house in Grafton Street, 'I apologise for the bad behaviour at your dinner last night, but I could not help it.'[41]

Hatfield House, splendid today though surrounded by urban sprawl, must have been truly magnificent in the 1900s and it is easy to understand how Kitchener developed a passion for it, and wanted to reproduce parts of its design in the various houses which he tried to erect in his attempt to create his own immortality. Not so easy to understand is the relationship between the two people, which was to escalate so rapidly after he went out to India. Reading his letters to her it is tempting to conclude that he was simply using her, and it is true that after 1906, when she had helped him win the battle with Curzon, there appear to be hardly any more letters – she had served her purpose.

Chapter Two

Viceroy and Sirdar

Lord Curzon's first and judicious biographer, the Rt Hon the Earl of Ronaldshay, makes no mention of the scheming methods which Curzon employed in order to ensure that he became Viceroy of India. Later biographers have told the story well enough but none of them has fully explained how it was that while Curzon managed to get on his side Queen Victoria, Lord Salisbury, and his son Lord Cranborne, Balfour, Brodrick and Curzon's other long-time friends, yet a mere six years later all of them (except the Queen and Salisbury, both dead) should have turned so violently against him. The conventional wisdom is that it was Curzon's own pride and prejudices which alienated them, but this really will not do as an explanation, since Curzon the Viceroy was not much different in character from Curzon the brilliant Undersecretary of State.

In June 1895, shortly after Curzon's marriage, Lord Salisbury came back into office and asked him to accept the Undersecretaryship of Foreign Affairs. He was also made Privy Councillor, the youngest in living memory. Nevertheless with Salisbury in charge of the Foreign Office as well as Prime Minister, this was not an appointment in which Curzon could show much initiative, although he did attend Cabinet meetings in Salisbury's absence abroad, when his unrivalled knowledge of Far Eastern affairs was so very evident. It was therefore probably more than politeness which caused Salisbury to thank him for 'the unremitting labour and brilliant ability with which you have conducted the business of the Foreign Office in critical times, and defended it with so much success in Parliament'.[1]

Curzon's indefatigable efforts to place himself on the Viceregal throne were means to a worthy end, so are not exactly reprehensible, but they show a thickness of skin which is not necessarily attractive. Curzon told two conflicting stories about his earliest determination to go to India as Viceroy. The first was when Curzon was Secretary of the Eton Literary Society, and Sir James Stephen came to the school to lecture. 'He told us,' Curzon wrote later, 'that there was in the Asian continent an empire more populous, more amazing and more beneficent than that of Rome. Ever since that day, and still more so since my first visit to India in 1887, the fascination, and if I may say so, the sacredness of India, have grown upon me.'[2] Curzon began to talk to his friends about one day becoming Viceroy, and the likelihood of this happening as part of the climb up the ladder to the Prime Ministership, was commonly discussed. Later, in 1898, Curzon came up with a different account. On visiting India, he had discovered that the army architect of Government House in Calcutta, which had been built 100 years earlier, had used as a model drawings of the house where he, Curzon, had been born, Kedleston Hall, in the country outside Derby. So he told the people of Derby (in a speech) that it was the fact of that resemblance which first turned his thoughts to the government of India. 'If fate were propitious, and I were held deserving of the task, I should like to exchange Kedleston in England for Kedleston in India.'

But by his own admission it was one year earlier, one morning in April 1897, while reading the *Morning Post*, that his mind powerfully concentrated on the subject, for he saw a report that the Marquis of Lorne would soon receive a peerage. He knew that this was an indication that Lorne was to be Viceroy, to take the place Curzon felt was destined for himself. He hurried to his desk to write a long letter to Lord Salisbury, then Prime Minister, setting out at length his own qualifications for the appointment. It was well-known that the ineffective incumbent, Lord Elgin (grandson of 'Marbles' Elgin) was due to retire in January 1899 and a number of names were already being canvassed, Curzon's among them. India was a troubled country, there had been terrible droughts and riots, British officials had been murdered, and the seige and relief of Chitral had roused the popular imagination, so a strong, firm man was needed to rule the country. Lord Balfour of Burleigh, then

Secretary of State for Scotland, was a front runner, as was Lord
Minto, another Scot. Curzon was younger than any of these but his
qualifications are described by his first biographer as 'brilliant
imagination, specialised knowledge, outstanding personality, self-
confidence, and assiduous industry combined with great gifts of
speech and writing'. Despite these qualities Curzon's parliamentary career had not matched his political progress because, despite
what *The Times* perhaps over-generously called 'a brilliant maiden
speech' he was not a House of Commons man and out of office 'his
record as a backbencher was unexpectedly meagre. He spoke
infrequently, even on imperial affairs' so it is probably true that
Curzon's eagerness to become Viceroy of India arose from an
awareness that, despite his polished manner, he would win fame
more easily outside the House than in it. Another factor in his mind
may have been that, if the Conservatives[3] lost their hold on the
government, which seemed increasingly likely, he would be condemned to several years on the backbenches. In the world at large
his energy, imagination and attention to detail might bring richer
rewards, and he still saw his final goal as the Premiership – as early
as 1891 he boasted of one day becoming Prime Minister, when
having dinner with Oscar Wilde and W. S. Blunt in Paris.

Curzon was by no means unaware of these qualities in himself
and he wrote to Salisbury, determined to make sure that the great
man kept them in mind. He recalled that he had visited India four
times, travelled extensively in the region, and written at enormous
length on the subject. He went on, 'I have long thought that were
the post in India to fall vacant while I am still a young man – I am
under 40 – and were it offered to me, I should like to accept it.'
Going on in this vein for some time, Curzon realised that he had
gone over the top and exclaimed, 'I seem rather to have been
putting my wares, such as they are, in the shop window . . .' He
concluded, 'I have only decided to make this confession to you as
my chief, in great trust and humility, not with a view to soliciting
any opinion or reply, but simply, if at a later date etc., I would be
grateful if my name were at least considered.'[4]

This was of course, utterly disingenuous, 'Not with a view to
soliciting any reply'! Curzon was sleepless with anxiety as he
awaited the response, and he knew full well it would be a difficult
one because Salisbury simply hated being pestered for preferment,

whoever the applicant. He considered it bad form, and said it made him quite 'sick and disgusted'.[5]

The reply, when it finally came, was evasive, so Curzon wrote once more, this time in pencil: 'Ill – from Reigate. I cannot think that personal ambition is at the bottom of any keenness I may exhibit in the matter.'[6]

This again was hardly frank, but Curzon considered himself uniquely qualified for the post, as indeed he was. As a matter of fact, Salisbury, despite his distaste for Curzon's pushiness, came to agree that Curzon should go, and early the following year he wrote to Queen Victoria in his favour, saying, 'He is a man in many respects of great ability, as well as of extraordinary industry and knowledge . . . His only fault is occasional rashness of speech in the House of Commons.'[7] (T. P. O'Connor, MP, said that Curzon had 'little tricks of condescension – the Johnsonian pomposity of his rhetoric'[8].)

The Queen – now eighty years old – replied to Salisbury as follows: 'The future Vice Roy [sic] must really shake himself free from his red-tapist narrow-minded Council and Entourage. He must be *more independent, must hear for himself*, what the *feelings* of the natives really are, and do what he thinks right and not be guided by the *snobbish* and vulgar, over-bearing and offensive behaviour of our Civil and Political Agents, if we are to go on peaceably and happily in India, and to be liked and beloved by high and low – as well as respected as we ought to be – and not trying to trample on people and continually reminding them and making them feel that they are a conquered people.' As he read the letter, Curzon realized that the wind was blowing in his direction. The Queen went on, 'They must, of course, *feel* that we are masters but it should be done kindly and not offensively which alas is often the case. Would Mr Curzon feel and do this? Would Mrs Curzon who is an American do to represent a Vice-Queen?'[9] Curzon made every effort to use the influence of his friends, and also wrote another long and warm letter to Lord Salisbury. Mary Curzon wrote to her parents, 'George will do with his career what he chooses, and NOTHING ON EARTH can alter his iron will. I have long since realised George's iron will and never crossed it.'[10]

Those who were against Curzon's appointment pointed out that he was a sick man and when Salisbury spoke informally to Curzon in the middle of June, he said that there would be two conditions: first that the appointment would be subject to a satisfactory medical report; and, second, his latest literary work could not be permitted to appear. As regards the former, Curzon managed to persuade his doctor Sir James Paget to write, 'I hereby certify that I have examined the Rt Hon George Curzon and I can find no sign of disease about him, and were I making a report to a life assurance office, I should recommend him for insurance at the ordinary rate for a 1st Class Life.'[11] As to his book, Curzon was much irritated at its censorship, as it was ready for publication, and he not only had to pay back a £1500 advance, but also charges of £153.19s. Money had been a considerable worry to him during the three years of his marriage as he had overstretched himself by buying No. 1 Carlton House Terrace, yet after only four months they had to let it for £2000 a year and take a lease on a smaller house at nearby 4 Carlton Gardens, owned by his friend Arthur Balfour.

Mary was not happy at this time, indeed she was unhappy and lonely for much of the early years of her marriage with recurrent headaches which started with her pregnancies. Curzon was working long hours on his parliamentary papers, and writing his books. 'He sits and sits at those Foreign Office papers until I could scream! I feel he is working himself to death, but he will do it,'[12] she wrote. But as soon as the news was announced that he was to go to India, her loneliness seemed to lift from her, and, lionised by their friends, the couple embarked on a round of social activity which was to continue for many months. Mary was even able to help him financially, as her father provided £3000 towards the considerable costs of the Viceroyalty in addition to the marriage settlement of £3500 a year. Nevertheless, Curzon remained hard up, and immediately on arriving in India was forced to ask for an advance on his salary. While Curzon would have liked to inherit the family money, he did not want to inherit his father's title, as this would have kept him out of the House of Commons. Salisbury found a satisfactory solution by recommending to the Queen to create Curzon an Irish peer.

Mary Curzon was to be such an inseparable part of the Viceregality, or at any rate certain aspects of it, that from this point in the story until her death just after they returned from India, it is impossible to think of Curzon without thinking of her too. There is no doubt that they were deeply in love and had a strong physical attraction for each other. Their first child was born after a difficult pregnancy for Mary. They had been living at a house called The Priory, near Reigate, when on Christmas Eve 1895, a miscarriage was diverted, just in time. Mary was hurriedly moved to London. Curzon had a coach she travelled in filled with a bed of white roses made by the gardener who was later to acquire a fame of his own, Fred Streeter. The child, their first daughter, was born at 4 Carlton Gardens, on 20 January 1896. Then, shortly after Curzon's appointment to the Viceroyalty was announced, a second child, Cynthia Blanche, was born on 28 August 1898. The couple ardently wanted a son, not only because Curzon had the strongest feelings about carrying on a family heritage which stretched back to the Norman Conquest, but because Mary, too, was excited about her newly acquired title, writing, 'Oh the ladyships! I feel like a ship in full sail on the high seas of dignity.'[13] Curzon once said, 'I pray in these same words every day: "May she bear a child to the honour and glory and to the good of Thy Kingdom, and may it be a male child".'[14] His prayers went unanswered, as Mary, always frail, was not to have another child for nearly six years, and then it was a girl.

But to return to 1898. Mary Curzon wrote to her father: 'George is going to be made Vice Roy [sic] of India as soon as the House of Commons rises. It cannot be known before, as George will at once have to vacate the Parliamentary seat. It takes my breath away, for it is the greatest position in the English world next to the Queen and the Prime Minister, and it will be a satisfaction, I know, to you and Mamma that your daughter will fill the greatest place ever held by an American abroad. Heaven knows how I shall do it, but I shall do my best to be a help to George and an honour to you and Mamma, and I shall be ready to put my trust in Providence and hope to learn how to be a ready-made Queen.' The appointment was publicly announced on 11 August 1898.

It was received with rapturous enthusiasm by his friends, but not without criticism from the world at large. Even *The Times* was non-committal. A leader concluded: 'We sincerely hope, for Mr Curzon's sake and that of the Empire, that Lord Salisbury's very interesting experiment will succeed.'[15] Curzon's father, who did not fully appreciate his son's achievements, tore himself away from grouse shooting and wrote, 'I begin to realise what a splendid position you have deservedly won. Congrats pour in from every quarter, and the country generally are as proud of you as I, your father, am, and more I cannot say.'[16] And Lyttleton summed up the friends' views when he wrote, 'Here is the top place of the Empire for you my dear. I knew you would get it . . . So here's to you, old boy!'[17]

More important, what were the responses of those who were later to turn against Curzon? Salisbury's son, Cranborne, was in favour, and so was his wife, later to become Kitchener's ally. Brodrick, one of Curzon's oldest friends, was delighted, and wrote in enthusiastic terms. Balfour, too. He was probably the pivotal figure in the Souls, that club of aristocratic intimates of which Curzon was also a central member. (The other club in which Curzon was prominent was the Crabbet which met at the home of Wilfrid Scawen Blunt). The Souls got its name from someone saying 'you are always talking about your souls'. Balfour thought the name 'meaningless and slightly ludicrous'.[18] Other members included St John Brodrick, the Tennant sisters, the Elchos, the Pembrokes, the Grenfells (later Desboroughs) and the Lyttletons. The Souls gave a farewell dinner for the Curzons at the Café Monaco, at which Balfour spoke generously. There was no element of jealousy here – all his friends expected Curzon to reach dizzy heights, and they knew him to be taking on what was his due. This was also the first moment when as his biographer Ronaldshay says, 'By an ironic decree of Fate, in view of what the future held in store, both he and Lord Kitchener stood prominently together in the limelight. The victor of Omdurman and the Viceroy-designate of India were singled out as "the most remarkable and conspicuous figures in public life" at that time.'[19]

The background to Kitchener's achievement in the Sudan is well-known, although the true scale of his own contribution is commonly over-estimated. Briefly, the ruler of Egypt had attempted to gain control of the Sudan in the 1870s first by employing the great explorer Sir Samuel Baker and then a Royal Engineer's officer, Colonel Charles Gordon, and the latter eventually became governor general of the Sudan. Gordon left the Sudan in 1880, returning at the request of Gladstone's cabinet two years later with rather muddled instructions to evacuate Egyptian forces from the

Sudan. He was totally unsuited, temperamentally, to the task, and was killed by the rebel forces, led by the Mahdi, in Khartoum on 26th January 1885, with the British relieving forces only two days away after a dilatory progress down the Nile. The whole nation, from Queen Victoria downwards, nurtured a powerful feeling of guilt that this typically botched British enterprise had ended so badly, and they yearned for retribution.

Kitchener had been preparing for the Sudan campaign to avenge Gordon for some years, and in 1896 the British Government had finally given the order that he could proceed, albeit cautiously. He was responsible not to the War Office, but virtually direct to Lord Salisbury, the Prime Minister, whose son, Lord Edward Cecil, Kitchener took on his staff. Lord Edward was entrusted with writing the weekly reports from the front to Salisbury, although Kitchener found them colourless and tried, without success, to make them more dramatic. Kitchener had already been knighted for services in Egypt, and when his forces won two engagements against the Dervishes at Firket and Hafir, he received a KCB.

This was in 1896, the year of Queen Victoria's Diamond Jubilee, and Kitchener came to London to obtain agreement for his plan to push on across the desert to Khartoum. He lunched at Windsor with the Queen and presented her with some trophies, and she noted in her diary that he was 'a striking, energetic-looking man, with a rather firm expression, but very pleasing to talk to'.[20] He alarmed a maid of honour, though, by talk of murder and execution for natives. However, when he returned to Egypt his plans for attacking Khartoum and the Mahdi were delayed and he became most depressed. His biographer Philip Magnus describes how he might remain morose and silent for hours on end. He was difficult with his staff, and often vented his spleen by bullying them as other men bully their wives. This was made much worse by his total incapacity to delegate even simple things – another fault he shared with Curzon.

He normally rose at least an hour before dawn and liked to get through three hours' work before breakfast. Later, in the evening, he would work again, after a gin and soda, and then he would dine in the mess with his staff. It was at this time, says the biographer, Royle, that he began to be affected by attacks of migraine and bad indigestion, ailments which made him even more sullen with others. Those with whom Kitchener worked also continued to find him devious; Cromer grumbled to Salisbury: 'The only fault I have to find with him is that it is sometimes difficult to extract the whole truth from him. He is inclined to keep back facts which he does not wish to be known.'[21] Another writer said of him, 'The Sirdar disliked channels. He was not only Commander-in-Chief, but Chief Staff Officer as well. He scarcely ever issued a written order, and confined himself to curt telegrams, the forms for which he carried in his hat . . . He had practically no staff and did everything himself. . . He hated the written word, and how the ultimate historian will tell the story . . . I cannot tell . . . But if the Sirdar did not write or speak much, he used to think. I never knew a man who more visibly, continually and deeply thought. The whole expedition was a picture in his mind. He was it. He sat there and pondered and thought it out. The orders had to be obeyed . . . He was hard on men who failed him. He seldom took into account, or even enquired into, the reasons for failure . . . I never saw him look at or speak to a private soldier or take the slightest trouble to ingratiate himself with his troops.'[22]

Then, on Good Friday 1898, his army was permitted to attack the Mahdi at Atbara – with the bands playing and pipes skirling. 'Kitchener was extraordinarily calm during the battle. He had a very slight knowledge of tactics, which he left to Hunter and Gateacre . . . to the best of my knowledge, Kitchener only issued three orders during the fight.' So wrote Lieutenant-Colonel Charles à Court Repington CMG, Commander of the Order of Leopold, Officer of the Legion of Honour, in his memoirs published after Kitchener's death. Another writer described the appalling scene after the Dervishes had been massacred by superior British fire power – 3000 dead in half an hour 'many mangled into mere fragments of humanity far beyond recognition'.[23]

Kitchener was much criticised for the fact that he suffered 600 casualties and because after the victory, he rode forward on a white horse with the Dervish commander, Mahmoud, dragged behind in chains. But criticism was forgotten when three months later, he was marching on Omdurman with an overwhelming force. Gordon was avenged, and Kitchener achieved notoriety by ordering his former ADC, Gordon's nephew, to dig up the Mahdi's body from his tomb. The head was brought to him, just as Gordon's head had been carried to the Mahdi, and Kitchener planned to have the skull polished as a decoration for his desk, but instead kept it in an old Kerosene tin. This caused an outcry and even Queen Victoria was outraged, so Kitchener had the skull buried secretly in the desert by night, although later Wingate, Kitchener's successor in the Sudan, claimed to have acquired it and used it as an inkwell.

Kitchener's victories owed a not inconsiderable debt to the skill of a 29-year-old Canadian officer in the Royal Engineers who had worked with the Canadian Pacific Railways, Edouard Girouard. Kitchener interviewed him in London in 1895, and the following year sent him to Wadi Halfa with instructions to build over 100 miles of railway, with hardly any trained staff to assist him. With Kitchener's support, Girouard achieved the impossible, enabling Kitchener to win battle after battle as his troops progressed towards Khartoum, surprising the Mahdist forces with superior firepower supplied from the railway. Whatever the morals of a type warfare which was 'carnage set to the tune of brass bands and bagpipes'[24] it was in fact a Canadian engineer who enabled Kitchener to become that new symbol of national reverence, Kitchener of Khartoum.

By his victories he had avenged Gordon's death and allowed the British nation to feel self-respect again. He became a national hero, rewarded with a peerage, the Grand Cross of the Bath, the thanks of both Houses of Parliament, and a money grant of £30,000. He took the title of Lord Kitchener of Khartoum and of Aspall in Suffolk, which had been his mother's home. The only discordant note in all this came from those who believed that he had acted brutally, as indeed he had, even by the standards of the day, and those like Haig, who thought he was an inexperienced commander with 'no plan or tactical idea for beating the enemy'.[25] He returned to London to a hero's welcome, and, as we have seen, arrived in the capital just as Curzon too was being given a hero's celebration by his friends, the Souls, as he prepared to leave for India. Amongst those who sent him greetings letters was Curzon, who wrote, 'Welcome home after your great exploits. It is a great thing that the nation should have heroes, but a still greater [one] that it should recognise them as such . . . I hope to see you before long, but at any rate at your Banquet on the 4th.'[26]

Kitchener's appeal both to high-ranking men and to women

needs some explanation. His biographer Cassar says, 'No one can claim that Kitchener possessed a charming personality,'[27] but it is hard to believe this. Many people, from King Edward VII to Curzon's wife Mary, fell under his spell. As far as the women were concerned the attraction does not seem to have been sexual in the heterosexual sense. One of the most attractive of the Souls, for example, said that Kitchener 'abided in darkness as to her charms'. But there was a side to his character which was, no doubt, strongly feminine in nature, but directed by an iron will which ensured that it was never used except to some purpose. 'His charm was never wasted on underdogs.'[29]

In contrast, he was most assiduous in his attentions to the influential, as is shown by his letter book for 1909 in which, over a period of eight months, he writes twelve letters to General Ian Hamilton, ten letters to his friend Ralli, nine to Renshaw (his friend and solicitor), five to the Marchioness of Salisbury (formerly Lady Cranborne) and five to Maxwell. Other letters went to the Duke of Connaught (the King's brother), Viscountess Helmsley, Lord Roberts (his superior during the Boer War and Britain's most senior soldier), Sir Schomberg McDonnell (formerly the King's private secretary), the Earl of Dudley, and numerous generals. But the person he wrote to most often, every other week, was the man for whom he had the strongest emotional attachment, young Major Raymond Marker. The strange story of Marker will unfold in the next chapter.[29]

It was probably during this period in London at the end of 1898 that Curzon first broached to Kitchener the possibility of his coming to India as Commander-in-Chief. Curzon knew that there were senior Army people in India who would not like the appointment, but he was sure himself that Kitchener's record and prestige were such that he could ignore this criticism. For example, he telegraphed the Secretary of State: 'The Hon Sir E. Collen [formerly Military Member of the Council of India] hearing rumours of Kitchener's appointment to India, represents to me that, in his opinion, such a nomination without any knowledge of frontier, country, or army, would be disastrous at this juncture. He strongly urges claims of Palmer as possessing great experience, progressive ideas and anxiety for reform.' Curzon added, 'I feel it my duty to pass on their views,'[30] but he took no notice of them.

It may also have been that Curzon heard rumours about Kitchener's alleged homosexuality, fuelled by those in the Army who were jealous of his rapid promotion, and also of his predilection for surrounding himself with young men who were a law unto themselves. One of these was Girouard, who had built the railway in the Sudan, who was noted for his iconoclastic attitude, and had no hesitation in laughing at his superiors. He wore a monocle to correct a deficiency of his left eye and was a colourful man, quite ready to contradict Kitchener who normally inspired awe if not fear. In the course of time, Kitchener's group of young men came to be nicknamed 'the Boys', or 'the Band of Boys'. They formed a staff of sorts in the Sudan and then in the Boer War, when, as will be seen, Marker joined the group. Other members at various times were Douglas Haig, Birdwood, Hector MacDonald, Smith-Dorrien, Henry Rawlinson, Oswald Fitzgerald, Hubert Hamilton and, the most famous of all, Frank Maxwell, 'the Brat', who was a kind of court jester, although of a unique variety as he had won the Victoria Cross. He had been in the Bengal Lancers with Marker and Fitzgerald and was regarded as shallow and not very bright, and it is interesting to note, later, how Hamilton speaks slightingly of his abilities, while at the same time being clearly very fond of him. Perhaps he encouraged paternal feelings in his senior and brother officers. We shall see later how 'the Boys', led by Hamilton, played a major part in the campaign against Curzon.

Chapter Three

The Curzons and Marker

When the Curzons arrived in Bombay, the landing stage was carpeted in red, and as they drove through streets filled with crowds and lined by soldiers, with the golden umbrella, the symbol of sovereignty, held above their heads, bands along the route played *God Save the Queen* – or, as Curzon may have thought, *God Save the King*. That night there was a dinner for a hundred people and a reception for 1400 more, and this time the Curzons stood on a carpet of gold. The next morning the Viceregal train which was to take them to Calcutta, was painted white. On their arrival at the capital of the Indian Empire, they found that 200,000 people lined the route, and their escort to Government House was a squadron of cavalry, a company of infantry, and the Viceregal bodyguard of 120 lancers. The cannons sounded a salute.

Kedleston had been the model for Government House, but the latter was a meaner residence, although larger. It was built of painted brick, not stone; it was out of proportion, being three storeys high, and the grand rooms of Kedleston were reduced, at Government House, to somewhat stark and poorly furnished apartments. For instance the dome, one of the glories of Adam's splendid erection, was in India sealed off and used as a storage space for trunks. Mary told her parents, 'I never knew a more inconvenient house than this. The distances are perfectly awful between my room in one wing and the children's in another [the two children were then three years and six months old]. To get to them, I have to go along my corridor, through an immense drawing room, across a ballroom of several acres, through another huge drawing room, down another corridor, eventually to their day nursery.'[1] The kitchen was 200 yards from the nearest corner of the house, in a Calcutta backstreet, and all the food had to be carried across the garden in dishes concealed inside wooden boxes. The garden housed flying foxes, jackals and civet cats. Mary once woke to find a cat five foot long drinking the glass of milk beside her bed.

Curzon made changes, installing electric light and fans. But it was not until 1905 that a single bathroom with running water was installed; in the interim, if the Viceroy or his lady wanted a bath, one man heated the water, another fetched the tub, a third filled it, a fourth emptied it. The Curzons were, fortunately, only at the house from December till February each year, being at Simla (north of Delhi) for the hot season, or on tour. During the three months in Calcutta, it was traditional to hold a State evening party, a garden party, a fortnightly dance, two Levees for men only, a Drawing Room for ladies, official dinners of up to 120 people every Thursday, and smaller lunches and dinners several times a week. There were also many outside receptions and social events to attend. It is doubtful if the Royal Family in England today has as full a schedule – and Curzon was also expected to administer India, a land of 300 million souls, in his spare time.

The immense relief at leaving Calcutta engulfed them both. Mary liked Barrackpore, a large country house 1500 miles from Calcutta, which had been built by Wellesley and enlarged by Hastings as the Governor General's summer residence. The Curzons could travel there by steam launch from Simla in a few hours, landing in the garden 'by the shimmering tomb of Lady Canning',[2] and walk up the gravelled terrace, through gardens which contained a Gothic ruin, a mock-Georgian church, bamboo pergolas and a golf course.

Simla had been the summer retreat of the Viceroy, since 1829, and in 1864 it became an annual routine. A town grew up around the small rustic retreat producing what Nigel Nicolson describes as 'the domestic felicities of Surrey under the shadow of the Himalayas'.[3] Curzon first heard of what he considered its suburban infelicities from Mary, who wrote to him in Calcutta:

> You never saw a quainter spot, the houses slipping off the hills and clinging like barnacles to the hill-tops – and then our house! I kept

trying not to be disappointed. At first you only see the ugly side. Every rich male in America builds *exactly* such a house. The inside is nothing fine, but nice, and oh! Lincrusta you will find turn us grey! It looks at you with pomegranate and pineapple eyes from every wall. Dead-beat as I was, I tore around the ground floor with Irene [her daughter] and I missed the dining-room but thought the ballroom was certainly what it intended to be, and the sitting-room nice . . . There are plenty of little guest-rooms, tiny bedrooms with drawing-rooms out, and the plan of the house is in many ways absurd, and everything suggests cheapness and lack of space and air but you can't have palaces on mountain-tops, and a Minneapolis millionaire would revel in this, and we shall love it and make up our minds not to be fastidious. The fireplaces, corner-cabinets, papers, curtains and furniture reek of Maples [a London furniture store], but a look out of the window makes up for it all, and I can live on views for five years.

Curzon never grew to like Simla, writing, after three years, that 'One of its loathsome features is its sinister novelty, always having to begin again with each year a new set of idlers, gossips and liars. I do not think there is a more pitiable position in the world than that of the Viceroy and his wife set down for seven months amid that howling gang of jackals.'[4] He therefore much preferred to go to Naldera, a rather grand tented camp seven miles from Simla, where the family could eat out of doors, and Curzon could work in the open. Even Naldera had its disadvantages, because the dawn chorus woke Curzon shortly after he had got to sleep, and there were frequent calls to return to Simla for a round of official engagements, similar in style to those at Calcutta, but with a less interesting range of guests.

Throughout all this, Mary supported Curzon in a remarkable way, and there were many reports commenting on her regal bearing, despite the various illnesses to which she became prone, particularly, after childbirth, her headaches. She wrote to Brodrick: 'The lot of a Viceroy is one of absolute aloofness and everyone is in mortal fear of the august being. As a Yankee I don't understand it, but I manage to assume the necessary amount of awful respect for His X when we appear in public.'[5]

She told her father: 'George never does any social functions of any sort [in Simla] and they all devolve on me. I do them all. He has not gone out once since he came back, so I go through all the needlessly long list, bravely making his excuses and telling no one how he suffers and works . . . So I go out to races, parties, concerts, weddings, prize-givings, polo matches and Lord knows what. It is all work and very little pleasure . . .'[6] And to her mother, 'No one knows how I loathe Simla and its cruel climate. I never feel well here . . .'[7]

In March 1901 Mary Curzon went to England with her children for a six-month holiday. She sent Curzon three kinds of support. The first was gossip: 'Arthur [Balfour] is wizened, worried and exhausted; Henry Asquith obese and hopeful about his political future . . . with amorous interest in various people, and his reckless consumption of champagne, and his loss of that old granite sense of right and his abomination of the disreputable. He is said to be in love with Pamela Plowden and goes to her room at night. Can you conceive of anything more grotesque than Henry as a lover of girls?'[8]

Second, she sent him encouragement: 'If you will keep your health, as I pray God you will, you have the whole future of the Party in your hands. Arthur will not take the trouble to lead . . . No one has anything like your vigour, and there is an apathy in London about everything and everybody. It was illustrated by Arthur saying of bridge, which he now plays the whole time, "I like it because it saves the effort of conversation." Inertia seems to have attacked them all. They will need you to come back and wake them up . . . So don't wear out your big brain. Keep it young, and let it go to bed at 12.30. And angel, take sulphonal as little as possible.'[9]

And third, she sent him love: 'I want you, beloved Pappy, so desperately, and rebel against this separation. I do love you – but what is the use of a loving woman 4000 miles away from your arms? I do feel in my heart that in our life there is a sense of comradeship almost as great as love . . . Take [a woman] away from it all and give her a blank six months in search of health, and she must feel she has lost her anchorage.'[10]

There was one other function she fulfilled, and that was as an unofficial channel of communication from the ministers who were ultimately Curzon's masters. Both Lord George Hamilton, then Secretary of State for India, and St John Brodrick met her regularly when she was in England and wrote to her too. Here is an example of a letter from the former which not only suggests their intimacy, but also shows how Hamilton could avoid the unpleasantness which Brodrick was later to manufacture with such dexterity.

Dear Mary,

I fully appreciate your motives in writing to me, and am grateful to you for so writing. George in his last letter to me wrote strongly on what he described as the hostile and suspicious attitude of the [India] Council here, and gave what he considered to be a summary of their hostile actions. Now to be quite frank with you, I am sure that he would not have written his complaints in such forcible and disturbing language if he had not been unwell and suffering from overwork and the strain it imposes. I do not always agree with the decisions of the Council, and from my constant communication with George I can better appreciate his objects than those who only see his official despatches. But George has had his way more than any Viceroy of modern times, and when you consider the magnitude of his reforms, and the inevitable personal antagonisms that such changes arouse, it is marvellous that the instances in which he has been checked have been so few ... I have a deep and growing admiration for your husband's talents and force of character. But in public life you must give as well as take. The Council here are the final authority on all Indian matters. They are most distinguished and experienced men and they cannot be expected to acquiesce in everything suggested to them without comment or query.

Try to get George to give himself a little more rest and holiday. It is the isolation that aggravates his sense of being checked and unsupported, and the activity and power which makes him forgetful of the duties and responsibilities of mundane bodies such as the India Council ...

Women can at times mould and change the whole aspect of things. I know of nobody more capable of performing such a feminine duty than yourself.[11]

Curzon's period of office in India, which was the longest of any Viceroy before or after him, was infused with devotion to the concept of Empire. 'The Viceroy is expected to preserve temples, to keep the currency steady, to satisfy 3rd class passengers [on the railway], to patronise race meetings, to make Bombay and Calcutta each think that it is the capital city of India, and to purify the police.'[12] So Curzon half-jokingly told the Byculla Club on the eve of his farewell to India. His biographer Ronaldshay, who knew India well said: 'The history of British rule during this time is the story of Lord Curzon's daily life and work . . . For seven years he converted what had been a practically unchallenged bureaucracy into something closely resembling a benevolent autocracy . . . He dominated the Administration in a way which few, if any, of his predecessors had done, and which it will never again be given to any Governor General to do.'[13]

This stress on his administrative capabilities is fair, but his other strength, the mouldling of foreign affairs, must not be forgotten, although it was at the basis of his disagreement with the Cabinet at home. Only the briefest outline of his administrative activities is possible here. He set himself a programme of twelve great reforms which he believed would satisfy the country for the next twenty-five years. These included the reform of the administration system itself (about which his criticisms were pungent and unpopular) and the education system. He wanted to improve the continuity of office in the Civil Service, he moved the Punjab government offices from Simla and wished to change the Bengal system of local government and the municipal government of Calcutta. Major agricultural reforms included not only programmes to prevent famine and improvements in irrigation, but also fundamental changes in the structure of land ownership with reform of the debtor system by establishing Agricultural Co-operative Credit Societies. He introduced the Land Alienation Bill and set up Agricultural Institutes; and there was the Assam Labour bill. As regards the economic health of the country, he made changes in the currency system to stabilise the rupee; industry was overhauled, a Mines Bill was introduced and protection sought for the sugar industry. Measures to reduce corruption in the police were developed. He tried to improve transport systems, setting up a Railways Board and urging the extension of the system to the frontier (this was blocked). There were hundreds – probably thousands – of lesser measures. These ranged from the institution of an Imperial Library (he claimed that when he arrived pigeons were flying about amongst the books) to proposals for maintaining the breed of the Burmese pony. He wrote on the file: 'I agree. The Burma pony is a damned good little piece of stuff.'[14] Then there was his passionate interest in the archaeological remains of India, almost all of which he inspected personally.

He said, 'I regard the stately or beautiful or historic fabric of a
bygone age . . . as a priceless heirloom, to be tenderly and almost
religiously guarded.'[15] His programme of restoration was unparalleled.

To turn to his views on defence and foreign policy; he began to
introduce army reforms before Kitchener's arrival, and formed the
Indian Cadet Corps to involve the famililes of the native princes in
military affairs. He made a close examination of the frontier
problem, inaugurated a North West Frontier Province and
changed the system of frontier posts saying, 'I want to have all my
troops ready when we call on them for the big things instead of
being watched on the small things.'[16]

He tried hard to improve relations with Afghanistan (1902) with
Tibet (1903) and Persia and the Gulf (1903-4), where the Muscat
agreement was intended to protect Britain's interests. His policies
for partitioning Bengal will be touched on later. These policies
caused friction with the home government, but Curzon believed he
was right, telling Balfour, 'My only discredit will have been to be a
little previous.'[17] He is sometimes believed to have been a militant,
but it is fairer to say that he saw a strong hand to be necessary if
peace was to be maintained. He told his friend Selbourne that his
aim was to hold up the flag: 'For myself I am quite happy to be
doing it in my obscure way here. If, while the Empire is troubled
abroad, any man can keep India quiet (for you scarcely realise at
home what are the possible elements of commotion here) still more
if he can foster its loyalty and add to its contentment, he is
rendering a service which no one can measure.'[18]

Inevitably such a great reformer was highly unpopular with
those whom he stirred up, particularly when his manner was not
the most tactful. Balfour told Lady Elcho that friends coming back
from the Durbar, the lavish celebrations in Delhi marking the
coronation of Edward VII, thought 'George was the most unpopular Viceroy ever seen. Whether this was because his reforms are too
good or his manners too bad seems doubtful.'[19] And Gertrude Bell,
who was also at the Durbar, made a more careful if less witty
comment to her stepmother, 'I am gradually coming to the
conclusion that he is something of a great man, but there is no
doubt that he is extremely unpopular.' An officer at the Durbar
told her, 'You get sharp words and bad manners from him, but you

find that the thing that needs doing gets done without months of official letters, and yards of red tape . . . All the frontier people are fire and flame for him.'[20]

Curzon's aims have been summarized by Edwardes as seeking 'to bring to India a new sense of purpose or, rather, a sense of the old purpose writ large and expressed in the vocabulary of the new century . . . His aim was to overhaul the machine so that it might push India into the modern world. He believed in looking to the future . . . With this as the firm foundation of his policy, he tried to restore to British rule in India the creative energy of the first era of reform; he tried, too, to purge it of that contempt for even the best of Indian civilisation and culture which had corroded and helped to destroy the reformist purpose . . . The ideal of early reformers had been to make Indians into liberal Englishmen; Curzon wanted to make them into scientists and technicians [who] could transform India. Curzon's was a vision of startling modernity, and one which today underlies the whole philosophy of economic planning in the underdeveloped countries of the world. In this sense, he came to India too soon, but in the political sense he had arrived too late.'[21] He had, says this historian, the feelings of a national autocrat with no faith in democracy, but it was too late to ignore the demands of educated Indians or those of revivalist nationalism. Because he did so, Curzon failed to see the road which India would come to take.

Amongst the actors in the drama of Curzon's downfall, none had a more important role than Raymond Marker. It was Curzon of all people who first chose him to play a part. The facts are briefly outlined in this cutting from a Ceylon newspaper, which Marker sent home with pride to his sister Gertie.

The new Viceroy has chosen as one of his Aides-de-Camp Captain R. Marker, that popular officer of the Coldstreams, who was here for two years as ADC to Sir West Ridgeway, and was such an all round favourite – whether at viceregal functions or in the sporting fields of the Island . . . He has our warm congratulations, as also, we may say, has Lord Curzon.[22]

Marker was known to Curzon as a pleasant intelligent officer who had the added advantage of being an old Etonian. What he did not know was that Kitchener had twice tried to recruit Marker as one of his 'Boys' in Egypt, but Marker, who was ambitious, had preferred to go out to the East. It was the Kitchener connection which was to be the most significant, and, for Curzon, the fatal one.

Marker went out to India with the Curzons and we hear, in a characteristic letter to his sister how he 'spent the afternoon driving about [Marseilles] with Lady Curzon making various last purchases which she wanted for the nursery department chiefly'. Marker began to dislike Mary Curzon, although he was too polite and too diplomatic to show it, and he was also the butt of Curzon's criticism. The Viceroy described one such incident: 'This morning we had a coronation service in the Park at 9 a.m. My leg ached as if it would drop off, but of course I could not sit down alone in view of the crowd. At the last moment, that great, long-shanked idiot of an ADC suddenly without any instructions or warning darted through the crowd and placed in front of my seat the green baize foot stool. I could have killed him with rage.'[23]

These irritations were to turn into a more profound alienation, by the end of the first Viceregality. But from early 1899 both Curzon and his ADC were busy on tours of inspection and preparations for the new administration. There were the social duties in the month of January 1899, the number of meals served to visitors, guests and residents in Government House was over 3500. And there were the social pleasures – tennis, polo and the endless dinners. On 8th June 1899, Marker writes to sister Gertie 'on Monday we had the Eton dinner here, fifteen of us' and there was the amateur production of *The Liars* in which he played a leading role. His letters to Gertie, written regularly each week, and always filling exactly four sheets of paper of the same size, give no hint that he did not enjoy the hectic life at Government House, Calcutta, then in Simla, and on tour.

Nevertheless, he tried hard to be sent on service to the Boer War, the more particularly when he heard that his brother had been posted there. One reason was, that promotion in the Army was dependent on some active service, and Marker was ambitious for his career. In the latter part of 1900 his wish was fulfilled and he was posted to South Africa. He was engaged on general duties for a few months, and then, in March 1901 came the breakthrough. He wrote home: 'My dear Dad . . . Yesterday I received a telegram from Lord Kitchener asking me if I would like to be his ADC.

Needless to say I accepted, but I never had a greater surprise in my life as I never dreamt of his ever doing anything for me after I had twice gone elsewhere when I might have gone [to him] in Egypt, and in fact I never thought he would remember my existence. I rather surmise that it means he is going to India as C in C and needs an ADC who knows the ropes of the place. If this is so it will be rather a startler for my former Lord and Lady when they find me turning up again like a bad penny.'[24]

The first hint that Marker found Army life more congenial than being ADC to Curzon comes in a letter to Gertie about six weeks later, after he had joined Kitchener. 'Managing a bachelor establishment run by soldier servants is considerably easier than satisfying viceregal whims in the midst of luxury!'[25] He was not to return to India until the end of 1902.

Back in India, Curzon did not see his life as one of luxury. He wrote: 'It is supposed to be a mark of efficiency and even greatness to get your work done for you by other people. I frankly disagree. I say that if you want a thing done in a certain way, the only manner in which to be sure that it is done, is to do it yourself. I assert that every really great man from Caesar to Napoleon has been a master of detail.'[26] He often stayed at his desk most of the night, hardly ever dictating, even drafting acknowledgements and purely formal papers for others to sign. The fact was, as he discovered, his administrative back-up in India was inadequate. 'Applying the test of salaries, we find that there are only 1200 Official Employees in India drawing salaries of £800 or over a year; while of those drawing £60 or more a year which is going very low, we find there are only 6500 English Officials in India. In other words, there is but one English Official to every 46,000 natives.'[27]

Neither of the Curzons was physically well. George's back was a perpetual worry. 'I am very tired after a 15 mile ride on an elephant this morning; one of the most horrible forms of locomotion, and to anyone like myself, with a weak back, of actual pain, that you can well imagine.'[28]

Mary's problem was sick headaches which made the official life difficult to face. She told her mother: 'Yesterday I had one of my headaches, but in spite of it I went on board the Admiral's ship. George also, and I smiled when I could have sobbed with pain. When I came back [to Government House] I had to be carried upstairs. The Doctor thought I was mad to go out to dine. I nearly fainted twice dressing and nothing but my will carried me through. I thought at times I should die, as when I arrived I had to shake hands with 70 people, and after dinner talk with each lady. The only thing I ate was a water biscuit and a teaspoonful of brandy.'[29]

Curzon was in the middle of his celebrated row with the maharajas which erupted at the end of 1899. He was determined to show the princes 'where their duties lay'. At Gwalior, where he was to make a speech, he took the opportunity of reading them a lecture. This was not a tactful thing to do, not least of all because Gwalior himself was a model prince, practically running the state himself, whereas Curzon's target was 'absentee amusements'. The speech was regarded by Curzon as an example of his 'familiar technique of plain-speaking combined with perfect courtesy'[30] but others did not see it in that light. 'The Native Chief', he lectured them, 'has become an integral factor in the Imperial organization of India. He cannot therefore remain a frivolous or irresponsible despot. His figure should not merely be known on the polo-ground, or on the race-course, or in the European hotel [Monte Carlo was a happy hunting ground for some of them]. These may be his relaxations, and I do not say that they are not legitimate relaxations; but his real works, his princely duty, lies among his own people. By this standard shall I, at any rate, judge him.'[31]

Curzon himself was pleased with his speech which he described as 'a brilliant success . . . I regarded the occasion as one of some importance, and I pitched my remarks therefore in a high, but I hope not exasperated, key.'[32]

In due course, Curzon had his views embodied in a formal document, which was published in the *Government Gazette*, and was regarded therefore as a manifesto for the ruling chiefs. He concluded it by noting that 'the desire of a Prince to visit Europe could only be gratified by formal permission from the Government of India'[33], that is, by George Curzon himself. This circular met with much criticism, and not only in India. Mary summed it up thus: 'What George has not realised is that the people at home thought he had taken on too much power in the matter of the Maharajahs. The people of England look upon it as if the edict were published saying Dukes must not go to Monte Carlo to gamble!'[34]

Curzon was not satisfied with ticking-off the maharajahs. He also admonished the British officials in a circular which said, 'I must chide many of you for general slovenliness in matters of dress. Some officials have even been known to attend official functions in trousers! Kindly remember that knee breeches and stockings should always be worn on such occasions. You simply may not take refuge in the less dangerous but irregular trouser.'[35] This, and his actions against the army, caused him to be unpopular not only in India with the British, but at home, where relatives received letters full of rumours which they passed on to the newspapers. Curzon was particularly incensed at 'the ridiculous lies about Colonel Sandbach, my military secretary, who one paper said had resigned because I insisted that he stood behind my chair at mealtimes. What rot!'[36] Much later still, in 1905 a most unfortunate incident took place when Curzon presided, as Chancellor, over the seventh convocation of Calcutta University. He determined to speak about Truth in public life. 'Do not exaggerate, do not flatter; do not slander; do not impute; but turn naturally to truth as the magnet flies to the pole.' But what caused a furore was when he went on, 'I hope I am making no false or arrogant claim when I say that the highest ideal of truth is to a large extent a *Western* conception.' Of course, he did not mean to suggest that Europeans were universally truthful, or Asiatics less so – that would have been an insulting proposition. But he did not think, he said, that in the East, craftiness and diplomatic wile had been held in high repute. 'We may prove it by the common innuendo that lurks in the words "Oriental Diplomacy".'[37]

This convocation address to the Bengali students was taken as an attack upon the character and scriptures of the entire nation. '. . . a more unscrupulous and mendacious agitation it is impossible to conceive,' whined Curzon.

It is lack of self-criticism, an inability or a refusal to see other's points of view, particularly those regarded as intellectually inferior, that is the most unattractive of Curzon's characteristics, and which, coupled with the physical stiffness of a man held upright by a surgical corset, ensured that the epithet of 'superior' would stick to him for life.

Chapter Four

Curzon and the Army Wait for Kitchener

'Good Lord, the things that the soldiers do in this country nearly turn my hair gray.'[1] So Curzon thought after only a few months in India. The Army, for its part, was to feel much the same about him. This feeling arose partly from Curzon's inability to forgive weakness in others. As he wrote to Hamilton, then Secretary of State for India: 'If I were asked to sum up in a simple observation the most remarkable discovery that I have made since I came to India, I should unhesitatingly reply, the Frailty of Man.'[2] But the Army was a special case, the frailest of the frail. Soon after his arrival in India, a private of the Scots Fusiliers siezed a dumb-bell and battered a punkah coolie to death. (The punkah coolies, who had the task of mechanically cooling the soldiery, were constantly subject to physical abuse for not fanning energetically enough and Curzon was to alleviate their plight by introducing electric systems.) The soldier – after considerable delay – was brought to trial and promptly acquitted. Curzon vowed, 'I mean, as far as one man can do it, to efface this stain, while I am here!'[3]

He put his faith, therefore, in the reforms which Kitchener would be able to make if he came to India as Commander-in-Chief. As early as August 1900, he was complaining to Kitchener: 'I see absurd and uncontrolled expenditure, I observe a lack of method and system. I detect slackness and jobbery. And in some respects I lament a want of fibre and tone. Upon all these matters, I shall have many opportunities of speaking to you, and of suggesting abundant openings for your industry and force.'[4] Curzon did not then know that it would be 1903 before Kitchener finally reached India. Meanwhile, he had already taken matters into his own hands, and reaped a sour harvest as a result.

In Rangoon, the capital of Burma in 1899, a squad of West Kent Regiment soldiers emerged drunk from an illegal liquor den to find a Burmese woman on her way home to her family. They dragged her to a nearby open space and raped her in turn. Her screams brought other Burmese to the scene, and the soldiers made off. At the subsequent court martial, the native witnesses were frightened into withdrawing their evidence, and the accused soldiers were acquitted. The military authorities on the spot showed a disposition to hush the whole matter up, and the civil officials were apathetic.

The Viceroy heard about it and ordered a full summary of the evidence. He read it and was outraged. He was determined 'not only that the offenders should suffer the punishment which they deserved, but that it should be made manifest to the world that official laxity in bringing to account persons guilty of offences against the people of the land would not be tolerated'.[5] The culprits were dismissed from the army and sent back to England in disgrace. High military officers were severely censured and the colonel of the regiment was relieved of his command; the regiment was banished for two years to Aden, all leave was stopped and the sergeant major in charge of the squad reduced to the ranks. The civil officials were severely sentenced.

Curzon wrote to the Secretary of State: 'It may well be that . . . there will be a great outcry on the part of the Services against the apparent harshness of the verdict, and even a formidable attack upon myself.'[6] When he issued an order in Council expressing 'a sense of profound horror and repugnance'[7] he was indeed criticized. A writer in the *Contemporary Review* said it was written in terms quite out of proportion to the offence and 'Bore the unmistakeable imprint of His Excellency's attitude towards Sin.'[8]

The Army did not like Curzon's attitude but it is incorrect to assume, as some do, that he acted high-handedly and without due authority. Kitchener's biographer, Sir Philip Magnus, was particularly outraged but the official papers on the subject do not support this view. The Rangoon rape occurred in the middle of 1899 and

Curzon made his recommendations for action to the Home Government in October, and disciplined the civilians at that time. While Magnus says he acted with 'rashness and arrogant temper' punishing 'for reasons which the Army considered inadequate' the records show that many months later Curzon was still awaiting a decision from the War Office on the recommendation put to them by the Commander-in-Chief, India. From the documents it is quite clear that Curzon acted correctly and moderately.

Curzon believed, as he wrote to Godley (Undersecretary at the India Office) that, 'A great deal will depend on Kitchener. Hitherto I have not met one soldier in India who is on my side. The majority of them openly denounce me, and unblushingly proclaim the law of licence. I do not suppose that any Viceroy has ever had to bear the brunt of such a campaign of malice and slander . . . the majority of them look upon me as anathema.'[9]

Kitchener's biographer, Professor Cassar, who fails to understand Curzon, refers to all this by saying, 'He took no trouble to conceal his contempt for the military profession.'[10] This is untrue, and anyway Cassar's own description of the behaviour of the Indian Army makes it clear that Curzon was totally justified in his criticisms. Following the death of Lockhart the Commander-in-Chief in 1900, and pending Kitchener's arrival, which he thought would not be long delayed, Curzon continued to deal with Army matters, and as his Commander-in-Chief he chose the senior army officer in India, Sir Power Palmer, to act provisionally. Curzon still believed that the Army was in 'grave need of reform'[11] and he remained convinced that Kitchener had the reputation and personal characteristics necessary to reform it. In one of his regular letters to the Queen, on Indian policies, Curzon wrote that it was 'essential that a strong man in the prime of life should be appointed to succeed'.[12]

It is important to note that Curzon continued to support his candidature for Kitchener over a period of three years from 1899, even though various attempts were made to persuade him that Kitchener was unstable. For example, Lansdowne (Secretary of State, War Office) wrote in a private letter of 26th February 1899, 'I fear things are not going very smoothly in Egypt, and I don't like the reports which reach me about the temper of the Egyptian Army, and the way in which K of K is handling it. He has become altogether too '*Zaberdastic*' [sic] and Cromer has found it out.' This was surprisingly frank, as Lansdowne's wife Theresa was one of Kitchener's warmest admirers.

Rennell Rodd, an old friend of Curzon's wrote to him from Cairo, 'We have heard a rumour that something has been said to you about Kitchener which has given you a very bad impression . . . Kitchener has many faults – they are mostly on the surface and are easily detected. He does not inspire friendship or sympathy, he is not straight in the sense that, having had everyone's hand against him for so long, he tries to achieve his objects in roundabout ways, mistrusting the direct and open method; he is secretive and not frank; he drives men hard and is a regular Jew over a bargain – in the interests of the work in hand, not his own, for in his private life he is liberal and even lavish. He is almost wholly devoid of charm, though there is a certain attraction about him, which many of his officers feel the power of; he is even, if one must say it, unscrupulous in his methods and intolerant of any weakness or failure in others. I do not believe he will make a good C-in-C for the reasons above cited and because he does not appreciate the value of high moral standards in government.'[13] Despite these rather strong words, Rodd concluded that Kitchener 'remains a man of remarkable ability.'

It would be very surprising if Curzon himself had not heard criticisms of Kitchener because they were widespread. Cromer had complained about his harshness, and Esher who met him in 1899 wrote in his diaries that he was 'not attractive. None of the men who served with him were attracted to him.'[14] General Rawlinson said 'He is an absolute autocrat – does exactly what he pleases,'[15] and Sir Power Palmer called him 'Kitchener of Chaos' and predicted general disaster.[16] Indeed Curzon wrote, 'The news [of his appointment] will be received here with weeping and gnashing of teeth. The Indian soldiers generally will alternate . . . between rage and alarm.'[17]

Another factor – besides Kitchener's personality defects – had now entered into the equation, the disastrous turn which the Boer War had taken in its first year. The most respected and senior of British soldiers, Lord Roberts, had been thought too old for command there and Buller, a VC, had been sent in his place. But by the infamous Black Week of 9-17 December 1899, the situation was so bad that Roberts had to be persuaded to take over control and in the following February he arrived in South Africa. Kitchener was highly respected by Roberts at this time – although later he had reservations about him. Salisbury too, had a high regard for Kitchener after his Sudan victories, as well as a personal friendship developed by Kitchener during his visits to London; he had stayed at Hatfield during two months' leave in the summer of 1899. The upshot was that both Roberts and Salisbury insisted that Kitchener should at once be withdrawn from Egypt, that his potential posting to India should be deferred, and he should be sent to assist Roberts, as Chief-of-Staff, or, effectively, second-in-command. Kitchener made a rapid journey to Gibraltar and joined the boat on which Roberts was making his way to South Africa, so the two men were able to discuss plans and strategies on the long sea voyage. Curzon and India were for the time being forgotten. Though none of them knew it at the time, it was to be two years before Kitchener arrived in India.

What kind of man was Kitchener, flushed with his successes in the Sudan and in London society, as he went into the third chapter of military success which was further to enhance his fame? The artist Mortimer Menpes, famous later for his Durban paintings, went out to South Africa to sketch the man whose 'brick-red face reflects the desert, having been dyed by many suns until the skin becomes hard'. He looked the part of a ruler, said Menpes, but 'wherever he was he seemed isolated, as if an invisible wall hedged him about'. Menpes adds, 'You couldn't imagine anyone calling him by his Christian name. The man does not want to be popular, in fact he never thinks about it . . . There is not one atom of sentiment in him.'[18]

Menpes clearly admired Kitchener, yet he does not scruple to say: 'He does not mind how long he waits to gain his ends, but he is as relentless as fate . . . Kitchener makes demands on his friends, and if one of them ceased to be equal to those demands, from reasons of health or otherwise, he would disappear . . . Failures are guillotined without mercy . . . No officer in the British Army, not even Lord Roberts himself, is held in such mortal fear.' Menpes quotes an anecdote to support this – how Kitchener would 'charge into a club or hotel in Cape Town suddenly and with a few words would sweep off all the young staff officers idling away their time there, giving them the choice of starting back to England or be at the front within a few hours'.[19]

Before he left Egypt for South Africa, Lord Cromer had noted these same characteristics of ruthlessness and had written Kitchener a private letter which said, 'I have been at this sort of work for some forty years and know something about it. I think therefore you will not mind my speaking frankly to you. In the first place, pray encourage your subordinates to speak up and tell you when they do not agree with you. They are all too much inclined to be frightened of you . . .'[20] Cromer then advised Kitchener not to be dogmatic about non-essentials and to keep a sense of proportion, and, third, not to be secretive and to consult others.

Kitchener worked loyally with Roberts in South Africa but he made enemies amongst the Army commanders, initially for his inept conduct of the battle at Paardeberg which convinced many of them that he would pay any price in casualties for ultimate victory. The test came when in November 1900 Roberts returned to England. Kitchener's biographer Royle paints a damning picture of Kitchener's abilities and says that the arrival of that more capable and efficient soldier, Ian Hamilton, as his second-in-command proved a godsend to his reputation with the Army. He was also unpopular with civilians, particularly with Alfred Milner who was there as High Commissioner, and who said of him, 'Kitchener will be impossible for me to work with. I can see he is absolutely autocratic and observes no compact'[21] and later wrote to Joe Chamberlain, when the Liberals came to power, 'I think [Kitchener's policy] is fatally wrong and [his methods] are – no "think" about this – very crooked.'[22] Finally, Milner could hardly wait for Kitchener to leave South Africa.

There were several reasons for Milner's attitude. Kitchener relentlessly pursued Roberts' policy of burning farms, removing stock and crops, and he also set up the concentration camps which were to be such a black mark on British methods of pursuing the war. His plan was that 'all men, women and children, plus all stock and Kaffirs from the farms will be brought into camps administered by military officers and later by civilian authorities'.[23] The conditions in these camps, in which women and children died in tens of thousands, leaked out and caused a public outcry not only in South Africa but also in Britain. There were several investigations, including one by John Buchan, who said that the camps 'make my hair grey . . . they were terrible'.[24] But Kitchener ignored criticism. Indeed, when Milner went home on leave, and Kitchener took over his civilian role in addition to his Army duties, he became more autocratic than ever, and the death toll in the camps actually rose, particularly among children, one in three of whom died. The toll of casualties in the camps, mainly women and children, was three times the Boer casualties in the war.

Milner wrote a long letter to Chamberlain requesting Kitchener's removal from South Africa. 'He has probably more than the ordinary soldier's contempt for the opinion of a civilian, and although he is always perfectly friendly and ready to listen, I find discussion of these matters with him quite unprofitable. My view is this . . . It is impossible to guide a military dictator with strong views, and strong character. He can only conduct the war in his own way . . . If I may make a suggestion? Is it not possible to tell Kitchener that he is wanted in India, and that, as a *military business*, the command of the Army there is, at present, in the opinion of HMG, a bigger thing than continued chasing of Boer guerillas?'[25]

Kitchener himself became disillusioned. He wrote in a letter to Roberts, although he crossed it out, that he 'hated the whole country, the people, the whole thing, more every day'.[26] One of his generals, Sir Bindon Blood, said that strain 'has told severely on him, that he takes little exercise, that he is very thin, and of a bad colour, that there is probably something wrong with him'.[27] And Kitchener finally wrote to Brodrick at the War office: 'If you think that someone else would do better out here, I hope you will not hesitate for a moment in replacing me.' But this may have been Kitchener's 'resignation ploy' in operation.

Over this lengthy period while Kitchener was in South Africa, Curzon continued to negotiate actively for his appointment as Commander-in-Chief in India, and support came from others, although there were reservations, as Lord George Hamilton's telegram of 5th April 1900 shows:

> Kitchener is very unpopular; his manner is most ungracious and he is very inconsiderate in his treatment of subordinates.

and in a private letter to Lord Lansdowne,

Lord Roberts recommends Lord Kitchener for C-in-C. He makes this recommendation after some months personal contact. Remembering Omdurman and other similar incidents, I am averse to the suggestion, but before the matter is decided here, I should like your opinion.[28]

Curzon replied:

Your private telegram of yesterday. Lord Roberts' advice based upon double experience of Indian Army and African campaign, carries great weight. Lord Kitchener's appointment would be unpopular with Indian [Army] Officers, but would not be condemned by public opinion in India. I should be willing to work with him cordially; but would like to know if it is intended to make the new C-in-C a Member of Council, and who would be the new Military Member? For my purposes, a capable and fearless Military Member is even more important than an energetic C-in-C; but in the public interests, it is desirable that the two should not quarrel.[29]

Yet there was still doubt about Kitchener's suitability. Salisbury told Lansdowne, 'Her Majesty takes a very strong line against . . . and swears nothing shall induce her to consent to it, because his manners are too ferocious.'[30] By November 1900 Hamilton was telling Curzon: 'Lord Roberts will be back in the middle of December. I will then telegraph decision as to C-in-C but he could not take up his appointment until spring at the earliest.'[31] Yet in the following February Curzon is told: 'This question is discussed in my letter to you of February 7th and will be further examined in my letter of February 14th.'[32] By the end of February, Curzon was told that it had been agreed by Brodrick (at the War Office) and Lord Roberts that 'Sir Power Palmer is to stay until March 1902 and to be succeeded by Lord Kitchener'.[33] The proposal, though, had still to be submitted to the cabinet, and in March Hamilton was telling Curzon: 'Please keep very confidential the idea that Kitchener may become C-in-C next year. It is very undesirable that this should be known in South Africa at present.'[34]

Incidentally, it was just at this time that Kitchener, from South Africa, was arranging for the loan of fifty-seven officers from India without any reference to the Government of India, or to Lord George Hamilton who commented, 'This is clearly irregular and should be stopped.'[35] It was typical of conduct to come.

Over all this time, Curzon was writing letters to Kitchener, saying how pleased he would be to have him in India, but the letters were delayed by the subsequent news holding up Kitchener's appointment. For example, in August 1900: 'I know well from our conversations before I left England how greatly set your heart has been on Indian service ... [I write] to assure you of my support in what you will find in many respects a difficult venture, and to write to you as a personal friend a few lines upon the task which lies before you . . .' After doing so, Curzon adds, 'You will find in myself a Viceroy who has perhaps a greater excuse than some of his predecessors for interesting himself in military questions, seeing that I know something of the Frontier (which is the principal military interest of India) and that I take its management [i.e. The Frontiers] exclusively into my own charge. I hope not to give you much scope for military activity there (though with so ticklish a problem one never dares prophesy) but the main guarantee for peace is a close and cordial co-operation between the civil and military authorities. I will not conceal from you that there are many respects in which army administration in India seems to me capable of great reform and in regard to which I look forward with much confidence to your vast energy and great experience. Its absurd and uncontrolled expenditure . . . I detect slackness and jobbery, and in some respects I lament a want of fibre and tone.'[36]

How Kitchener must have bridled at the words 'I take its management exclusively into my own charge' but when he received the letter it was accompanied by another, written at the end of March 1901, six months later. Curzon then added, 'I regard military administration in India as bound up in interminable writing and over-centralisation from which I have been doing my best to relieve it. I believe it is nothing like so bad here as it is at home, but it is in my opinion bad enough. Another blemish here (I say it in the strictest confidence) is the mild jobbery in which all the great military panjandrums indulge. Each one rolls the log of the other. Now I set my face against this like a flint, for in the last resort the Viceroy can stop anything.'

Curzon concluded the letter: 'The co-operation of the Viceroy and the C-in-C is the only preventative of these evils that I have described, and I can honestly say that I shall look forward with keen anticipation and bright hopes to your appearance.'[37] But this was to be further and further delayed.

As we shall see in the next chapter, the man who, writing nearly forty years later, used hindsight to take the credit for Kitchener's delayed arrival in India was none other than Curzon's schoolboy friend, Brodrick. He then claimed that he had 'done all in my power to prevent Kitchener going till Curzon had left India.'[38] This, as we shall discover, was moonshine. One of Kitchener's biographers Cassar ignores Brodrick's claim and merely implies that Curzon wanted Kitchener in India at all costs, regardless of his need for home leave, after the rigours of South Africa. The records do not support this version of events, any more than Brodrick's. They show that from late in 1900 onwards, Curzon and Lord George Hamilton, the Secretary of State, were both engaged in trying to get Kitchener to India as soon as possible.

Curzon had a confidential talk with Blood (on Kitchener's staff in South Africa) in December 1901, who, when they met in Simla, put it to the Viceroy that while Kitchener could be released from South Africa in February or March 1902 he needed a period of home leave. Curzon wrote to Kitchener unequivocally accepting this: 'He [Blood] expressed a strong opinion that you would be the better for a new month's holiday at home, an opinion with which I strongly agreed.'[39] But when he wrote in March 1902, Curzon felt bound to say, 'The only doubts I begin to entertain is whether we shall see you at all . . . although I hope to see you lead the troops at the great Imperial Durbar at Delhi on January 1st, 1903, I feel no sort of confidence.'[40]

Kitchener did not acknowledge these letters, and although Curzon had struggled to get him to India before the hot season, he wrote: 'Who in the world can begrudge you your very modest holiday. I would only like it if I had the requisite authority to impose upon you the duty of utilising it in order to bring out a chatelaine to Snowden (Kitchener's residence in Calcutta).' Curzon continued: 'The Viceroy and C-in-C are brought a good deal in contact with each other . . . You may rely on me to do all in my power to make your path smooth.'[41]

Kitchener finally replied in October: 'My best salaams to Lady Curzon and to his Excellency. I am looking forward with great pleasure to serving under him in India.'[42] So much for the insinuations by Kitchener's biographers that Curzon wanted to get his new Commander-in-Chief to India regardless of his need for a holiday. Meanwhile, Curzon himself had run into further trouble with the Army, and, as he wrote to Kitchener, there was 'a tendency on the part of the military authorities, if anything unpopular is done, to which they have themselves consented, or which may even have emanated from them in the first place, to shrug their shoulders and shift the burden on to those of the masterful Viceroy'.[43] This trouble was the case of the 9th Lancers.

The 9th Lancers was one of the smartest and most celebrated regiments in the Indian Army, and its officers had powerful connections at home. On the night they arrived back from South Africa, 9th April 1902, they held a party with the Black Watch at which a native cook was beaten up by two troopers. He died nine days later. A court of enquiry of officers of the regiment said that they were unable to identify the culprit. A week later another coolie was murdered, supposedly by the regiment. A relative of the dead man wrote to Curzon about it two months later. Curzon spoke out harshly: 'I will not be party to any of the scandalous hushing up of bad cases . . . or to the theory that a white man may kick or batter a black man to death with immunity because he is only a "damned nigger".'[44] He decided, with the agreement of the Commander-in-Chief, since no culprit had been found, to punish the whole regiment. All men on leave in India were recalled, and allowed no more leave for six months. As a result, Curzon was freely called 'a nigger lover' in the messes and clubs. As will be seen, the case of the 9th Lancers did not end there. Curzon realised what he had done, writing: 'Anyone who dares to touch a crack regiment of the British Army – even though it contains two murderers – is looked upon as though he has laid hands on the Ark of the Covenant.'[45]

He therefore anxiously awaited Kitchener, saying, 'As soon as I meet Kitchener, I shall have a very frank interchange of opinion with him . . . The way in which I have been made the scapegoat of the sins and blindness of the Army in India is a crying scandal. I have borne it without a word, though at any moment I have had it in my power by simply stating the facts to hold the Army and its officers up to public opprobrium. But their honour has been dearer to me than to themselves and for nearly four years I have borne such a weight of calumny and misrepresentation such as no one can imagine.'[46]

Chapter Five

Curzon and Brodrick

As the winter morning sun trickled through the windows of Downing Street, Arthur Balfour lay in bed, as was his habit each morning, wondering which letters, if any, he should attend to. His fingers toyed with several from his friend Curzon, received some months before, and he came to the conclusion that despite his dislike of correspondence of any kind, something must be said to Dear George. Three and a half years of Curzon's term of five years as Viceroy had passed before Balfour became head of the Government in the summer of 1902 and it was not until 12th December that year that he came round to answering Curzon's letter of congratulations received on his own appointment, when Curzon had said, 'You have not a more faithful or devoted henchman anywhere than myself.'[1] Balfour wrote:

My dear George,
Truly I am severely punished for the dilatory manner in which I carry on my private correspondence! Had I written to you, as week by week I intended to do for these many years, [*sic*, months?] in answer to your delightful letter, I should not now find myself in the position of having to make my first epistolary communication to you on a subject respecting which we unfortunately disagree. But I am not going to argue it, I am only going to dogmatise. I cannot really assent to your view that because the position of the Sovereign was (in your view) affected by the course to be taken at the Durbar in reference to taxation, you were therefore justified in carrying on an independent correspondence on a point of high policy without the knowledge or assent of your colleagues ... [Curzon had written

direct to the King]. However, I regard all this as ancient history. What is not ancient history is our admiration for your great services as Indian administrator. You seem to think that you are injured whenever you do not get exactly your own way! But which of us gets exactly his own way? Certainly not the P.M. Certainly not any of his Cabinet colleagues. We all suffer the common lot of those who, having to work with others, are sometimes over-ruled by them. I doubt whether any of your predecessors have ever received so large a measure of confidence from either the S. of S. or the Home Government. I am ready to add that probably none have ever deserved that confidence more; but do not let any of us forget that there cannot be a greater mistake committed by a British statesman than to interpret any difference of opinion as a personal slight, or as indicating any want of confidence among colleagues.

Dear George, I do assure you that no one has marked with greater pride or greater pleasure your triumphant progress, and the admirable courage, energy and sagacity with which you have grappled with the immense difficulties of your task, than your old friend and colleague.

I have differed from you on this point or that point; I may have (who knows) to differ from you on others. But nothing will for a moment diminish either the warmth of friendship or the enthusiasm of my admiration.

yours ever,

A.J.B.[2]

Curzon replied soothingly that 'it was the greatest pleasure to see your handwriting again'.[3] The complaint about Curzon's written tone was repeated three months later in a PS to a letter about Curzon's proposal that he should stay on for a second term after the end of 1903 when the Viceroyalty expired.

There can be no doubt in my judgement, that it would be of great advantage to Indian administration that your work there should not be brought to a summary conclusion at the end of this year. You have proved yourself not only a great administrator, but a great reformer, and in the latter capacity you have sown much valuable seed, the early stages of whose growth it is of great importance that you should have an opportunity of superintending. Your plan however is not without difficulties. (1) the uncertain future of the Government, (2) the parliamentary difficulties have been occasioned as much by matters personal to St John B [Brodrick] as by the merits of demerits of his military policy.

P.S. George Hamilton — by-the-way — has shown me a private letter of yours in which quite a surprising number of pungent adjectives are applied to the Asiatic Policy of the Government. If anything were to be gained by it, I suppose I could find some not less pungent method of describing the alternatives proposed from India. This however is hardly worthwhile. I only mention the subject as an additional ground for thinking that much would be gained by a few hours of conversation.[4]

By June, they had solved the problem of Curzon's return for leave (in his absence Ampthill, the Governor of Madras, would act as Viceroy) and the second term of office to follow, but they had not solved the problem of the 'questions of style' in Curzon's letters, and Balfour returned to the point once more:

So much for business. Now I am going to enter a very humble protest against your epistolary style! You and I are old and devoted friends, why should you adopt towards me the tone of your last communication? I mean your letter of April 30th. In it you speak with apparent indignation of my having described the scheme for prolonging your Viceroyalty as "your plan" and "your suggestion". Why of course it was your plan and your suggestion. Look back at your letter of Feb. 5th, in which it was first broached. But why should it not be your plan? I think it is a very good one, and am certain that the person responsible for it had no reason to be ashamed of his handiwork, and no one thinks that your desire to stay on (and whatever you may say, it is and ought to be, your desire) is prompted by any motive whatever except the good of India . . . But why should the man who volunteers upon a service of difficulty, if not of danger, quarrel with those who describe the enterprise as "his plan"? You have often reproached my slackness as a correspondent and I plead guilty to the charge. I admit that I always take up my pen with the utmost reluctance and lay it down with a sigh of satisfaction. But I sometimes think that the weakness has its good side. You do not share it; but are you not sometimes tempted to use your extraordinary readiness of composition in a way which does not facilitate the co-operation of those who should find it specially easy to work together, since they are not only colleagues but life-long friends? Differences of opinion among these there must occasionally be. It is much more difficult to conciliate those differences by correspondence than by speech. Even if we were sitting together round a Cabinet table we might not absolutely agree; still more difficult is absolute agreement when we are separated by thousands of miles. But do remember that so far as the Cabinet is concerned you have had an absolutely free hand in Indian administration, that we have admired you and supported you through your most honourable labours, and that if we have differed and perhaps still differ about certain questions of foreign policy, this is neither due to weakness of purpose on our part nor to any want of regard for you.

Well, this is a long screed from one who is no letter writer; but (if things go awry) it may be the last I shall address to you as P.M. Hence perhaps its abnormal proportions. But whatever the fortunes of the minority or the Party, at all events you have the satisfaction of knowing that your Indian administration has added great lustre to a Government which I believe will be thought in time to come to have done much for the country; and as this is so, why should I wrangle with you over questions of style.

My dear George, take care of your health,
    and, Believe me,
        yours ever,
            Arthur James Balfour[5]

Curzon answered instantly.

My dear Arthur,
    I am much obliged for your letter of June 18. I am sorry that you were offended with the style of my letter of April 30. When I wrote it – and I did not write it in a hurry, for I kept yours for ten days – I was hurt not at the style but at the tone of yours to which it was a reply, and which seemed to treat me grudgingly. I thought that I was submitting to a sacrifice – and I think that if you had five years of the strain in India you would think so too . . . Your letter seemed to imply that the Govt. were doing me a great favour . . . I dare say I did you a complete injustice; but honestly this was in my mind and it coloured my answer.

As regards correspondence in general, I write freely to the Sec. of State and other friends. I do not know how they use my letters. Sometimes I know that things that I never meant to be seen by anyone else have been shown and have done harm. I am very defenceless in this respect, but I think it a sound rule never to be offended at anything in a letter which one was not meant to see . . .

I think you assume too readily that because in the discharge of my duty I sometimes put forward advice in respect of Foreign Affairs, which is not accepted by the Cabinet at home, therefore I am seriously offended, or there is a grave discrepancy between our respective principles and points of view . . .

I have another point of view. I think it the duty of Ambassadors, Proconsuls, Governors, etc. to be a little ahead of the Governments whom they advise. The inclination of the latter is always to go slow, sometimes unnecessarily slow. The way has to be shown to them, even if they decide perhaps quite rightly not to take it . . .

Some of the things that I have put forward and that you have rejected – e.g. Tibet – will of a surety come; and my only discredit will have been to be a little previous.

Apart from these small differences, my dear Arthur, which are the incidents of public life, I have never been indifferent to the support which has on many occasions been given to me by the Government, and which I am confident that, within reason, I may always be hopeful of receiving from yourself.

yours ever

Curzon[6]

Balfour was one of Curzon's oldest friends (although there was a difference of ten years in their ages), and perhaps he was the only living Englishman whose mental abilities Curzon fully respected. Birkenhead said of Balfour that he had the finest brain that had been applied to politics in his time. Furthermore, there was a gentleness about him which was very appealing. His biographer Kenneth Young writes: 'There *was* a feminine streak in his character; at Cambridge where . . . he received the nickname "Pretty Fanny", later still, when he first entered the House of Commons, observers thought there was about him "a distinct flavour of effeminancy". Nor did he ever marry. But there was never any suggestion of the homosexual about Balfour; his heterosexual proclivities may have been low-powered, but they were certainly present. He was not a man who needed to assert his masculinity to prove that it existed; but neither did it occur to him to conceal the "femininity" which is part of every masculine character, as a certain masculinity is part of the female.'[7]

Curzon's verbal attacks tended to be directed not at Balfour but at those he considered intellectually below him – Godley and later Brodrick were regular targets. In the case of the latter, there was another element which entered into the feelings Curzon entertained towards him. The competitive instinct in some men can override almost every other emotion, and this was true in Curzon's case. He had always felt competitive towards Brodrick who, when they met at Eton in 1874, was higher up the school and who, when Curzon reached Oxford, was already President of the Union. Fortunately for him, he only achieved a second class degree, or Curzon, who did likewise, would never have forgiven him. Brodrick for his part knew at once that he had met in Curzon someone infinitely superior, and this was a judgement which met with Curzon's approval – he recognised it and used it. Curzon was, therefore, amazed when in 1898 the Government appointed Brodrick to be Undersecretary of State at the Foreign Office, a position which Curzon himself had held with distinction until his appointment as Viceroy. He knew that Brodrick could not do the job competently, and lost no opportunity of showing this when stories of his failure began to reach him in India.

In 1900 Brodrick was moved back to the War Office which was considered a safe place, as he had been Financial Secretary there fifteen years before, rising to Undersecretary in 1895. But the fact is that as Secretary of State, he was well above his level of competence and it was recognised that he would have to be moved again. One of the main charges made against him was his tactlessness and his habit of making gaffes for which he was much renowned amongst 'the Souls'. Rose in his biography of Curzon lists several of these. His other faults were listed in a letter from Curzon's old friend 'Rom' McDonnell written to Curzon in October 1901: 'St John is working like a horse and I think is very much better than in August when I found him very shaky and nervous – no wonder, poor old boy. I do no think he leaves enough to others, which is a bad thing – it is of no use to keep a pig and do all the squealing yourself. I am always afraid lest this passion for seeing and doing everything will not break him down. He exhibits however occasionally a most infernal impetuosity which I fear will land him in trouble some day: I don't know if you ever remarked this in him. It has become much more apparent lately.'[8]

In early August 1902 Curzon received a letter from his friend Sir Clinton Dawkins, containing the astonishing news that the Cabinet was considering sending Brodrick to India to replace him as

Viceroy, while he, Curzon, would take over at the War Office where Brodrick was proving a fumbler. In early 1903 Lord Knollys (the King's secretary) sent him the same story. Curzon wrote privately to Lord George Hamilton at the India Office asking for private opinion about Brodrick's competence (observing that his tactlessness and clumsiness even 'his dearest friends know to be ephemeral'[9]) and the reply he received, dated February 13th, was brutally frank: 'Brodrick's deafness has greatly grown upon him and that, combined with a certain tactlessness, prevents him from understanding the gist of personal conversations, and to this physical failing rather than anything else may be attributed the very unjust opinion which, I fear, normally prevails concerning him.'[10]

Hamilton wrote again: 'He is so deaf that he does not hear other people's opinions, and he is in addition very self-opinionated himself.'[11] Armed with this negative opinion, Curzon decided to give Hamilton his frank opinion on the Viceroy question. It should be noted that letters took about three weeks to reach their destinations. He wrote: '[I hear] from an authoritative quarter in England . . . that the idea has seriously been entertained of sending Brodrick out as my successor to India next year, because he is thought to have failed at home, and of bringing me back to clean up the mess he is supposed to have left . . . My answer would be No No A Thousand Times No.'[12]

There were those in London who would have agreed with him. Balfour's Private Secretary, Jack Sandars, said Brodrick 'had unhappy genius for producing strained situations'; but Curzon was incensed not only with the absurd suggestion that someone as intellectually inferior as Brodrick should take over from him in India, but that he himself should make a move which would be, at best, sideways. However, the reply from Hamilton was reassuring: 'Brodrick has ridden his horses to a standstill . . . I do not believe it would be politically safe to put him in a position of such unique authority as the Viceroy of India exercises, and where his discretion would be so unfettered. Therefore, from every point of view, I consider it would be for the advantage of India that you should stop on.'[13]

Other opinions support the views that Brodrick was actually incompetent. Miss Emily Hobhouse, who interviewed him about

concentration camps in June 1901 told her brother she had
obtained a strong impression of 'his gentlemanly incompetence –
slippery and pleasant, mediocre and agreeable, ready to listen,
ready also to drift'.[14] And Curzon's biographer Dilks says Brodrick
was *persona ingratissima* with the King.

Kitchener, who was in close correspondence with Brodrick
throughout the South African war, also spoke slightingly about
him. And even the Dictionary of National Biography says, 'To the
general public his most notable reform was the introduction of a
new forage cap for the Brigade of Guards, which was in no way his,
but which came to be known by his name.' He adds that he failed to
'impress his personality upon the country'.[15]

In another letter from Sir Schomberg McDonnell, Curzon was
told that the Government was in disarray and that 'the phenomen-
al feature of the whole business, is the hatred of St John: granted
that he is tactless and rude, and that the indecent rejoicing over his
second marriage has shocked many of his friends – that does not
account for the malignity with which he is regarded by his own
party in the House of Commons; men cannot be got to admit now
that he was even able; and in his office he is even more detested
than in the House. It is a curious business and not quite compre-
hensible . . . George Hamilton is quite stale; Gerald Balfour is quite
useless at the Board of Trade . . . Eddy Stanley is a standing joke at
the War office . . . I don't think my dear old George that you will
have much difficulty in running into your own place when you
return; already people think of you as the next PM. You have a
reputation for *strength* which is everything now; at this moment the
public chooses to think that Arthur Balfour is weak and not
hardworking, whence most of the difficulties, *outside* the House,
arise . . . We hear that you are to have an extension; and if your
health will stand it I hope it is true: it will be time enough if you can
come home when the General Election takes place . . .'[16]

And in a later letter written in the autumn, McDonnell says,
'The principal point of interest in the construction of the Ministry
is the position of St John. He will have to leave the War Office . . .
and is almost sure to go to the India Office . . . I wish you were here
to take the Colonies.'[17]

Balfour's biographer, Kenneth Young, writes of 'the raging
unpopularity of Brodrick'[18] at the War Office. This was partly due

to the Elgin report revealing inefficiency and even corruption during his period of office. On 3rd February 1903, Balfour writes to Lady Elcho, 'Never before has his stock been so low. I really do not think it is his fault, but whether his fault or not, his unpopularity now is the most serious menace to the Government . . . It naturally depressed the poor old boy and my thoughts continually referred to 1900, and the sleepless nights which Hilda [Brodrick's then wife] endured, through fears that St John would not be Secretary of State for War! NB *Never* wish for anything over much!'[19] And so it became accepted that it was safer to move St John on to the India Office, particularly as his long-standing friendship with Curzon would, it was suggested, be an advantage. The opposite proved to be the case.

One of the most serious attacks on Brodrick's character was made in Peter Eleming's book *Bayonets to Lhasa* (1961) in which he gave his view of Brodrick as 'shabby', 'spiteful', 'stuffy', 'inept', 'callow', and 'a deceiver'. Before examining the Lhasa incident, and Brodrick's part in it, we may first turn to what Brodrick – or Lord Midleton as he had by then become – wrote about his relations with Curzon and Kitchener in 1939. 'I took over the India Office from Lord George Hamilton in October 1903, with very serious misgivings,'[20] he claims. No prior independent evidence for this exists; indeed after his feeble efforts at the War Office he was lucky to be moved to the India Office as, according to Curzon's biographer David Dilks, the King indicated he must leave the War Office. But Brodrick naturally makes no mention of his failure. 'I was leaving an office in which I had spent twelve years in various capacities,' he continues, 'which I thoroughly understood, for duties which were novel. But, apart from this, the attitude of George Curzon since he went to India five years before had become increasingly trying to his friends.'[21] This is putting too strong an emphasis on the complaints Balfour had made, but to Brodrick, attempting thirty-five years later to justify his treachery to his friend, it is an essential part of the story that it should be Curzon, not he, who has abandoned his friends.

Brodrick goes on to paint a glowing portrait of Curzon and claims, 'I had been his confidante, and he had consulted me at almost every great step of his life. Indeed, he wrote to me before he went to India, "you have been the good genius of my life for twenty years!" There was no question of jealousy or competition, as our political paths were wholly different. But I was very conscious that while in India he had drifted away from all of us.'[22] It must be clearly said that there is no evidence whatever that Brodrick was conscious of such a drift at the time – none in Brodrick's own letters, none in the letters of friends, none in their conversations with Curzon's wife. And since they urged him to return home to take up his place in politics there, to be, eventually, the leader of his party, is it likely that they would do so, if they were feeling estranged?

But Brodrick, oblivious of the facts of the case at the time, rushes on: 'Writing after thirty-five years' interval,' he says, 'it is impossible for me to allude to Curzon's period of office in India and the unhappy termination of it, without giving a full account of the difficulties which arose between him and the Home Government, as the issue has some historical importance. Even if I desired to leave so unpleasant a subject where, so far as the public was concerned at the time, it stood, I am bound by a pledge given ten or twelve years ago to Balfour [that is, in 1926 or 1928] who was Prime Minister during Curzon's Viceroyalty that, since he was himself unable to complete his autobiography, I would take care *to give to the public whatever was requisite to make clear the position of his Government in these proceedings*.'[23] [my itals]

This pledge – if pledge it was – appears to have been recorded or noted, because Balfour's biographer, Kenneth Young, mentions such an agreement, but Brodrick's motives could be put down to a desire to clear his own name at the expense of Curzon and of Balfour, both dead.

'In deference to Balfour's wish, some years ago,' claims Brodrick, 'I wrote a considered account, which was reviewed by the then head of the India Office and accepted in every respect by Balfour himself, and was printed in the India Office as a State Paper.'[24]

In a letter to *The Times* when his memoirs were challenged by Younghusband, leader of the ill-fated expedition to Tibet in 1904, Brodrick said that what he had written was based on 'an official record, drawn up and printed, at Lord Balfour's instance, after careful review of the correspondence by Indian officials, in case at any time doubt should arise as to the action of his cabinet.'[25]

His memoirs continue: 'The case for a considered statement now

– apart from the fact that after thirty-four years and the interposition of the Great War, there can be no international trouble through these revelations – is emphasized by the account given of these Indian difficulties in the *Dictionary of National Biography* [by Harold Nicolson] and by the appearance of Winston Churchill's brilliant work, *Great Contemporaries*. His comments which, though I must challenge them, he was justly entitled to make on the facts before him, bring out the very danger that Balfour foresaw, namely the belief that Curzon's removal had been due to one issue alone.'[26]

This State Paper, dated May 1926, is entitled *Relations of Lord Curzon as Viceroy of India with the British Government 1902-5* and is according to Brodrick franked 'seen and approved by the Earl of Balfour, June 1926'. It appears to have been neither seen nor approved by anyone else. This curious piece of special pleading, then, forms the basis of the charges Brodrick was then about to make, although sadly for him, it is impossible to accept the accuracy of a State Paper which set out the 'facts' so clearly according to him.

Churchill had written 'there is I believe at this distance of time no question that Curzon was right . . . In the climax, the Government – of Curzon's own friends – and the Secretary of State, Mr Brodrick, almost his best friend, pronounced against him, and pronounced against him in error.'[27] Churchill's book, published in 1937, must have greatly rankled Brodrick, and Brodrick is now telling us that firstly his own views of the facts were printed in 1926 (just after Curzon's death) as a State Paper, secondly Churchill did not know the facts when he wrote *Great Contemporaries* in 1937, and thirdly, all the historians and biographers have been at fault in believing that Curzon resigned over the Kitchener affair whereas, says Brodrick, he was removed on many issues, not this one alone.

Brodrick sets about establishing that Curzon's health 'affected his judgement and prejudiced his mentality in all personal matters . . . Short of profligacy or alcoholism, I do not think any man could have done more than he did to shatter his health. He broke all known rules and derided advice.' Brodrick produces amazing evidence for this. 'I never stayed with him in a country house without being worn out by late, serious and intimate talk.' This disease, says Brodrick, 'instead of passing away, as it did with others, got a firm hold.'[28] What the disease was, and which other politicians had it, is not specified in this strange accusation. Is Brodrick talking here only about Curzon's back? It is not clear.

'After he joined the Government in 1891 things got worse, and he had so bad a collapse in 1898, just after he had been appointed to the Indian Viceroyalty, that Balfour told me he and Lord Salisbury were considering whether the appointment could be carried out. I persuaded Balfour to wait a few days. He then called at Carlton Terrace, and found the object of his solicitude had got up and was in the neighbouring house, which he had just bought, engaged in transferring the wine to the bins of his new dwelling with his own hands.'[29] What kind of impression is Brodrick trying to make here, manufacturing facts to suit his story? The truth is well known, that Curzon was asked to obtain a medical opinion as to whether he was fit to go to India, did so, and was given a clean bill by the specialists (see p. 30). Brodrick goes on to say that Curzon rejected his advice to take things easy, even after Lady Curzon had asked him to intervene, with the result that 'the tension of nerves and absence of consideration for others which resulted from it, prevented his ever getting the best service from those under him and cancelled his magnetism'.[30]

Brodrick now turns away from this attempt to establish that Curzon was sick, to reveal 'new matter to those outside Balfour's Government who valued him [Curzon] most; they [the new facts] at least from a record of most earnest efforts by intimate friends and admirers to save him from himself as far as their duty to the country made it possible'.[31] The implication clearly is that Brodrick knew his patriotic duty while Curzon did not. Brodrick goes on to allege: 'In the India Office, and especially in the Council of India in Whitehall, in which was centred an unrivalled array of past administrative experience, there was anxiety at the contempt which he showed for any advice or check, however legitimate, from any quarter, and at his disposition to secure the appointment of men entirely subservient to his views on his own Council.'[32]

There are two charges here. The first, that Curzon was contemptuous of advice; this, if true, would be revealed in the correspondence between the Viceroy and Lord George Hamilton, Brodrick's predecessor as Secretary of State, and particularly in the private correspondence between them. Anyone reading the steady stream of letters which passed between Hamilton and Curzon will find no contemptuous rejection of advice. Curzon often disagreed with points of policy, but was loyal in carrying them out if the decision went against him. And, when Curzon went into the wilderness in 1906, Hamilton remained one of his most steady supporters. Hamilton, after Curzon's downfall, wrote to him: 'Our relations were, I think, as little controversial as was possible, considering the difference of our surroundings and temperament. It will always be one of the retrospective pleasures of my life to look back upon our co-operation in India's welfare.'[33] It is however true that Curzon was contemptuous of advice from Brodrick, who he said knew nothing of India. The second charge, that Curzon employed sycophants, is also nonsense. He had argued with Ampthill, but agreed that he should go to the Council of India, the governing body, as Viceroy in his absence. He did not get sycophantic behaviour from Elles, the Military Member, or Ibbotson, another Council Member, even though, it is true, his strong intellectual powers were liable to render his critics less vocal than they might have been with a smaller man.

Brodrick then goes into detail about the disagreement between Curzon and the Government over the matter of the former's wish to have the King announce a remission of taxes at the time of the Durbar in January 1903. Following this, he continues, 'the Cabinet had found it necessary to check the aggressiveness of his policy both as regards Tibet and Afghanistan.'[34] Dealing with the latter first, Brodrick with customary hindsight refers to Curzon's unfortunate 'special obsession as to the advance of Russia in Central Asia [which] marred his judgement'.[35] But if this was an unfortunate obsession, it was shared by other men of distinction including Brodrick's own hero, Kitchener, and by Balfour.

It is true that Brodrick believed at this time that Curzon was unpopular with the Cabinet, because in the autumn of 1902 he warned Curzon that if he elected to resign on the issue of the Durbar (the Government wanted the Indian Government to foot the expenses for the British guests) the Cabinet would not press him to stay. This advice was not wanted and Curzon furiously told Mary, 'Observe the amicable way in which he informs me that all the Cabinet, including himself (a humble participator) were quite prepared to throw me overboard. What a light it throws on human nature and upon friendship.'[36] This was perhaps the first rift in the lute, and Curzon signalled his displeasure by suspending his weekly letters to Brodrick for three months.

To return to Brodrick's book of reminiscences, he even makes the curious claim that Curzon's famous visit to the Amir in 1894 described in *Tales of Travel* 'had done more harm than good' relating Curzon's account of it at a dinner party at Brodrick's house, when, asserted this master of hindsight, 'my dinner party were aghast.'[37]

To complete the picture of Brodrick's new relationship with Curzon, it will be helpful to move ahead in time from the events of 1902-3 (the Durbar) and go forward to the end of the following year when Brodrick took over as Secretary of State for India. Far from cementing an old friendship, the result of Brodrick's move was to be disastrous, and in his memoirs, Brodrick claims that he found that Curzon was so unpopular in the India Office that he had to act to save his old friend from further errors.

Brodrick claims that on taking office in October 1903, he found that men like Arthur Godley, afterwards Lord Kilbracken, permanent head of the India Office, and Ritchie, head of the foreign department there and all the other heads of the India Office, together with the Cabinet and the Council of India, 'were now beginning to regard a Viceroy who was always making crises, and whose protests were couched in most unusual language, as a serious danger.'[38] There is not a shred of evidence for this in the written, printed or personal papers now preserved. What did happen when Brodrick took office was that he found a ready opportunity to attack Curzon and from that moment his conduct became what Fleming, in his detailed study of the Lhasa affair, concluded was 'curiously unattractive'.[39]

What he did was to immediately set about trying to stop the Younghusband sally into Tibet. Colonel Younghusband was Curzon's protégé, selected by the Viceroy to lead a military and diplomatic 'invasion' in 1904. This was Curzon's project, which he had persuaded the Government at home, against its better nature, to support. Fleming's belief is that Brodrick's attitude to Curzon and to Younghusband arose from some 'subconscious impulse'.[40] He begins his case by commenting on Brodrick's friendship with Curzon as exemplified in his letters to Curzon. These 'full of solicitous admiration, reflect a kind of hero-worship untarnished by envy . . . there is no hint of rivalry or jealousy. It would be slightly unfair to Brodrick to suggest that theirs was a jackal-lion relationship, but the world saw a marked difference in their statures, and both were faintly aware of it.'[41]

At the end of October 1903, Brodrick found himself 'set in authority over his paragon', says Fleming, 'and it is difficult not to suspect that his first official action in his new appointment was prompted by a strong though perhaps subconscious impulse to assert his newly-won dominance . . . It cannot be proved that Brodrick's precipitate, and, on the face of it, uncalled for action was prompted by the desire to thwart and humiliate his oldest friend, but his conduct throughout the Tibetan affair was disfigured at times by a kind of spite for which it is hard to account save on psychological grounds.'[42] Fleming says Brodrick's precipitate and uncalled for action was a 'callow telegram' to Curzon which 'boded obstruction and interference'.[43] Curzon stood his ground and Brodrick then sent a further telegram which said that His Majesty's Government 'accordingly sanction the advance of the mission'[44] to Tibet, but went on to make certain reservations which Younghusband was to call 'curious' because they 'described with so little precision the real purpose of the advance'.[45]

It is hard not to escape the view that Brodrick was a mealymouthed middle-of-the-roader who, having had an unsatisfactory stay at the War Office, was anxious to ensure that in his new role at the Indian Office, he would always toe the line which his superiors in the Cabinet wanted to be followed. Peter Fleming records how Brodrick's first reaction in 1904 to Younghusband's successful negotiations in Tibet was enthusiastic, sending him 'hearty congratulations' but this was immediately followed by 'misgivings' as 'things got really bad at the Foreign Office' when the Russians and the Germans objected to British actions at Lhasa. Brodrick's attitude hardened 'with a rapidity for which it is hard to account' and his 'intention to make Younghusband a scapegoat emerges'.[46] Brodrick claimed that 'Younghusband had "sold" us' and wrote to Curzon saying, 'it seems impossible to avoid throwing over Younghusband to some extent'.[47] Fleming goes so far as to say that 'Honour has several meanings and many unbecoming things have been done in its name'[48] and he clearly means that both Brodrick and Balfour, then Prime Minister, acted dishonourably in wanting to 'throw over' Younghusband. He says: 'There begins here to emerge an atmosphere of conspiracy' and claims Brodrick was 'taking no chances'. He was out for Younghusband's blood and was now 'vengeful' and had 'for not easily fathomable motives embarked on a vendetta against him'. This took the form of not only publicly criticizing Younghusband's actions but of recommending him, for those very actions for 'a shabby and inadequate' decoration. An interesting sequel to the matter of the decoration is that when Austen Chamberlain took over the India Office in the 1914-1918 War, he took the trouble, probably at Curzon's suggestion, to call for the Younghusband papers and, having studied them, arranged for Younghusband to be awarded the decoration which Brodrick had refused him twelve years before, the KSIE (Knight of the Star of the Indian Empire).[49]

Brodrick's behaviour throughout 1904 became even more unattractive. He prepared an India Office despatch printed as a secret document and addressed to Curzon, which concluded with a paragraph which seems to be aimed as much at Curzon as at Younghusband. 'Questions,' wrote Brodrick, 'of Indian frontier policy could no longer be regarded from an exclusively Indian point of view, and the course to be pursued in such cases must be laid down by HMG alone.'[50] A Blue Book was then prepared, based on this despatch, for presentation to Parliament, and Brodrick used this, says Fleming, to pursue his campaign against Younghusband. He did this by writing to the editors of several leading newspapers, sending them an advance copy of the Blue Book together with what we would now call a 'handout' composed by himself, trying to influence what they should print. At least one editor was indignant and a question was nearly asked about it in the House of Commons. The result was that the press campaign had the opposite effect from that Brodrick intended. *The Times* wrote, 'It will be an evil day for the Empire when Ministers at home shall set about to discourage by churlish strictures the readiness of public servants abroad to assume responsibility in cases of extreme difficulty and urgency,'[51] and in India the *Pioneer* strictured 'the unseemliness of the language employed' in the Blue Paper, and concluded, 'Sir Francis Younghusband has been disowned by the Secretary of State; but it is Mr Brodrick himself who stands discredited.'[52] This was not the last occasion on which

Brodrick's unseemly language was to be publicly criticised, as we shall see. We shall also see that Fleming is correct when he says that, 'One has the impression that Brodrick, impelled by some strong but almost certainly subconscious impulse, was striking at Curzon through Younghusband.'[53]

Curzon, when he wanted to annoy, particularly by the written word, had few equals. As the time for his return to London grew nearer, he set about annoying Brodrick. For his part, Brodrick continued to turn the other cheek, partly because he knew that Curzon was a formidable adversary, and also because he realised that he was exhausted, alone (Mary Curzon was in England), and that in addition to his own back problem, Curzon was deeply worried about his wife's health. Brodrick therefore showed considerable forbearance in his letters, although in his 1939 Memoirs he claims that Curzon was so hurt by the 'rebuff' over Lhasa that he made his dissent 'so forceful' that 'strong representations were made to the Prime Minister that it would be unwise for Curzon to be reappointed to the Government of India after his leave expired'.[54] It is most unlikely that this is true, or, if it were, that Balfour paid any attention to it, despite the fact that there was a real difference of opinion between them on the way to handle Tibet. Yet, wrote Curzon to Brodrick, 'I can scarcely believe that many people really think that, after five years characterised by the caution I have displayed on the North West Frontier, I should want to snatch a doubtful laurel by a policy of precipitate and emotional aggression on the North East.'[55] Brodrick replied:

> My dear George, Thank you for your long letter of 27 written in the train in a marvellous hand under the circumstances. Godley has shown me a letter of yours of the same date in which you complain a little, as you have done in writing to me, of our hurrying you too much for replies, especially at a time when you are far off from your officials. I need not say I will do all I can to avoid this occurring in future. In reality, it has not been altogether my fault.
> . . . as I write, it seems as if war was very near.[56]

Brodrick also expressed worries about the confidentiality of their correspondence but Curzon was terse in his reply. He wrote, 'The compositors who set up the type as a rule can neither speak nor understand the language which they are printing.' Then, driving in the knife, he adds, 'On the other hand, can you give a similar assurance that my letters to you are not seen by others at your end?'[57] A month later Curzon hardly improved the tone: 'At about the time when you and I are, as I hope we shall be, seated side by side on the top of the pavilion at Lords, looking on at the Eton and Harrow match in the forthcoming summer, three years will have elapsed since we first sent your predecessor the Minute.'[58] (to which no reply had been received).

Brodrick also tried to ingratiate himself by implying that he had used his offices to acquire for Curzon the office of Warden of the Cinque Ports. At first Curzon was inclined to turn down this honour, commenting that although it carried with it residence at Walmer Castle, 'I believe that the great relaxation there is golf.'[59] Later, when he accepted it, he turned this point to advantage, writing to Balfour that, 'One of the prospective pleasures of the place is that excellent golf links are, I believe, outside, and we may therefore, be able to create a reasonable excuse for persuading you to come down.' Balfour had a passion for golf, even writing about it for the *Badminton* library. Curzon also added that Balfour would 'not find the *enfant terrible* as bad as you think'.[60]

As England loomed nearer, Curzon's letters to Brodrick mellowed a little. 'I am writing to you, as I often have to do, in a tent . . . It is hard work writing as midnight draws on, after spending a whole day on the back of an elephant, one of the most physically exhausting experiences in the world. It seems difficult to realise, after an unbroken experience of nearly five and a half years, that this is the last weekly letter that I shall be writing to the Secretary of State.'[61]

What Curzon did not realise was that his account at the bank of goodwill had nearly run out, and Brodrick, a weak, pompous, humourless man, would come under another more powerful influence which would turn him away from Curzon and make them enemies for life. This influence was that of his new wife, Madeleine Stanley, a woman of twenty-seven who the widower Brodrick married when he was forty-seven years old. The marriage, only a year after the death of his wife, was not universally applauded. Sir Schomberg McDonnell wrote 'the indecent rejoicing over his second marriage has shocked many of his friends'. His new wife's father was the youngest son of Lord Stanley of Alderney – a family connected by marriage with some of the leading families such as the Harewoods. But her father had died when she was only five, and her mother married again. Churchill records that Brodrick's new mother-in-law 'moved in military circles'[62] and so did her new husband Francis Jeune, a QC who became a judge, and a lawyer of such eminence that he was considered a potential solicitor general. He became Judge Advocate and was heavily engaged in Army matters; he had to confirm or quash the findings of every general court martial. Jeune came to know Kitchener well during his visits to London, and he was a frequent visitor to the house.* Mother and daughter brought their pro-Kitchener prejudices heavily to bear on Brodrick in the years 1904 and 1905, and when Frank Maxwell was ill in 1905, Lady Jeune nursed him in her house.

On the subject of Kitchener, Brodrick writes even more evasively in his 1939 memoirs. He claims that Kitchener's appointment to India 'lay with the War Office, and although Curzon did not know it, I had, on strong public grounds, done all in my power to prevent Kitchener going till Curzon had left India'.[63] It is true that technically Kitchener's appointment 'lay with the War Office' of which Brodrick was then a weak and vacillating Secretary of State, but the fact is that with other such powerful influences at play as the King, Roberts, Curzon himself, and Kitchener with all his allies like the Salisburys, Brodrick was a very small fish. And what could be the *strong public grounds* that Brodrick hints at? If they were so strong they should have been minuted in the state papers of the time, but they are not. In his memoirs, Brodrick implies that the reasons were Lord Roberts' problems at the War Office, where he 'had not thought out the military problems of War Office organisation and required a vigorous Chief-of-the-Staff at his side . . . I knew and told Curzon that my efforts at the War Office would suffer irrevocably if I did not retain Kitchener, but it would have been impossible to put forward my grave misgivings as to their personal relations. No one in the Cabinet knew either of the men as well as I did, and I would have wagered half my fortune that there would be a clash between them.'[64]

*In her book *Memories of Fifty Years*, Brodrick's mother-in-law names Kitchener amongst her close friends and makes the claim that 'I have reason to believe on good authority that Lord K danced for the first time in his life at a small dance I gave a few years ago.'

What nonsense this is. Kitchener had no intention of going to the War Office, then or later, and he would have resigned rather than do so. Brodrick says nothing about this at the time although he claims that 'to avoid a serious difference, after consulting Lord Salisbury, I referred our rival claims to Kitchener's help, to the decision of Lansdowne and Roberts, as being the most recent military and civil opinion about India. They decided unhesitantly that Kitchener must go.'[65] As regards the 'grave misgivings' Brodrick kept quiet about these at the time, if indeed he felt them, because he was far from being on intimate terms with Kitchener, apart from obsequious letters weekly during the latter's service in South Africa.

But though Brodrick claimed that he wanted Kitchener to go to the War Office, there is a letter from Mary to Curzon written in April 1901 which suggests exactly the opposite: 'St John,' she says, 'did nothing but talk of the huge sacrifices he was making to give you Kitchener – only friendship and love for you had induced the sacrifice. If he hadn't been where he was [in the War Office] you would never have got him.'[66] This is at total variance with Brodrick's 1939 claims.

To conclude this general critique of the views of the man who – after Kitchener – was the most influential of the campaigners against Curzon, we may note the irony if not the insincerity of the telegram that St John, on his appointment to the India Office, had hurriedly despatched to his friend the Viceroy. 'Judging from the past, I am likely to be in sympathy with you. I trust this arrangement will commend itself to you. Apart from personal affection, no Member of the Cabinet more fully realises the greatness of your work in India and his own inexperience. Be sure of all possible support from me.'

Part Two

The Battle

Chapter Six

Kitchener Arrives in India

Kitchener's triumphant return from the Boer War would have been enough to turn the head of a man with only a fraction of his vainglory. On landing at Southampton, he was given the freedom of that city; he went on a special train to London, stopping at Basingstoke to receive their freedom too; at a beflagged Paddington station, there was a welcoming party which included the Prince of Wales, the Dukes of Cambridge and Connaught (both royal) and Lord Roberts, Commander-in-Chief of the Army. Then there was triumphal procession in open carriages to St James's Palace for lunch. The coronation of Edward VII had been postponed because of his appendix operation, so the welcoming crowds occupied the coronation stands. Then he went to the Palace where his old friend the King presented him with the Grand Cross of St Michael and St George, and, for good measure, the Order of Merit, today reserved for those who make rather different contributions to the nation. He was promoted to full general and created a viscount, taking amongst his titles that of Aspall in the County of Suffolk, his mother's home. Parliament gave him thanks and £50,000 ('You should have had £100,000 and an earldom' said his friend Ralli, and Lady Cranborne agreed). In addition to these public gifts, Kitchener had helped himself to a good deal of private loot from South Africa, including statues of the Boer leaders which he had removed from their cities to decorate the grounds of the large country house he intended to buy and beautify. These were discreetly returned to South Africa by the Government in 1909'.

Trevor Royle, Kitchener's latest biographer, asserts that his subject had 'begun to display a proprietorial interest in other people's possessions. If a piece of porcelain or other small and costly object took his fancy, he would admire it and then expect it to be presented to him; that courtesy not being forthcoming, he would simply pocket it, no matter whose home or official residence he happened to be visiting.' And 'Loot like blazes'[2] he told his staff. Lord Hardinge, in his memoirs, recounts too how Kitchener incurred the undying enmity of a Nawab by selecting the very best sword which had been in the Nawab's family for generations.

It is tempting to wonder what occupied Kitchener's thoughts on his journey to India as the train carrying him across Europe steamed towards the Mediterranean. Unlike Curzon, who scribbled out his thoughts to all and sundry, Kitchener believed, like Tallyrand, that the gift of speech was given in order to enable us to conceal our thoughts. As a result he found letter writing genuinely difficult. 'He sweated blood over them and became exhausted by them.'[3] Why was this? The man who wrote about him with the greatest understanding was that wise soldier and author, General Sir Ian Hamilton, formerly his second in command in South Africa, who said that Kitchener's actions were 'the outcome of a never-ending struggle between his commonsense and a mania for secrecy which almost always got the upper hand'. Hamilton believed that Kitchener 'longed to exhibit himself to the world, but could not because he was afraid of it, afraid of what it might think of the inner thoughts and restrained passions of Herbert Kitchener'.[4]

This is one of the most revealing comments ever written about Kitchener and one of the truest. Falsehoods abound. The most common of these is the myth that Kitchener was a great organiser, and administrator. Cromer for instance had described him as 'a first-rate military administrator'[5]; Hamilton dismisses this as 'a bit of cheap rubbish' and explains, 'Although Lord Fisher [the Admiral] and a hundred others said, when they sought for some catch-phrase to explain K's success, that he was an organiser, history has now revealed to us what is the absolute, stark truth: he hated organisations; he smashed organisations if they were ever imposed upon or inherited by him.'[6] This was because he did not trust others because he could (rarely) explain his thoughts to them, being so occupied with the concealment. Balfour called his an

'Oriental mind'* and Hamilton, who knew this method of working so well, explains, 'He should see *everything* of importance first, should make *every* plan.' Ian Hamilton goes on to explain, 'If there was any criticism [afterwards] of his rejection of the accepted system, or the total reorganisation of an HQ he had inherited, K could always turn to his critics and say, "Well, it works doesn't it? And works a damned sight quicker under my system than under yours!" '[7] This assessment by Ian Hamilton is repeated by Magnus, another of Kitchener's biographers, who comments that 'Kitchener's thoroughness constrained him to swing his boot into any system of administration, *and to rend in pieces any established chain of command.* His system was, in reality, the negation of any system; and his drive prompted him inexorably to centralise every species of authority in himself. After he had done so, he performed miracles of improvisation, and extracted from subordinates whom he trusted and occasionally loved, much more than they or anyone else believed that they had to give.'[8]

To return to the speculation about Kitchener's thoughts, it seems certain that a predominant preoccupation was 'How he was to operate in his new post?' Hamilton said, 'He made up his mind to run for the India Stakes without a handicap.' He determined to do away with 'the accepted system' because, quite simply, he 'mistrusted a subordinate's ability to make a proper job of one of his, K's plans . . . since he found it quite impossible to get close to most people to see whether they were to be trusted or not.' And once Kitchener made up his mind to succeed in a campaign, Hamilton confirms, 'he had all the moves, places and columns in his head, rather like a chess player.'[9]

The theory that Kitchener was brooding over the organisation of the Army in India suffers from one unfortunate handicap. His biographers† prefer to assume that he knew nothing of the organisation of the Army in India until after his arrival, and would (perhaps) not have accepted the appointment of Commander-in-Chief had he been aware of the system which prevailed since the

*When Kitchener heard of this accusation he replied, 'Yes, I suppose it is so, but I am an old man now and I cannot change my habits – it is too late now'. [Esher]

†Brig. Gen. Ballard's biography, not well known, does say, 'Even before he left England, Kitchener had been warned by the Adj. Gen. that the Mil Dept was obstructive.' (p.197) Smith-Dorrien's book concurs (p.298, 307)

Indian Mutiny. The fact is that Kitchener was well aware of the position, as is explained in a memorandum written by Lovat Fraser of *The Times of India* and deposited with Curzon's papers in 1908. It reads:

> On June 22 1903 I met Sir Archibald Hunter, LGC Western Command in the Bombay Yacht Club. Sir Archibald Hunter was my personal friend . . . He said that during the campaign in South Africa he had several times discussed Indian Mil. Admin. with Lord Kitchener and had impressed upon him that the Mil. Dept. was unnecessary and obstructive, and ought to be swept away. There can be no doubt that the first suggestion of this kind was put into Lord K's head by Sir A. H. who had been his most trusted Lieutenant in Egypt and who had commanded at Quetta. I believe Sir A. H. told me that before Lord K. came to India, he placed his views concerning the Mil. Dept. before Lord Balfour and Lord Lansdowne and received general promises of support in any reforms he proposed. Sir A. H. said that Lord K. believed the abolition of the Mil. Dept. would be a simple matter, and he never dreamed of serious trouble, otherwise he would never have come at all . . . He told me Lord K. had consulted him throughout and had sent him every single paper for his advice and suggestions . . .'

Kitchener stopped off in Egypt for a few days, telling Lord Cromer that he intended, when he arrived in India, to break up the existing system of military administration. Cromer, who was well aware of Kitchener's ruthlessness, and was later to decline a suggestion that the latter should succeed him in Egypt, lost no time in passing this information on to Brodrick in London.

Aboard ship and heading towards India, Kitchener employed himself in strewing the Red Sea with the 'collected correspondence' of a quarter of a century.[10] He also studied Hindustani, for he was a keen linguist. In contrast he was not much of a reader, and we are told that he travelled with bound copies of *Country Life* and novels by Stanley Weyman. He landed at Bombay later in November, and on 1st December 1902, he finally met Curzon in India, and gave no sign that he would be troublesome. The Viceroy was immediately taken in, and wrote home praising 'his honesty, directness, frankness and his combination of energy with power'.[11] In fact, Kitchener had already made plans for his views to be received direct at the most senior level in England – top secret letters 'under the guise of legal documents'[12] were to be sent to Lady Salisbury by Kitchener's military secretary, Hubert Hamilton. It can only be presumed that he made this arrangement because he was already determined not to 'play second fiddle' to Curzon.

Indeed, it is quite clear that Kitchener could play second fiddle to no one, and the effort to do so to Roberts during their brief period in South Africa had convinced him that he should never try again. The system of control of military affairs by 'the civilians' in India was anathema to him, and if it was embodied in Curzon, then Curzon must be quashed, removed or destroyed. Sir Walter Lawrence, Curzon's private secretary, writing after Curzon's death in 1928 in his memoirs *The India We Served* relates how Kitchener spoke to him about 'the system' in London in the summer of 1902, and later, after the Durbar, asked him to take breakfast in the Fort at Calcutta where 'he handed me a lengthy note proposing the abolition of the Military Department'. Lawrence glanced at it and made a few comments, whereupon 'he put the note back in his pocket and said he would wait for a year'. But in May (i.e. less than six months later) Kitchener was telling Lady Salisbury he would resign 'if Curzon gets a year's extension as everyone here seems to think probable . . . I could not stand the position I am placed in for another year'.

What was this 'system' or organisation in India which Kitchener was determined to abolish long before he arrived there – and thought it would be an easy task to achieve? It is a complex one to explain, and amongst the principal reasons that Curzon failed to defend it was that he never really bothered to explain it to the Home Government. Finally, after his fall, the ex-Viceroy did sit down in 1906 to produce a pamphlet, which he had privately printed, and circulated to his supporters.[13]

'The essential point, the pivot and centre of the system,' Curzon wrote, 'is that the supreme Military authority is the whole Governor-General [the Viceroy] in Council, i.e. the Government of India as a whole.'[14] When each Viceroy first took his seat in the Council Chamber at Calcutta, his Warrant of Appointment was read out to the assembled dignitaries:

We do hereby give and grant unto you our Governor-General of

India, and your Council as the Governor-General of India in Council, the superintendance, direction, and control of the whole Civil and Military Government of all our territories and revenues in India . . . and we do hereby order and require all our servants, officers and soldiers in the East Indies . . . to conform, submit and yield due obedience unto you and your Council.

These words repeated the provisions of the Charter Act of 1833, and it was thus nothing other than the sacred constitution of India which Curzon was seeking to uphold in his long dispute with Kitchener and eventually with the Cabinet in London. In all civilised nations, he believed, the paramount military authority resided in the Government as a whole, and not in any member of it. This is why Curzon was always careful to ensure that it was he and the Council who made decisions and proposals. 'Any claim that the Commander-in-Chief in India should be given *carte blanche* or a "free hand" in India, or that he could be invested with quasi-dictatorial powers, is utterly unconstitutional.'[15]

The scheme of government devised in India to carry out these intentions of the constitution was a form of cabinet government, the various branches of the administration being divided between different departments and 'ministers' who collectively with the Viceroy (the latter being in effect Prime Minister and Foreign Minister, as Salisbury and Balfour had been at home) constituted the Governor-General in Council. Military affairs, which of necessity occupied a more prominent place in the government of a dependency than was the case in England, had two representatives out of a total of eight Members of the 'Cabinet' Council. One, the Military Member, corresponded in certain respects, but not all, to the English Secretary of State for War. The other, the Commander-in-Chief, was also on the Council, but to emphasise the difference he was not an ordinary member, but an extraordinary member – that is, first he was not head of a department, and, second, the Viceroy might exercise his discretion in appointing him a member or not. In practice he was invariably appointed.

Now, what were the powers of the Commander-in-Chief? Curzon explained that he occupied a position altogether greater than had been enjoyed by a corresponding figure in England, even in the days when a member of the Royal family was Commander-in-Chief or even in the time of the Duke of Wellington. Alone with the

Viceroy and the two Governors of Madras and Bombay, he had the title of His Excellency. 'He has emoluments and surroundings equal to those of a head of an administration. He is the executive head of the army, and has its entire promotion in his hands. He is responsible for its recruitment, organisation, training and distribution in time of peace, for all schemes of military offence, or defence, for the mobilisation of the Army for war, and for its direction in time of war. Endowed with all these powers, a Cabinet Minister, and second member in the Council to the Viceroy, a member of the Legislative Council, Inspector-General of the Forces, and Chief of the General Staff, all in one, he wields an authority and enjoys a prestige greater than that of any other military officer in the British Empire.'[16] Such was Kitchener's position from 1902 onwards.

'The cardinal factor and the principal source of his power lies in the fact,' wrote Curzon, 'that he is what no English Commander-in-Chief, as such, has ever been – namely a Cabinet Minister. Thus, not only can he claim access to the Viceroy on any subject or at any time – it is inconceivable that such a request could be refused – not only can he insist, apart from personal intercourse, upon any military case being referred officially to the head of the Government, but he can demand that it should be taken to the Cabinet [Council]. If overruled he can dissent from the decision of Council and have his dissent recorded in the shape of an Official Note; and he can claim that this Note be appended to the despatch reporting the decision of the Government of India to the Secretary of State [in London]. To speak of an officer enjoying such advantages as being habitually hampered or overridden is therefore to impugn not the system but himself,'[17] added Curzon in a direct reference to Kitchener. Curzon liked to recall the past history of Commanders-in-Chief to show that Kitchener's power in 1905 was greater, not less, than his predecessors – three Viceroys had been their own Commanders-in-Chief; others overshadowed their Commanders-in-Chief by accompanying them in camp or in the field; and as recently as 1895, the Commander-in-Chief had only had control of the Bengal Army.

The Military Member's functions were threefold. Curzon explained: 'Firstly, he is directly responsible for military administration, i.e. the control of the departments of supply and transport, ordnance, remounts, clothing, medical stores, military works, and marine, and military finance, that is, the keeping of the accounts, the preparation of the military budget, and the submission of each case in its financial aspect to the Finance Department [of the Council].'[18] Secondly, the Military Member, like the heads of other departments, was the head of the office that performed the Government's military business, preserved its records, conducted its correspondence and issued its orders. The third, or advisory aspect of his duties arose from this – he had to advise on any proposal from the Commander-in-Chief or from the Secretary of State in London before submitting it to the Council. Curzon pointed out that 'were there no Military Dept. and Military Member, the Viceroy and his Council would have no alternative but to accept whatever proposals might emanate from the office of the Commander-in-Chief, which is concerned neither with the political nor the financial, but exclusively with the military aspect of schemes – or else to assume without knowledge and without advice, the invidious responsibility of refusing them.' To finally clarify this, Curzon said, 'It is not the Military Member, but the Government of India (of whom he is only the official mouthpiece) that is and must always continue to be omnipotent in military affairs, and the "wishes" and "decisions" even of the Commander-in-Chief can only be carried out if they win the approval of that paramount authority.'

This distinction 'between executive and administrative functions is a recognised feature of sound military government in all civilised countries' said Curzon, 'partly because to place them upon the C-in-C in a country of any size and with an army of the scale of that in India would mean an inevitable breakdown.'[19]

The procedure actually worked like this. The Commander-in-Chief had an office, Army Headquarters, headed by an Adjutant-General and a Quartermaster-General. One or the other of these two would submit a proposal of military policy such as expenditure, in writing to the Government of India. This would be received by the Military Department as would a despatch from the Secretary of State from London. The Military Department would note on the proposal, and this note would be confidential and not seen outside the department.

In the preliminary stages, this work would be performed by junior officers, 'And indeed, all the work of the department was performed by officers of inferior rank to the C-in-C for the simple reason,' noted Curzon, 'that there is no military officer in India who is not in that position.'[20] (Kitchener hated his plans being commented upon by those junior to him in rank. Accordingly in May 1903, Curzon issued instructions through the Military Member prohibiting the noting by junior officers upon proposals emanating from the Commander-in-Chief himself.) The case having been prepared by the Military Department, if it involved expenditure it would go to the Finance Department, and then to the Viceroy, or to the Viceroy direct. If both Military Member and Viceroy agreed, and in financial cases the Financial Member, then the matter was settled. If there were disagreements, the Viceroy sent the case back to the authority with whom he disagreed, 'Or, very likely, if the matter is of no importance, he will see the dissentient parties together about it.'[21] In the last resort it was always open to either party, as already explained, to take the matter to the final tribunal. In practice, as can be seen from the files in the India Office, as the files went round and round, the words 'Agreed' or 'Noted' are the most frequently used.

This system somehow had acquired the name *dual control*, but Curzon pointed out, 'If it is a dual system it is dual in precisely the same sense as the entire civil administration in India is dual.' He added, 'This so-called dual control is only division of labour under a nickname. Two men and two organisations were appointed to perform a task which is beyond the power or capacity of one . . . In so far as control is involved in military affairs – and resented – it is not dual control but civil control. The authority who protests against dual control will usually be found to mean in the last resort he objects to control of any description.'[22] This was the crux of the matter.

It would be naive to suppose that Curzon did not have some flicker of appreciation, from the start, that Kitchener hoped to sabotage the existing system. Amongst his papers is a handwritten note probably from his secretary, Lawrence, dated January 1903 at Delhi (i.e. just after the Durbar) which says, 'I gather that what Lord Kitchener would like, would be to have the whole Army, executive and administration, under himself, for this is really what his views come to. This was the case in Egypt under him, and no doubt works for a small army. But with an army of 250,000 of all races and creeds, serving under various conditions, and under a settled government, I have no hesitation in saying that it would be beyond the power of any one man.'

There is also already, a few weeks after Kitchener's arrival, a critical note in some of Curzon's comments. For example he wrote to Hamilton: 'Our "Hercules from the Himalayas" as Rosebery persists in calling Kitchener, greatly to the fury of the latter, has an opinion about [Brodrick] which it would be hardly wise to repeat on paper.'[23] Later, in answer to Hamilton's query about whether Kitchener would make a suitable Viceroy, Curzon wrote, 'His whole heart is in the Army and he thinks and talks about nothing else . . . Moreover Kitchener has no grasp of administration . . . In my view he confuses finance with arithmetic.'[24]

In another letter to Hamilton he said, 'Kitchener cannot understand why the Viceroy should be splendidly housed and equipped while he is accommodated in what by comparison is a bungalow . . . He frankly dislikes Anglo-Indian Society . . . He is bored with Simla.'[25]

Curzon wrote again to Hamilton, 'I suspect he is one of the keenest wishers for my retirement in December next . . . and with a new Viceroy, ignorant of India, and probably less strong-willed than myself, he will be the ruler of the country in everything but name.'[26]

Later Curzon said: 'Kitchener is mad keen about everything here. I never met so concentrated a man. He uses an argument. You answer him. He repeats it. You give a second reply, even more cogent than the first. He repeats it again. You demolish him. He repeats it without alteration a third time. But he is as agreeable as he is obstinate and everyone here likes him.'[27]

Curzon also has possessed some appreciation, from the start, that Kitchener could be a potential competitor in India – even if he did underestimate the extent of the threat. An indicator that he did so is the matter of their respective signatures. Curzon was, officially, Curzon of Kedleston, and there were complaints from his Curzon relatives whenever he signed public letters with the name 'Curzon' alone. He persisted in doing so, for he realised that when Kitchener arrived, he would be competing with a signature which read 'Kitchener of Khartoum'. So he wrote to Kitchener almost as soon as he landed in India asking 'How are you going to sign? . . . I hope that unless you have strong views to the contrary, that you will sign "Kitchener" and will instruct the Department to that effect.' Curzon attempted to justify this by telling Kitchener that 'the additional labour with the thousands of signatures that I have to write, would be prodigious'.[28]

One of Kitchener's first duties on his arrival was to officiate at the magnificent Delhi Durbar which Curzon had organised to celebrate the coronation of Edward VII. The wits called it The Curzonisation. Kitchener's position was largely decorative, yet as he rode his white charger into the Delhi arena at the head of his troops, the artist Mortimer Menpes, now in India to record the great Imperial event, wrote, 'It was impossible that the thought should not enter the head of anyone with the smallest imagination that the man who now fulfilled the role of C-in-C was destined one day to sit in the seat of Viceroy.'[29] Marker wrote to Gertie about the ceremony, 'The Durbar today was wonderfully done and organised and such a sight as never was or will be again, I imagine. The Duke of Connaught [the King's brother and representative] was extremely well received, but I fancy the Curzons' nose must have been somewhat out of joint by the feeble reception they got.'[30] This latter comment by Marker was less than frank. The problem of Curzon's lack of public acclaim rose because of his action over the 9th Lancers. Despite their punishment, he had insisted that the regiment took part in the Durbar parade, by telling the Commander-in-Chief who thought they should not, 'My dear fellow, have you taken leave of your senses? I need all the cavalrymen I can get.' He only had 35,000 in all.[31]

But Curzon should have taken his advice, for when the Lancers advanced into the arena, they were greeted with enthusiastic applause by all the Europeans present, including Curzon's own guests from England. He wrote that night, 'As I sat alone and unmoved on my horse, conscious of the implications of the cheers, I could not help being struck by the irony of the situation. There rode before me a long line of men, in whose ranks were certainly two murderers. It fell to the Viceroy, who is credited by the public with the sole responsibility for their punishment, to receive their salute. I do not suppose that anybody in that vast crowd was less disturbed by the demonstration [of the crowd] than myself. On the contrary, I felt a certain gloomy pride in having dared to do the right. But I also felt that if it could be truthfully claimed for me that I have loved righteousness and hated iniquity – no one could add that in return I have been annointed with the oil of gladness above my fellows.'[32]

Curzon had warned Kitchener before his arrival that he would continue to exercise his Viceregal authority as far as the Army was concerned, particularly in strategy on the frontier, which he knew intimately. Kitchener immediately set about undermining Curzon's authority. Curzon had already, in 1902, before the arrival of Kitchener, been alarmed by the military failure of British forces in the South African war, and began putting forward a scheme to reduce the garrisons retained in India for the preservation of order amongst the native population. 'These same troops can be released to form a field army for the purposes of war,' he wrote.

Kitchener pretended not to know about this, and wrote home, 'On my arrival . . . I discovered that Curzon had tied up all the available soldiery in garrisons to prevent native uprisings. I informed the Government that there was little danger of this. It was my view that these same troops could be released to form a field army for the purpose of war.'[33]

He told Lady Salisbury that the use of the army to hold India against the Indians 'is a wrong policy' but he did not say that Curzon thought so too. She was expected to pass on his criticisms to her friends in the Cecil clique, telling them, for example, that the army was scattered 'all higgledy-piggledy over the country without any system or reason whatever'.[34] Together with Marker, the new Commander-in-Chief embarked with a small escort on a series of tough frontier tours, riding mules or ponies throught the difficult terrain, quite ignoring Curzon's hints that frontier policy was a political matter for the Viceroy to decide.[35]

Marker was delighted with his new responsibilities and rapidly took the Chief's side in any conflicts with Curzon. Kitchener had ensured his loyalty on their arrival in India, by noting him as qualified for a Staff appointment without having to go to Staff College – a considerable plum. As he talked to Marker, Kitchener vented his dissatisfaction with the system under which the Army was administered, and which was referred to by almost everyone as dual control. In the Kitchener papers at the Public Records Office in London, there is an undated, unsigned single sheet of paper which was probably produced at Kitchener's initiative at a very early date, and which sums up his views precisely.

Three Essential Principles of Sound Army Administration in India

1. Dual control in the Army and the reduplication of work in the Military offices must cease.
2. The chief Military adviser must have direct access to the Viceroy and Government of India, without the intervention of an independent Military channel which only causes mis-interpretation and distortion of the views put forward.
3. That under the supreme control of the Viceroy and the Government of India the power of control over the army must be conferred where responsibility is to lie.

Within about a month of his arrival in India, Kitchener was writing as follows, to Lady Salisbury:

What you say about our being the most un-military nation in the world is most true and I greatly fear that when we meet a really military enemy our house of cards will tumble down. It looks as if the whole people were cheerfully running along a narrow edge of rock leading to a known chasm . . . I wonder why we are such an unmilitary people? Can it be that fear of Oliver Cromwell still exists, or is it that the civilian authorities are jealous of any independent military administration? Efficiency for war really depends on a mass of technical subjects, armaments, supply of food, transport, training, command, discipline tactics, but beyond all these, we have to deal with the human nature of a collective body of men which is quite a different thing to the human nature of an individual. To make an army efficient, you must be able to feel the pulse of a whole army collectively and intuitively . . .

I find things are about the same out here as at home. Curzon is all that one could wish and as kind as possible, but the system under which a Member of Council is made responsible for the administration of the Army independent[ly], while the latter has only executive functions, is extraordinary. A machine is handed to the Commander-in-Chief for him to work by turning the handle, but he must not interfere in any way for the defects in the complicated machinery. I asked the Viceroy why he liked the system and his answer was: "If the C-in-C had anything to do with the machinery, he would become too powerful so to keep him down we take his power away and run another man as well. Between the two, the civil elements get control."

When one sees the deplorable state of the organisation of the Army, I am astonished at the satisfaction expressed . . . With an army of 250,000 men, if Russia invaded India tomorrow, they could only put 60,000 men into the field to be followed some months later by 30,000 after which the field army would be exhausted. Is that satisfactory?

As to power, I do not want any more power outside the army, but I do want power to do good in the army. If I am incapable, why appoint me? If I fail, get rid of me; why keep on a dead level of inefficiency or drift backwards because you won't trust the person you appoint to do good . . .

The question of troops on the frontier is most important. Curzon has established an excellent militia recruited from the tribes, and I should like to see the numbers doubled.[36]

Although he did not like the 'system', Kitchener was not nearly so virulent in his attack on it during the early period of his arrival in India as he was later to become. His supporters would say that this was because he did not know its defects in these early days, but it would be fairer to say that he never really tried to understand it or use it (see Appendix 3). A long note he wrote in February 1903, in answer to a request for his views on possible changes from the military department, and a 1750-word letter he sent to Lady Salisbury in January give a fair description of his views. As in all his letters, he had little time to spare for social intercourse and from first word to last he is taken up with his views on military matters. The long note is, to begin with, historical, but when we come to page 11 we find a proposal on future relations between the Viceroy and the Commander-in-Chief which includes the sentence, 'Questions which affect the army in the administrative, political or financial aspect will be dealt with, as now, by the Military Department.'[37]

Kitchener then comments: 'I must say, when on my having been newly appointed C-in-C I read the above rule, that it caused a shock. . .all questions dealt with *by* not *through* the Military Department. This puts the C-in-C more than ever in the position of the fifth wheel in a coach, and accentuates very considerably all the drawbacks of the present position, so much so, that, were it law instead of a *proposed* regulation, I should greatly prefer the position of Military Member to that of being C-in-C.' He continued: 'In practice the C-in-C's opinion is no doubt solicited on many Army matters, and in most cases where political affairs affect the Army. But any opinions he may wish to offer . . . cannot reach the Viceroy without being freely criticised, from the lowest subordinate in the Military Department upwards. Each in turn has his say. Captains, Majors, Colonels – all no doubt clever with their pen, but generally having – even for their rank – comparatively small experience of the art of war.'[38] As we have seen, Kitchener could not bear to be criticised by those junior in rank, and as everyone in India was junior in rank, Curzon stopped the practice. Kitchener went on, 'When, once or twice, the C-in-C finds that his opinions are overruled, possibly owing to a subordinate officer's unanswered criticisms, he becomes naturally chary about giving opinions and feels somewhat hurt. Moreover, it is apparently quite impossible to keep these printed opinions secret, and in a short while it becomes known to the Army that the C-in-C has lost influence with the Viceroy.'[39]

Kitchener claimed that the 'great faults of the present system are the enormous delay and endless discussion which it involves' and added, 'To carry on war under this system of divided power and divided responsibility would be absolutely impossible and yet that *theoretically* is what is attempted. Fortunately our *practice* is better than our theory, and in war the C-in-C is in direct but entirely unofficial communication with the Viceroy, issues the necessary orders and asks formal sanction afterwards. Operations thus proceed unchecked . . . There is however a great danger involved in this system. It can only work as long as the Viceroy believes in and supports the C-in-C.'[40]

Curiously, this was the first and last time Kitchener was to use this argument, because, of course, he could never claim that Curzon did not support him. He ended his paper by saying, rather reasonably, that 'the problem is not an easy one, but I think the question to study is whether some office to supply these needs, but without the great disadvantages of the present system, could not be devised.'[41] Alas, he was never to be so reasonable again.

At a personal level, relations between the two men appear to have been on the surface surprisingly good, perhaps partly as a result of Kitchener's attentions to Mary Curzon.

From the moment of his arrival in India, Kitchener had taken great care to renew, and deepen, his friendship with Mary, and she reciprocated. In 1903 Mary spent much time recovering from illness in the tented camp at Naldera, where Kitchener was a constant visitor. 'A fine character with a perfect scorn of popularity,' Mary wrote to her mother. 'He and George both have indomitable wills, and it is frequently my diplomacy which keeps them friends.'[42]

In December 1903 she was back at Barrackpore, and was excused social duties. Kitchener was now her constant attendant, and his growing affection for her was reciprocated. Some of his letters to Mary were tender to the point of flirtation, while to her, 'He is a rugged sort of companion. There is a sort of bracing north wind of resolution and strenuousness about him, and a gentle spot about a woman which a woman is always quick to find.'[43] She told Curzon that these long hours spent with Kitchener were some of the happiest she had spent in India 'as his utter dependence upon me appealed so strongly to me – more so because liking me as a woman, he talked to me as a man.'[44] Having so little small-talk, he spoke to her mainly of his work.

Early in January 1903, an event of significance for Marker took place. Mary Curzon's mother and sisters, the Leiters, from Chicago, arrived in India for a third visit, and they made a great impact on the English community, and in particular on Raymond Marker. He wrote home excitedly to Gertie: 'I have become acquainted at last with Mrs Leiter – who is really a nice old lady and her "malapropisms" have been greatly exaggerated – I do not think she does more than the average in the way of saying unfortunate things. The more one sees of her family, the more I wonder why Lady Curzon should be so absolutely unlike the rest of them – for her knack of being disagreeable to the staff certainly does not seem to have diminished, though she has always been like honey to me.'[45] It was not, however, with Mrs Leiter that Marker wished to become acquainted, for he had fallen in love with her daughter, Daisy, and there was talk of their becoming engaged.

Marker had first met Daisy (her real name was Marguerite)

when she and her sister Nan came out to India alone in March 1899, staying on and off with the Curzons until the New Year following. They were a rather lively couple and even after seven weeks Mary was writing home that theirs was 'somewhat of a visitation' although she told her mother 'both are very nice and make no trouble'. Actually they were both rather naughty. They were flirtatious. Nan called the Captains Majors, and the Colonels Captains 'and mixes up their names, to our great delight'. As a result, the ADCs 'clamour to sit by her at table as she is so funny and sweet'. Daisy too was 'very sweet' and everyone liked her, and her flirtation consisted in annexing Captain Meade 'quite a harmless youth on the staff'.[46] Mary assured her mother that, despite this, Daisy was keeping in touch with her boyfriend at home in America, one Craig W., who also wrote regularly to her. This was innocent enough but 'a little cloud' arose when the two girls, much amused by the ceremony attached to the Viceregal office in general and to George's person in particular, decided to have a practical joke at his expense. They waited until there was a Viceroy's audience in Government House, and then calmly walked forward and prostrated themselves at his feet. They were amused, but no one else was. Indeed, they were sent to their rooms for some time as a punishment, like small girls (they were in their early twenties). Mary noted that, after this, Daisy stopped flirting, and she told her mother that she was 'now a thousand times more attractive because she is dignified' particularly when wearing her lace dress from Pagnier. The dignified life had other results, for Daisy put on fifteen pounds and 'her sit-upon is perfectly enormous and she is bursting out of her clothes. She is too big-looking for her best . . . as she is almost buxom'[47] reported Mary.

The buxom Daisy and Marker were brought somewhat close together towards Christmas as he and another ADC, plus the Curzons, took the girls on sightseeing expeditions to Agra and the Taj, combined with Viceregal duties. Indeed, Mary wrote home, 'We do everything for their enjoyment that mortals can.'[48] Since Marker's correspondence on the subject of Daisy is destroyed or suppressed, we do not know how far his feelings for her had developed at this period. However from what is said by 'the Boys' and from Kitchener himself, it was clear to everyone that Marker was in love with her and that she gave every outward sign of returning his affections. She 'had gone to the very extreme limits of what may be allowed in that direction with any sense of decency' exclaimed Hubert Hamilton, and even accounting for the difference in mores between 1903 and the 1980s, those are strong words. No one really believed that 'Miss Daisy was only amusing herself' with poor Marker, and the rest of 'the Boys' agreed with him that she was 'a straightforward honest girl'. Hamilton thought 'their tastes are so similar they would make a very happy couple'. When they parted in March 1903, she returning to America, 'the scene which took place on parting, when she declared she could never stand it again' and her attitude after that when 'she has written a few lines every day [that is, for nearly nine months] has admitted of only one interpretation if honesty and due consideration in one's dealings with fellow creatures have a place in our moral code.'[49] So wrote Hamilton, and the shock therefore, when Marker learnt that she would not after all marry him, was considerable. 'I have never seen anyone so completely knocked out.'[50]

The shock was particularly severe because the reason given by Daisy for her change of heart was that she proposed to marry 'Useless' Crawley, one of Curzon's ADCs. Hamilton could not believe it. 'I don't suppose for a moment that Daisy will marry "Useless" Crawley as the Army calls him, with his burden of debts. Picture him as the brother-in-law of our great Viceroy! But Crawley will serve a purpose in shaking off Marker.' But if Daisy's explanation of another suitor was nonsense, what was the real reason for Marker's rejection? Hamilton explains, 'Last year Lady Curzon didn't much like the idea of the match. Her ideas ran to Lord Kitchener or some worldly swell for Daisy, but before the latter left last March, she and Mrs Leiter had acquiesced in it subject to Mr Leiter's approval after seeing Marker.'[51] So far as we know, Mr Leiter never did see Marker, but perhaps his influence was decisive in feeling that Daisy could do better. Mary Curzon's dream of a match with Kitchener was presumably never pursued, and history would certainly have taken a different turn if she had brought it off. To return to the world of reality, somehow the Leiters persuaded Daisy that she would make a match if in fact she married not the much despised 'Useless' Crawley, but the Earl of Suffolk one of Curzon's ADC's. His debt were after all, of little moment to the Leiters.

'The Boys' found Daisy's conduct 'dishonourable and quite inexcusable'[52] but they blamed it not on her or on the Leiters but on the Curzons. Marker remained firm in his love, though, and said he 'was not prepared to condemn her for her caprice'.[53] Kitchener wrote to Lady Salisbury, 'Poor Marker is I fear very unhappy, however, I have no doubt it is the best thing that could have happened, as nothing less would have opened his infatuated eyes.'[54] Curzon's youngest daughter, Lady Metcalfe, has in the collection of her mother's letters from Lord Kitchener, the following, written when Mary was in London and he in Calcutta, on 25 January 1904.

I have been much astonished to hear from Marker the sad news about your sister's change of affections – Marker cannot believe it, and after this long and close intimacy, it certainly seems to us all almost incredible. He is however going home at once and I sincerely hope when he arrives it may prove to have been only a temporary caprice. It seems almost impossible that anything serious could have been brought about by 'Useless' Crawley as he is known in the Army.

I remember however what you told me about the engagement on our last drive and realised that there might be difficulties, though I felt all along that Marker so fully believed in your sister's affections that he would hardly come to grief – poor fellow I fear he feels it very much and is only buoyed up by the absolute belief in your sister's affection for him.

Kitchener told a different story to Marker, explaining that it was the Curzons who had put the knife into any relationship between Daisy and he, on the grounds that Marker was unsuitable socially, and Daisy was to be married to some of greater social standing. Kitchener also told Marker that he must get away from India as quickly as possible, and arranged a posting to London. Hubert Hamilton wrote another long letter to Lady Salisbury explaining what had happened to Marker, and hoping that she could speak about the matter to Lady Curzon, who was then on leave.

One of Marker's first actions on reaching London was to seek a meeting with Mary Curzon, no doubt in hopes of some further explanation of what had happened. It is not known what she told him, but Marker wrote to Kitchener about it (this letter is missing) and the Chief replied, 'I am glad Lady Curzon played up and think you are quite right to get away for a bit.'[55] After a short holiday, Marker returned to Whitehall, and soon became a trusted confidante of the War Office Minister, Arnold-Forster. But unknown to Forster, Kitchener had told Marker to keep him informed by telegram about all matters concerning the army in India, and not only to do so in code, but also to send them 'privately, and pay for them, charging me'.[56] Thus Marker became a spy in the War Office, crossing the road to the post office to send commercial cables to Kitchener, usually daily, often more, and receiving them back also in code.

Kitchener, for his part, was busy keeping his contacts in London alive, and, much as he hated letter writing, his style was warm and friendly, and he hardly ever crossed out a word. For example, to Eddie Stanley, who as Lord Derby was to say that Kitchener was his only real friend, he wrote:

> Dear Eddie, Very many warm congratulations on your entrance into the Cabinet [as Postmaster General] although I am sorry you leave the War Office. So many thanks for the sauceboat; I am now perfectly fitted out, and I think my dinners go rather well. I am just back from an interesting and I think useful visit to Gilgit and Chitral. I spent one night in China and saw all the passes.[57]

His correspondence with Lady Salisbury was already bearing fruit, Balfour writing to him, in December 1903, when he had been in India less than a year, 'My own personal conviction is (at least as at present advised) that the existing division of attributes between the C-in-C and the Military Member of Council is quite indefensible . . . I cannot say how thankful I am that we have got you, in this critical and in some respects transitional period, as our military advisor and guide on the problem of Indian Defence.'[58] Presumably he did not send a copy of this letter to Curzon, too. By October 1904 Balfour had slightly changed his view and was telling Lady Salisbury, 'Though I am at one with K as to his ends, I cannot express unqualified admiration of the means he employs to get them.'[59]

A case could be made out for believing that Kitchener established a relationship with Lady Salisbury because he knew that, one day, an entree into the Cecils' circle would assist him with his ambitions to be Viceroy of India, or Governor of Egypt and the Sudan. Even if this view is not subscribed to, it is clear that once he arrived in India he determined to use her to achieve his purpose of obtaining military autocracy. He started almost immediately on arrival, telling her 'there is some waking up to be done' in the Army and 'the Military Member is making difficulties almost insurmountable'.[60] He was not above a dig at the Curzons' expense, as when he gossips about the Durbar and advises that though Curzon should, in his opinion, have asked the Duke of Connaught (the King's representative) to accompany him in the first elephant in the procession, Curzon was proposing to take it for himself. 'I suggested to a solemn official that I should make Curzon honorary Colonel of a native regiment – not the 9th Lancers – so that he could wear the native dress and look his part better. They nearly all had fits . . .'[61]

More seriously, he sends her a twenty page typed document which he has produced, in answer to a proposed order put forward by the Military Department, and asks, 'I wonder whether you were terribly bored by the last letter I wrote you. If you were not and take an interest in some of my difficulties, you might I think like to read the enclosed minute I have written and propose sending in after I have shown it to the Viceroy next Sunday when I am spending the day at his country place.'[62] Was she flattered at seeing his papers before they reached even Curzon himself? Was she genuinely interested in his 'difficulties' or did she think he could not manage to achieve reforms if he could not get his way? We shall never know, because he destroyed her letters.

She may have enjoyed being drawn into a conspiracy. He makes it quite clear to her that she is his fellow conspirator. After being told off by Lord George Hamilton and Curzon for writing behind their backs, he sends her a copy of 'the wigging' warning 'of course there is nothing for it but to be very circumspect in future'.[63] But the next week he is plunging in again, saying, 'Notwithstanding the censure for writing too much, I think I must write you a short letter about defence of the frontier . . . I am sure that you will be careful that *nothing* comes from me and that my name is never used.'[64] He sends her copies of his letters to Curzon, but she tells him that some questions have been asked about his letters to her – we do not know by whom. Kitchener replied, 'I think you [had] better be very careful about the person who wrote to you about our correspondence. I have also been through a pumping process, which did not result in much advantage to the energetic pumper.'[65]

The following month, he was marking his letters 'Private' which was a wise precaution since they now contained the highly secret game-plan he had developed for a frontier war with Russia. He called it his *Kriegspiel* or *Three Volume Novel* and said, 'It will interest Mr Balfour, but I hope it will be kept *quite* secret. After you have read it, will you give it to Mr Balfour as a present from me?'[66] This must have been flattering to her, to be let into the inner thoughts of the Empire's greatest soldier. It was hand-written too 'as we have no confidential printing press out here'. Lady Salisbury not only read it, but wrote to him asking for figures – an approximately fortnightly state of the troops. It was the stuff of which espionage cases are now made. His letters to her were now fuller and longer than the four-page documents of Boer War days. There were intimacies too – he sends her an X-ray of his leg,[67] broken in an accident, and details of the injury. She in turn sent her photograph to 'the Brat' and to Hamilton who had also started corresponding with her, but is also enjoining secrecy, writing in December 1903, 'Lady Curzon is going home on 10 January. I need hardly warn you that every word is repeated.'[68]

Kitchener had also been warned that his direct correspondence with London had not gone unnoticed, because Lord George Hamilton wrote from the India Office to Curzon warning him that Kitchener was not playing the game by the rules. As a result, the Viceroy wrote to Kitchener formally:

> In his letter which came by yesterday's mail, the S of S mentioned that he had heard from members of the Imperial Defence Committee at home of 'schemes of wide reform and of great alteration' being put forward by you, as he assumed in private letters to the WO or the C-in-C . . . [After repeating Lord George Hamilton's warning, he says,] I give you this word of warning so as to regulate your correspondence with Lord Roberts. Confidential communication between you and him is not only according to custom but is most desirable. If however you adumbrate large schemes or ideas to him about which the Government of India have not been consulted [crossed out and replaced with] pronounced, then they when they

hear of it (as they are certain to do) are sure to think that you are going behind their backs, and they are apt to become antagonistic.[69]

Kitchener replied, also asking that his letter should be copied to Lord George Hamilton. Curzon answered:

I will gladly forward your letter to the Secretary of State. I do not think the situation is one of great difficulty ... It is desirable that you should be in frequent private correspondence with the C-in-C at home for the reason more than any other that has been pointed out by yourself viz that you do not happen as yet to possess the Indian experience of which he is the greater living master.
1. Where your ideas or proposals have not yet been submitted to or received the consent of the Government of India, you make it clear to him that you are expressing your own views solely.
2. At the other end, Lord Roberts and his officers do not quote from your confidential opinions as though they possessed an official character.
    Let me know if you think what I have said reasonable; because if so, I will send a copy of this letter together with yours to the S of S.

This was how Kitchener had replied to the charge that he had been incautious in sending his minute on the organisation of the Military Department to Roberts direct.

I have no doubt that the scheme of reform referred to by the S of S must be my minute about the organisation of the Mil. Dept. which you have seen and a copy of which I sent confidentially to Lord Roberts for his opinion. [This must be] my private and confidential opinion about the efficiency of the Indian Army for War about which I have mentioned points that occur to me. Of course, there have been other points of small importance such as promotions and appointments both at home and in India which have been referred to in our letters.
    I wish you would point out to the Secretary of State that my position out here is a somewhat peculiar one. I have not had long Indian experience, and I have no military advisors here who have. When therefore a question of grave importance such as the organisation of the Mily. Dept. occurs which I have been forced to take up by the appearance of the GGO [Order] on the subject, and which I recognise may possibly necessitate my having to resign my present

command and thereby cause the Government some inconvenience, it seems to me rather hard that I should be cut off from that advice and assistance that was promised me by the one officer who has had the longest experience in India and is more in touch with the Govt. at home than any other. I am quite ready to stand in the future alone, and to trust to the experience I have already gained, but I certainly thought it wiser to discuss subjects of this sort with others who would give me advice in a difficult situation that would be of great value to me. I have not marked this letter *Private* as you may like to send it to the S of S.

There, for the present, the matter ended, and on 5th June 1903 Lord George Hamilton wrote to Kitchener thanking him for the letter 'not only for the substance but also for the tone and spirit in which it was written'. These letters were important not only for revealing how Kitchener would undermine official channels, but also for indicating for the first time on a formal level his intention of changing 'the system'. Curzon was by now well aware of what was afoot, writing to Hamilton, 'He thinks that when I go, he will get rid of the Military Member, and with a new Viceroy, ignorant of India, and probably less strong-willed than himself, that he will be the ruler of the country in everything but name.' Nonetheless, Curzon was determined to keep Kitchener's ambition under control, telling Hamilton: 'I want you clearly to recognise that no effort on my part shall be wanting to prevent such a stupid disaster as the loss of Kitchener's services [by resignation]. I am regarding it from the point of view of the advantage of the Empire.' It was about this time that Curzon sent Hamilton his often-quoted description of the C-in-C 'just like a caged lion, stalking to and fro, and dashing its bruised and lacerated head against the bars'.

A few months later, when Parliament re-assembled after the summer, Lord Hamilton was gone from the India Office, to be replaced by Brodrick.[70]

Chapter Seven

Kitchener's First Feint

Curzon had mixed feelings as he surveyed the prospects for the year 1904. The Durbar had been an outstanding success and Kitchener had arrived. But Curzon was lonely without Mary, and he knew he was becoming difficult and tetchy as a result of all the overwork to which he had submitted himself. These should have been the last few months of his Viceroyalty, but there was so much left undone and still to do, and there was mounting tension in Afghanistan. He was torn between staying in India to finish his tasks, and returning home at the end of his period of office, because almost all of his friends were worried at the weakness of the Conservative Government under Balfour, and felt his qualities were needed in the Cabinet. Mary wrote to him from London: 'You do loom so great and big and strong out there in India, away from the miserable muddles here, where each day seems to add to the failures of your friends. . .Austen Chamberlain is an admitted failure; AJB hopeless and Joe [Chamberlain] run away from the muddle he has landed them all in [over Free Trade]. You are out of it – untouched by the strange ill-luck that pursues the party. . .Here you are looked on as a giant, and a frightening one.'[1]

This was all very encouraging, but in his heart of hearts he knew he had made enemies too. Curzon was not a man who could take criticism easily but as long ago as 1900 Brodrick had warned him of the problems:

My dear old boy, I have been meaning for a long time to write you a special letter, and have put it off. And now I shall take the plunge because I don't want to feel a humbug any longer . . . Once or twice you have alluded to the unpopularity your reforms are causing you in certain quarters, and the lies, as to your social proceedings, which find their way into the English press. You are only one third of the way through your time, and you have big schemes on hand – and I can't bear the thought of your being in any way handicapped. What I am going to say is told to no one else, not even my wife.

The fact is, you drive some hard and they resent it. You rebuke others and they cannot turn. You ignore a few and their mulishness reacts on others. But what distresses me particularly is your inability to be popular with others in the social life of India. After all, you and Mary started in excelsis. "We have got a young god and goddess come to rule us" they said. Now they fear you, I'm told. I don't know what it costs me to write all this . . .

And why not smooth everyone down a bit? I mention no names, but my informants are very diverse. . . I am very bold to write this but it is because I am always your affectionate St John Brodrick.[2]

Curzon should have remembered this advice – perhaps he did – four years later when he exacerbated another enemy by now letting rip at Brodrick for the tone of his letters, and he was also suspicious that those he wrote marked *Personal* were not being treated by Brodrick as such. Yet Brodrick had had the gall to ask him if he thought the letters he received were treated in confidence. Curzon asked Brodrick, 'I wish you will tell me frankly what form you think our correspondence ought to take. I have been in the habit throughout the last five years of addressing the Secretary of State weekly in my private letters with the utmost candour and fullness on every variety of subject, trusting to the confidential nature of the correspondence, but at the same time never pausing to think of the effect that might be produced were my communications to pass into wrong hands. [Curzon could have added that he wrote to Godley in similar terms.] Your view of the correspondence between the Secretary of State and the Viceroy seems to be rather different . . . I am led therefore to think that you do not attach as much value to the private correspondence between us as I believe has generally been the case.'[3]

Brodrick told Curzon that his letter 'shows me that you are dissatisfied with the character of some of my letters. You think I do not value yours, indeed you suggest that I do not even acknowledge receipt of some of them . . . I daresay George Hamilton's letters to you were more uniform than my own.'[4] Godley was also on the receiving end of some of this criticism. At the same time that Brodrick was making placatory noises, Godley was writing to Curzon:

> I have before me your letter . . . but, before I answer it, I must refer to mine of last week. I cannot help thinking, when I recall it, that I was perhaps betrayed into using a too contentious tone. If so, I sincerely regret it. I can assure you that in my correspondence with you I never for a moment forget that I am a small man writing to a great man . . . I had the pleasure of being allowed to call on Lady Curzon [in London] a day or two ago. She was very kind to me, and did not visit on my head the sins of the India Office, though, if she had done so, I should have had no right to complain. There is only one word, which, as a result of my conversations with her, I wish to say to you: and that is, to repeat what I have said in previous letters, that to the best of my knowledge and belief, my Secretary of State is perfectly loyal to you and most anxious to support you as far as he can . . . from one of your letters which he showed me, I gathered that his private letters to you had produced a rather unsatisfactory effect on your mind.[5]

Curzon, reading this, recalled that Godley had warned him in November 1903, 'I am quite sure that you would be wrong if you were to count on [Brodrick's] being either ductile or malleable.'[6]

Curzon had been particularly incensed at Brodrick's tone during the Younghusband affair, but at this stage it may well be that Godley was right and Brodrick's problems with his new relationship to Curzon had not yet surfaced. For Curzon, too, friendship with Brodrick, of such long standing, had not yet been overtaken by total irritation with the official tone the latter adopted.

Curzon wrote to his friend the merchant banker Sir Clinton Dawkins in March 1904 a letter which shows that he tried to analyse the changed relationship. Brodrick 'though personally very loyal and friendly to myself, does not at all like being merely my echo, and I think rather enjoys spreading the impression that I am a very difficult person to handle, and that it is a good thing for the

Cabinet to sit upon me from time to time. All this will disappear when I get home and meet these suspicious gentry at table'.[7]

Curzon was convinced that little of moment would occur in India while he was away and he had anyway briefed Ampthill exhaustively. The latter told Godley that Curzon's 'ideas and marvellous powers are certainly most inspiring and I have never had such interesting conversations in my life'.[8] As he left India, Curzon referred to his 'earnest longing to do his duty in a calling that I always think has been laid on Englishmen from on high'.[9] He knew too that this calling might well come to an end during his leave in London because Brodrick had privately warned him that the Government might collapse in the summer, and with it Curzon's plan for a second term.

There may also, in this increasing tension between the two men, have been an element of jealousy on Brodrick's part arising from the self-knowledge, even in such a pompous man, that he really knew very little about India. Certainly everyone was agreed that the written correspondence was causing friction, and that a good dose of personal contact would be the best cure. Godley wrote to Curzon: 'Since I last saw you, I have had the advantage of a long talk with Lady Curzon about many matters connected with India and I wrote to her yesterday. I think the conclusions of our conversation was really the most important part of it, namely that she thinks, as I have done for many months, that if you can come over here and see us all, it will make many questions infinitely easier to deal with . . . The distance of many thousands of miles, and the different way things look when they are explained by letter, counts for much. Your house, by the way, with its alterations, looks exceedingly well, and the two rooms to the Park remind one of that which you occupied in 1895.'[10] To one of his letters Godley added a PS: 'You are greatly wanted on the Front Bench just now.'[11] And Brodrick wrote, 'I do hope you will give me the first evening after your return in order that I may assemble all that are brightest and best amongst those who have missed you for the past five and a half years.'[12]

Curzon admitted that distance did not lend enchantment to the view: 'I think there is a great deal in what you say in your last letter as to the value of oral communications. You must remember that at the end we can have no idea what is going on except what you may choose to tell me in your private letters. I have never realised so forcibly as during the last year the extraordinary difficulties and disadvantages of trying to conduct a Government at this great distance, and without any power of personal explanation.'[13] Although there were daily – or more frequent – interchanges by telegram, letters took about three weeks to reach their destination, and the strain this imposed both on Curzon and on the India Office is clearly seen.

Curzon was full of high spirits at the prospect of leaving India and seeing Mary and the children once more – they had been away since before Christmas 1903. At the same time, he made the most careful preparations to ensure that while he was in England there should be no lapse in policies, or any problem which would disrupt the orderly flow of administration. Lord Ampthill, who was to act as Viceroy in his absence, wrote home to Godley, 'My conversations with Lord Curzon had the effect of rejuvenating and refreshing me in the most extraordinary manner, and although I was dead-beat when I arrived here, I have been able to start work feeling as fresh as if I had had a month's holiday. Lord Curzon's personality, ideas and marvellous powers are certainly most inspiring.'[14] Godley replied that, yes, indeed, 'Curzon has a touch of genius.'[15] Although no record of it exists, it seems certain that Curzon warned Ampthill about Kitchener's proposals for reform, because, as will be seen, when these were somewhat incautiously reintroduced as soon as Curzon had gone on leave, Ampthill did not fall into the trap laid open for him.

There was an element of jumpiness in Curzon's mental state at this time, as if he were not sure that he ought to leave India just when Russian manoeuvrings in Japan and on the Indian border caused concern. He telegrammed to Brodrick 'Owing to affairs in the Far East, do you think there is the least fear that I may be unable to come home this summer?'[16] but the new Secretary of State replied, 'In my opinion it is most important that you should return . . . Mr Balfour and others think that the opportunity of consulting you on Eastern affairs will be invaluable.'[17] Curzon continued to be gloomy about returning to London. He wrote to Mary: 'My idea is to arrive in London about May 18-20. But I don't suppose, darling, from the public point of view it makes much difference. I do not suppose for one moment that anyone will come down to meet us, or that the slightest notice will be taken of my arrival. Who cares for India?'[18]

Despite this forboding, the actual homecoming in May 1904 was a triumph. A crowd of friends were at the station to meet him and he was driven directly from Charing Cross to Buckingham Palace for an audience with the King. As he was driven down The Mall, he turned over in his mind the undoubted fact that the sound relationship which he had had with the India Office in Lord Hamilton's day had gone forever, and he wondered if he was right to tell the King that he would definitely be returning to India. Godley, whose correspondence with Curzon shows a spirit of frankness and amiability, had advised him some months earlier that there were strong reasons for thinking it would have been better if he had not exceeded the normal term as Viceroy.[19] During his visit to Lady Curzon Godley also advised her that the time had come for the Viceroy to leave India and he told Curzon: 'You are inclined when there is a difference of opinion to carry your protest beyond the recognised official limits, to bring pressure to bear to force the hand of the Government at home. You will say at once that the impression is most incorrect and unfair. Still I venture to urge you to remember that it exists.'[20] Curzon did not take Godley's warnings about Brodrick seriously enough. 'When he was appointed [Secretary of State] many of our mutual friends did not give the combination six months' Curzon had written. 'I replied that in view of our old relations, I saw no reason why it should not last for six years. Nor in anything that has yet passed between us do I see the signs of that disruption which you appear to portend.'[21] Curzon much preferred to listen to advice from those he considered his equals or betters – such as Balfour, rather than from Brodrick, whom he did not.

Curzon's confidence in his own grasp of affairs in India, and his strong sense of duty, overcame any doubts he had about the wisdom of returning to India, and he gave the King a pledge that he would return to deal with such difficulties as Afghanistan and Persia.

Godley seems, however, to have despaired that he was getting his message through to Curzon, writing that in his disputes with the Council during the London visit, Curzon seemed not to say to himself, 'I will prove to the Cabinet or to the Council of India, that they are wrong about this and that I am right.' but, alas, 'I have given my opinion, I have even reiterated it in two or three despatches. I am the Viceroy of India and, confound you, how do you dare to set your opinion against mine?'[22]

Curzon was contemptuous of the India Council in London which he regarded as low in intellect and lacking any depth of knowledge of India. His view seems to be supported by another man of considerable intellect, Maynard Keynes, who began his career in the India Office. He described its Council as 'Government by dotardry. At least half those present showed manifest signs of senile decay, and the rest did not speak'.[23]

In the early weeks after his arrival in London Curzon did not in fact spend much time with the Council or with Brodrick, as the latter was engaged in a feud with his successor at the War Office, Arnold-Forster, which overflowed into the press. Curzon attended a meeting of the Imperial Defence Committee (of which more later) but found that their discussion of Indian affairs was limited by the fact that barely one of them had been in India. 'The only representative of our interests is the Secretary of State [Brodrick] who knows nothing about India at all.'[24] The other body of men with whom Curzon had to deal, the India Council, were, Godley told Ampthill, 'a very good set, straight and patriotic, strongly conservative,'[25] but they were suspicious of Curzon's views, believing them to be unrepresentative and inflexible. Again, Curzon thought that any stiffness between them would be alleviated by personal contact but it is doubtful if this was the case. Curzon looked to the Secretary of State – after his experience with Lord Hamilton – to be his supporter in any difficulties with the Council, but this was not the role Brodrick had cast for himself. Indeed both Brodrick and the Council disagreed with Curzon on some ten issues in the first year of Brodrick's period of office. Brodrick complained to Balfour that Curzon was always trying to force through his opinions. 'These diatribes descend on me two or three times a week,' and 'Poor Ampthill writes that George's letters are a series of courts martial and reproaches and they look [forward] to his return as much as the boys at "Dotheboys" did to the return of Squeers after the holiday.'[26] Yet while Brodrick was whining to Balfour, he was buttering up Curzon with such phrases as, 'I sometimes wonder if you know how often I think of you and of the

difficulties you so courageously overcome.'[27] Curzon remained
cynical – it was during this leave in London that Curzon was much
humiliated by the treatment meted out to Younghusband which
has already been described in Chapter 5, and which was Brodrick's
first attempt to thwart Curzon's policies in India.

As those in London were making great efforts to repair the
problems of communication with Curzon, Kitchener was already
making substantial progress with his own highly-sophisticated
network of contacts at home. Letters and copies of his memos were
flying to and fro, to General Stedman, General Clarke, Lady
Salisbury, Field Marshall Lord Roberts, Brodrick, and Lord
Derby, all of them in key positions. His man, Colonel Mullaly, was
about to leave India for six months' duty at the War Office,
thoroughly primed as to Kitchener's point of view, although
Kitchener had asked that 'in regard to any aspect on which he had
not stated his own views, he asks not to be bound by Mullaly's
opinion'.[28] It was particularly important that the Home Government should be on his side as it now looked as if Curzon might
shoulder a second term, 'always,' said Kitchener, 'like the lover
who while protesting yet relents – always going, never goes.'[29]

Kitchener had, from the moment of his arrival in India, taken an
independent line about communication with London. To Lord
Roberts, his late chief in South Africa, and now in charge of the
Army at home, he wrote regularly to enlist support, as we have
seen, almost from the day of arrival. For example:

> I have been out with the army on manoeuvres for the last 12 days
> and I am sorry to say that I am not very impressed with its efficiency
> for the field. In fact, I fear that if the army were called upon to take
> part in war, it would come to considerable grief and we would have
> some unpleasant incident to meet. The value of these manoeuvres
> has been reduced to a minimum owing to transport and supplies
> being so arranged by the Military Department as to tie the whole
> forces down to fixed positions and only certain roads.[30]

5th February 1903:
> Eddie Stanley [later Lord Derby] will have shown you a scheme for
> reorganising the Army as a whole. It will be of enormous value to
> the Army efficiency out here if it can be carried out and I am glad to
> say the Mil. Member agrees in this.[31]

12th February 1903:

The Military Dept. having officially asked me my opinion on a recent GGO dealing with the organisation of the Indian Army I have been writing a minute on the subject on which I should much like your opinion. Please show my Minute to Johnny [Iain Hamilton]. I know he is very interested in the question.[32]

6th May 1903:

I enclose some private correspondence which has been going on between Curzon and myself. I hope you will think I took the right line. As Curzon's letters are marked Private, please do not show them to anyone, and certainly not to Brodrick. The position here is very galling, with the Military Member virtually C-in-C and supported at every turn by the Viceroy; it makes what would have been a pleasure a disagreeable duty. I hope to be able to stand it till next year; but as you will see from the correspondence, things may get critical at any time. If Elles [the Military Member] had any knowledge of what an army ought to be to hold its own in a big war, we might get on, but he is narrow-minded and bigoted to a degree.

I never sent you a complete copy of my reorganisation scheme, so enclose one now with Ch. 2 that I have just finished showing the deficiencies of the Army out here in case of war. The authorities that be will not like it.[33]

Kitchener returned to the attack as soon as Curzon had left for London, writing to Roberts in May 1904:

I do not know how the Mil. Dept. worked in your time, but now it is the Govt. of India and as such the Military Member is almost *de facto* and certainly *de jure* C-in-C. He also has the Supply and Transport Depts. under him, and through these are some absurd regulations, absolute dead letters, that can be quoted to show that the C-in-C has something to say in transport matters, you might as well make a regulation to the effect that 'the Army will always defeat the enemy' and then sit tight and do nothing, as depend upon the existing impracticable regulations which no one pays the least attention to . . . I hope you will discuss the question with Duff and Mullaly [both on Kitchener's staff and temporarily in London] who have had considerable experience of working the present position and know my views . . . The Govt. of India, through the fiction of keeping the Viceroy hidden behind them, [means] that the Mil. Dept. have abrogated to themselves all the power of the S of S at home before the Esher Commission, and no doubt legally, under the existing rules, they have right on their side . . .

I do not complain of being openly opposed or that my views are not sufficiently considered, but under the existing system it is an enormous labour to get anything done, and the Mil. Dept. can burke and delay to any extent questions which they do not like . . . I know how difficult it is to change a system that has been working so long in India, but unless something is done now, when serious war comes we shall be defeated through our own fault. *You can show this letter to anyone interested.*[34]

7th July 1904:

I hope something may be done to get rid of the dual system of Army administration and responsibility out here, it simply blocks everything. Do you think anything will be done . . . in the near future?[35]

27th November 1904:

Brodrick writes to me privately that you do not consider any change in the relations between the Mily. Dept. and the C-in-C should take place. I did not understand this from your memo on the subject, but owing to your opinion Brodrick intimates that no change will take place. I consider with the Mily. Dept. as it is, my time is being wasted out here, I can do practically nothing. I think you will agree that I do not mind responsibility but I must say that I do not like to think of the number of soldiers' lives that would be needlessly thrown away if we went to war with Russia with our present organisation at HQ. My opinion is that dual control should be abolished and the two departments should be brought together to work as one for the efficiency of the Army as a whole. If the Mily. Dept. cannot be brought to work with the C-in-C then I think the C-in-C should be abolished and the MD with a chief of staff should alone rule the Army. The responsibility for efficiency in the Army would then rest on one shoulders . . . I should much prefer to see a system introduced by which the Mily. Dept. would work with the C-in-C but as long as they remain absolutely independent and represent the Govt. of India I fear this is impossible. Under the present system of dual control, the friction between the two offices must I fear always continue as long as we have to deal with human nature . . . If nothing can be done in the matter I feel I am wasting [my] time and as soon as I can be spared I may be allowed to get out of this. Otherwise I like the country and the work and would not leave it. I feel that time is going on, and as I do not intend to be one of the old officers about the clubs in London, and as you know have no wish to go to the WO, I shall have to start some other work outside the Army when I leave India.[36]

Two years earlier, Mary Curzon had written to Kitchener, immediately after his arrival in India, 'I suppose you know that the prayer of the soldiers has been that the two giants (you and George) will fall out.' How ironic, now, to read that letter, which has often been quoted in part:

> I must send you a line of greeting – just to hope that you like your army and your men and the *mimic* warfare after the *real* you have been so deep in. I hope your talk at Bharakpore gave you as much satisfaction as it *did* George and as it *does* me. Do please take the army and all the Military straight into your heart. It will be a wondrous load off George. I have always felt that it was wrong in every way that he should have had as much to do with it as he has – but now there is a Chief at last who is supreme and absolute with his army in his pocket! It pleases me quite enormously to feel how much there is for you to do and I shall watch the two strong men, you and George, battling with the Indian Machines, Military and Civil, with intense interest. I suppose you know that the prayer of the soldiers has been that the two giants will fall out – and it will be a grief for them to see you work in harmony and to know the intense satisfaction it is to George that you are here at last. There is something else I feel I must say and that is that we do hope we shall see much of you in Calcutta and Simla, peacefully and intimately, and last officially. There is a lot of traditional and iron-bound isolation which encircles you and us, so we shall drag you out of your solitude, we hope, very often, and see you often when there is no society. Do you play billiards? If so George will seize you for many family games! *Please don't answer this.* It is only a friendly little line, not meant for a minute to bother you, or add to your labours. I think it rather unnecessary of the Duke of Connaught to come out and take me down to dinner just as we have finally got you here!![37]

Kitchener had a strong streak of mischief in his make-up and it must have amused him over the years to mislead Mary about his intentions, just as he enjoyed the sight of a holder of the Victoria Cross, Frank Maxwell, with his trousers pulled up above his knees, dancing about in a tub of *papier mâché* making material for the library ceiling of Kitchener's villa, Snowdon. The ceiling was to be an exact copy of the one at Hatfield, and Kitchener, whose expenditure at Snowdon caused some problems, decided to economise by using the files – which he called *bumph*. He was delighted at seeing 'Brat' Maxwell, and another of 'the Boys', Victor Brooke, pounding away at the masses of files which he could now never read. Kitchener was by now increasingly annoyed at the slow progress he was making in abolishing the Mil. Dept. He wrote to Marker:

> I am glad you saw Clarke [Secretary to the Imperial Defence Committee]. I wonder whether he will be able to do anything to improve the administration of the Army out here. I am pretty sick of the present state of affairs. The Military Member is the real C-in-C. I am merely his [supporter] and as to getting things done, it is almost hopeless. If my reorganisation scheme is accepted at home I am quite sure it will be wrecked out here by the Military in every detail. Peg away at this whenever you get a chance. *I see a possible chance of resigning before long but I fear it will be blocked as Ampthill would not like my going in his time.* Keep this to yourself.[38]

This possible 'chance of resigning' came about as a result of Kitchener's own underhand methods. What had happened was that Curzon had been invited to attend another meeting of the Imperial Defence Committee on 15th June 1904. This was an advisory body set up by Balfour at the end of 1902. One of Balfour's keenest studies was the defence of the Empire, and he believed that a very high-level committee of good minds, studying papers on various aspects of the defence of the Empire, regardless of narrow geographical limitations or specific military divisions, would contribute to the development of grand strategic plans. It met weekly, initially under the chairmanship of the Duke of Devonshire, and Balfour himself attended every meeting. One of the recommendations of the Esher Committee (officially known as the War Office Reconstitution Committee) set up in November 1903 was that the Imperial Defence Committee should have a permanent secretary, and the man chosen was Sir George Sydenham Clarke who had been secretary to the Colonial Defence Committee, and an Intelligence Officer in the Army with the rank of General as well as Governor of Victoria, Australia.

This formidable man set up his offices in Disraeli's old house in Whitehall Gardens, with easy access to Downing Street, the War Office, and other centres of power. As will be seen, Kitchener was soon to realise his significance. The Esher Committee recommended that the Imperial Defence Committee, though completely subordinate to the Prime Minister, was empowered to 'anticipate' his needs. Clarke took full advantage of opportunities to do so until, after Balfour's downfall, he was dismissed by the Liberals.

It is not clear why Clarke took Kitchener's side against Curzon. At first he appears to have realised the problems that would ensue if Kitchener got his way. 'K is an ultra centralizer and if he got his way, he would get everything into his own direct power . . . His influence is out of all proportion to his judgement . . . If the Press had not taught the country that K is a God-send administrator, it might have been possible to make progress in obtaining a staff qualified to direct operations of war.'[39] This was a sound assessment, but after talking to Mullaly, Clarke seems to have gone over to Kitchener's side.

To return to the invitation for Curzon to join the Imperial Defence Committee meeting during his leave, he received the relevant papers from Sir George, and, as he sat in Carlton House Terrace, one June morning, turning them over, he was astonished to come across a long memorandum from Kitchener. He immediately took up a sheet of paper and wrote to Balfour expressing his annoyance:

> I want to raise a point about the papers submitted to the points discussed in the forum of Imp. Defence. Yesterday Sir Geo. Clarke sent me a fresh batch of papers and among them greatly to my surprise I recognised a memo of Kitchener on the Admin. of the Indian Army. Let me tell you the history of that. When he came out to India in Dec. 1902, K. already had the first edition of this paper prepared. It had been written for him by someone before he started, and he discussed it at our first private meeting two days after he had landed. I urged him to wait until he had the machine in working order. A few weeks later at Calcutta he sent me the first draft and asked my confidential opinion (it was in a very different form from the present). I gave him my views and again urged him not to begin by trying to overturn our constitution before he had been a month at headquarters. The draft again disappeared. He arrived from a long

tour at Simla in May 1903 and he let out to my wife one day that he
had again launched it on its official career and had sent it through
the Adj. Gen. to the Mil. Dept. It had now assumed a second shape
different from the first. But also differing from its present form. It
contained a slashing attack on the Mil. Dept. and a proposal for its
practical extinction. Sir E. Elles the Mil. Member came to me in a
great stew, wanting to know if he should resign. I calmed him and
had a talk with K. I pointed out that he had not spent much more
than a month at the HQ and that his account of the proceeding of
the Mil. Admin. in India was quite incorrect, that I could not myself
support his proposals and that I had little doubt that they would be
rejected by Council. I again urged less precipitate proceedings. He
accordingly withdrew his memo which from that day to this I have
never again seen.

Suddenly it turns up, rewritten and re-expurgated in the papers of
the Defence Com. here. How it got there I do not know. But I ask
because I think you will agree with me that a point of great
constitutional importance is involved. The admin. of the Indian
Army is a matter which would materially originate in one of two
quarters (1) the S of S in Council, (2) the Govt. of India. That is
either the S of S might ask us in India to consider the matter, and
might submit concrete proposals to us – or the Govt. of India at the
instigation of the C-in-C or some other member of Council might
initiate proceedings and approach the S of S.[40]

Balfour replied at once:

I am in very close agreement with the opinions expressed in your
note. I did not intend K's observations on the relations between the
C-in-C and the Mil. Member of Council to be circulated to the
Defence Committee. Nor should I think of allowing the Defence
Committee to discuss it, or to pronounce an opinion upon it . . . We
are vitally interested in the success of such schemes as Lord K has
suggested, with, I believe, your full approval, for increasing the
proportion of our Indian Army which, in case of war with Russia,
would be available on the frontier. We are also bound to consider
such questions as the adequacy or inadequacy of transport, animals
and warlike stores immediately available in India for the purposes of
mobilisation, for these nearly touch our own arrangements . . . I
quite agree with you that it is not the business of the Defence
Committee to interfere with Indian administration, just as it is not
its business to interfere with War Office or Admiralty administration. It has no powers, it is merely an advisory body.[41]

Meanwhile, in India, Kitchener was taking advantage of Curzon's absence to press his case with Lord Ampthill, the acting Viceroy. He came up with an ingenious proposal that he should take over as Commander-in-Chief various responsibilities hitherto held by the Military Dept. Lord Ampthill's response was described in a private letter to Brodrick.

There is another matter in which Lord Kitchener is pressing me very hard concerning which Lord Curzon can tell you a great deal. He demands that the administrative control of the Supply and Transport Department should be transferred to the Commander-in-Chief. My colleagues appear to regard it as a comparatively simple and unimportant matter in which Lord Kitchener's personal views should be complied with, but after a careful study of some very able and exhaustive notes written by Sir Edmond Elles, who is of course firmly opposed to the proposal, I have come to the conclusion that it is a very large question, which has been so brilliantly debated in former days, as to whether the office of Military Member should be abolished or not. Lord Kitchener as you know, raised this question as soon as he assumed office but was persuaded by Lord Curzon not to press it officially. I see in Lord Kitchener's present proposal another means of attaining the same end. It is in fact the thin end of the wedge . . . I take it that it is now an axiomatic principle that the Executive and Administrative should be sharply divided in army affairs. Lord Kitchener's proposal is in effect to revert to the system of combining executive and administrative functions under one head, a system which no longer exists in any other army in the world, which India abolished fifty years ago, and which has at last been finally and emphatically condemned in England. I see no reason for making even one step in this retrograde direction. [If Kitchener does not accept this] we shall have to fight it out in Council, and I fear that this latter contingency is the most probable as Lord Kitchener is desperately keen on this subject. He refers to it on every possible and impossible occasion, and he even dragged it in the other day on some papers relating to the diseases of camels. I only hope that it will not lead to any serious disagreement between Lord Kitchener and myself.[42]

Ampthill wrote again to Brodrick:

I have failed completely in my endeavour to conciliate Lord Kitchener in the Supply and Transport question. He firmly declines to acceptt the compromise . . . I am sorry to say that the C-in-C has imported a personal note into the discussions . . . Lord Kitchener both in his official note and in a private letter to me hints that the question is one on which he might have to make his resignation depend, but as he said the same thing before on the larger question and did not act upon what he said, I can hardly believe he will be prepared to stand or fall by what is only a portion of that same question.[43]

And a few days later:

I have read with the keenest interest his [Kitchener's] memorandum [to Stedman]. It more than confirms the opinion I have already expressed . . . I do not think that Lord Kitchener has quite played the game in this matter. He gave Lord Curzon a pledge that he would not raise the matter again during his time, and yet before Lord Curzon had left India and without Lord Curzon's knowledge he sends home his scheme to the Prime Minister . . . Lord Kitchener should obviously have requested Lord Curzon to send his memorandum home officially . . . I shall of course behave as if I knew nothing about the memorandum and had never seen it, but it will be of the greatest use to me to know what has transpired.

Lord Kitchener in his present attack on the Supply and Transport Dept. disavows any intention of assailing the position of the Military Member. I am afraid that from the first I distrusted his sincerity in this matter, and it is now clear from the Memorandum that he is bent on the design of abolishing the Mil. Member.[44]

Kitchener's threat of resignation was, as we have seen, conveyed to London by Ampthill, and Brodrick, who should have known from his experience at the War Office that Kitchener's threats of resignation were a regular occurrence, at once began to show signs of fear. Indeed, it was from this time that Kitchener's power over the Home Government began to develop because of the latter's lack of backbone when it came to decision making. 'The Boys' back in India were pleased that Kitchener had at last shown signs of doing something, even if it was only to threaten. 'The Govt. would lose more votes by K's resignation than all their other bungling put together,' wrote Hubert Hamilton to Marker.[45] This was a lucid assessment of the Conservatives' position and there is no doubt that the pressure which Hamilton advised Kitchener to put on the

Government by offering to resign was based upon it. At the same time, Balfour's mentality was probably too complex to allow him to be moved by one simple link in a chain of complex events.

Brodrick now got in touch with Kitchener (although strictly speaking he should have addressed his correspondence to Ampthill in Curzon's absence) asking him what his views were on the broad question of the Army Admin. system in India. He added, 'I believe it is forbidden by practice for me to communicate with anyone except the Viceroy . . . but I want to break the rule on the principle that when the cat's away! You must not let it be known that I have written . . . reply sub rosa . . . when the cat's away!'[46]
Kitchener replied from Simla:

You ask me about the Army system in India; well it is one which patience may improve, but you require a vast amount of it. There is no doubt that if we had a big war on the frontier there would be a fearful crash and "show up" here. A system under which Transport, Supply, Remounts, Ordnance are entirely divorced from the executive command of the Army and placed under an independent authority is one which must cause an entire reorganisation as soon as war is declared, rather late to begin some people think. In the meantime, though, large sums are lavished on these services with a liberal hand. All these departments are to my mind quite inefficient to meet the wants of the Army, from which they are separated, and therefore out of touch, instead of being co-ordinated with the troops that must depend upon them in war time.

Money voted for the Army is wasted out here just as much, if not more, than at home; but they all seem to like it, and efficiency is about the last thing that appeals to anyone, except the Viceroy. What has been done in the past is right, and nothing must on any account be altered by horrid innovations coming from benighted England, be they Viceroys or Cs-in-C. Curzon had done a great deal, but there is still much to do.[47]

Kitchener also continued to press his case with others in London who could influence the outcome. A letter from General Sir E. Stedman (in the India Office) was of particular significance because Kitchener had no right to correspond with him behind Curzon's back – nor indeed had Stedman any business to follow up the correspondence, or to circulate it, which he did. When this

letter eventually came to light two years later, Curzon and his
supporters were to be greatly enraged at Kitchener's duplicity.
Stedman's reply was as follows:

> The despatch on dual control will be taken in hand on Monday.
> Meanwhile I have passed your typewritten letter to me of criticism
> on the Mil. Member and the Viceroy's notes to Sir A Godley to
> digest and when the despatch comes I will show it to Mr Brodrick. I
> have no official instructions about the technical treatment of the
> despatch but I believe the Cabinet will deal with it . . . I feel that
> your views will be supported *here* and if the Cabinet takes the
> decision into its hands they will also I think support them. The only
> man who will presumably oppose them is Lord Lansdowne [the
> Foreign Secretary] and he always has a cool and reasonable method
> of treating questions and an open mind. I shall not feel as happy
> about things if the Council of Imperial Defence is constituted the
> judge of the question but I think this very improbable.[48]

Kitchener was continuing to receive support from Sir George
Clarke who wrote (marked *private*):

> Thanks for yours of 9th with a copy of yours to Sir E. Stedman. I
> have shown it to Lord Esher who thinks it is absolutely unanswer-
> able. I hope to get Mr Balfour to read it today. It is most necessary
> that he should fully understand the immense strength of your case. I
> notice you have not quoted the opinions of Lord Roberts in 1889
> after he had been nearly 5 years C-in-C. I enclose the Minute.
> Surely the sentences I have underlined and others, constitute a
> powerful indictment of the whole system.[49]

Reference has already been made to 'the Band of Boys' with whom
Kitchener surrounded himself. 'The Boys' were hard at it on
Kitchener's behalf throughout the late summer of 1904. They were
headed by Kitchener's Military Secretary, Hubert Hamilton, who
was known to the others as 'Handsome Hammy' and had a
conventional army background. Birdwood, also one of 'The Boys',
said he was a 'typical Queen's officer' a mark of high praise.
Hamilton wrote to 'Conk' Marker regularly every mail with news.
For example, 'Ampthill is quite dependent on K and was quite
unhappy when he mentioned the idea of going on tour. K has been
wonderfully fit this year – in spite of the leg – no headaches and

always in good spirits . . . The absence of Curzon coincides with the absence of headaches!!'[50]

In another letter to Marker, Hamilton says, 'Frank Maxwell has just returned . . . He completely broke down . . . poor boy, I fear his brain is not his strong point.'[51] Maxwell was only in India for a short visit and returned to London in October. But Maxwell apart, the rest of the team was working solidly together. Birdwood was appointed to the HQ General Staff in India 'but he is to keep touch, the closest'.[52] In London, Marker sought advice about his relations with the press, and told Hamilton that Repington of *The Times* wanted to come to India to interview Kitchener on the subject of the Mil. Dept. One problem which Hamilton foresaw was that Repington who was not married to the lady with whom he was living, would travel with a 'wife (or lady or woman) who would be a difficulty, especially with K.'[53] Hamilton also told Marker:

> Further consideration made me mention your letter from Repington to K with result that I have wired you this morning, as per enclosed, and to Mullaly what follows your message. No one knows the whole subject so well as Mullaly and K's views on it, so that if Repington plays his cards well with M and if M is discreet without being needlessly secretive, R will get all he wants without coming out here. I am in great hopes you will manipulate this business with discretion – I am in no doubt about the discretion, but as Mullaly leaves on 29th. . .I fear you may not have the opportunity of prompt manipulation.
>
> K was rather funny and nice when I spoke to him. His first instinct was to shy at Repington – that is natural, but I pointed out the great importance of the question and R's power for good or bad. Then he came round and hit upon the Mullaly idea, explaining that while the matter is still under discussion he cannot himself resort to the press in any way. "Of course the thing is known more or less and can be discussed in the press and elsewhere, but people must get what material they can for discussion from others. I cannot give it. *Curzon knows that I am practically the only one who understands that he alone is the real obstacle, and if the reform I consider essential* is finally blocked why then I resign – I cannot go to the Press even then, or in the meantime to fight my cause. It would not be right and etc. etc."
>
> This indicates K's line sufficiently, and I quite agree, but it always amuses me when he promises to do "what would not be right"![54]

And from time to time Kitchener would himself write to Marker to ensure that the message was getting through clearly: 'What we should do under the present system if we had a serious war God alone knows. Disaster would follow; but then it would be too late to change. I have pointed all this out as you know, and proposed changes to do away with this dual system . . . If I cannot succeed I must resign as it is wrong the public should think all is well when it is not so.'[55]

Kitchener had been advised during Curzon's absence to be as tactful as possible with the acting Viceroy Lord Ampthill, and despite the difficulty about the resignation, there were times when Kitchener had him on his side. Hubert Hamilton wrote to Marker:

> We have had some little interest here of late. Council could not agree as to the composition of Brigades. K was for homogeneous Brigades in an Army to meet the Russians, but Elles adhered to the mixed Bdes, and had Lord Ampthill and Hewett [another Member of Council] with him. Consequently K had to canvass and explain to these two latter until he convinced them his proposal was sound and not attended by any danger, and then after 3 weeks' delay followed the defeat of Elles. This is typical of what is always going on under the system of dual control and until we get rid of it there can be no progress. In the meantime of course, K is becoming wearied and disgusted. However, his ultimate victory cheered him up . . .
>
> I shall hear next mail if you were able to bring Repington and M together. Mullaly is due back by next mail. He has worked so very hard and so well that one can't help regretting he is a bit difficult in tact and breeding . . .[56]
>
> [And later] I think you managed all right about Repington. K doesn't like him at all and would prefer to have nothing to do with him — so strange to find his qualities do not appeal to K.[57]

When Hamilton wrote privately to Marker in London he called the resignation 'K's ultimatum'.

> *No* one but Mullaly knows of it outside our family circle here — not even Duff and I don't know if the Viceroy even told Elles. But of course it will leak out in time. Of course K was immensely relieved when he had done it, and I think and hope the effect will be good. *It gave the Govt. a shock and may awake them to the folly of treating K like any*

ordinary creature . . . I think on the whole K has found this a dull season with Ampthill but he has got through it wonderfully well. I think he likes the excitement of Curzon in spite of his headaches.[58]

Hamilton wrote again to Marker:

I have had two good talks with Mullaly and gather the ground is so well prepared at home so far as the question of Army Admin is concerned, that at present the intervention of the press is not only unnecessary but might be inadvisable. In the meantime the ultimatum will have given the whole question another hard push in the desired direction – as yet we have felt none of the effect of the latter here but I am convinced we shall when Curzon arrives . . .

Lord Bobs [Roberts] . . . is also well-satisfied that when he was C-in-C in India everything was perfect, while as regards the present and future, he is always certain to make for the winning and popular side. Curzon is the real stumbling block – he finds the Mil. Dept. a most suitable personal buffer against the possible eccentricities of C-in-Cs. However I am hopeful that the ultimatum may bring things to a head in the near future.[59]

But by the end of the year both Marker in London and the team in India had to agree that 'the effect of the resignation is wearing off, the Govt., having got over the shock, don't care a straw about its cause . . . they are much too absorbed . . . in their efforts to cling to office.'[60] Was Balfour merely clinging to office, or did he genuinely believe Kitchener was right?

Following Kitchener's threat of resignation, Curzon had urgent talks with Balfour and on August 4th a hastily-called meeting was convened in the Prime Minister's office in the House of Commons, attended also by Lord Roberts, Brodrick, and Godley. While Lord Roberts and Curzon were in favour of retaining the present relationships in Military Administration, the others were for a change. Some weeks later, Balfour referred to this meeting in a thirty-page letter to Curzon which began by dealing with the question of the Afghanistan/Persian border.

I quite admit that no man living has so intimate a knowledge of Afghan affairs as you may justly boast of; and if these questions could be decided on authority alone, there is no man to whose authority I would more willingly defer than your own; and indeed, in everything which I am about to say, I hope you will understand that I am merely putting forward arguments as they present themselves to my mind, without in any way pretending to arrogate special insight or knowledge in connection with these difficult problems . . . There are many others who may justly claim to speak about them with knowledge. Is there a single one, not actually under the spell of your personality, who takes your view? I agree that true foresight is constantly found in the minority, and not in the majority, especially when the minority contains, or, in this case, consists of a man of genius: still, after giving the fullest weight to this consideration, the opinion of the majority cannot, I think, be wholly ignored. There is another matter on which . . . we have had some conversation already, but on which I am still anxious to press my views on you – I mean the question of military organisation in India.

There are aspects of this on which I should never think of putting my judgement against yours. You necessarily have an experience of the making of the system to which I cannot pretend. But there are some general considerations whose value seems to me to be almost independent of local circumstance of special knowledge which we cannot afford to forget. Hitherto, India, under our rule, has never really been threatened by an external enemy. The fear of Russian invasion stretches over many generations of Indian Administrators, and goes back to a time when, so far as I can judge, an invasion would have been wholly impracticable. No one however can say that it is impracticable now; and with the evidence of the magnitude of the Russian forces which can be accumulated and supplied at one end of a railway 7000 miles long, we have to recognise that since the extention of Russian railways to the Afghan Border, the problem of Indian Defence is different from that which had to be faced even 15 or 20 years ago.

This being so, we have sent out as C-in-C the soldier who certainly commands a greater amount of confidence than any other English General, Lord Roberts excepted. He takes the strongest view as to the impossibility of efficiently conducting a war with the present organisation of the Indian Military system, and I feel perfectly confident that he will not continue to stay in India if that system remains unmodified. I feel also certain that, if he resigns, he will make public the grounds of his resignation, and that the ground will be the one I have stated.

Now putting aside for the moment to intrinsic merits of the question, how is such a contingency to be met?[61]

One week later they had another meeting and Curzon urged that if the Government insisted, against his wishes, in having an official enquiry, at least they should follow the constitutional method of asking the Indian Government's opinion by a despatch. He must have realised that Balfour was not on his side in the matter although he still relied on his own powers of persuasion, particularly when Balfour wrote to him afterwards, in November, 1904, 'I cannot tell you how pleasant it was to have a long talk with you the other day, and, I will add, how useful.'[62] Curzon, who still thought nothing would be done, would not have been so sanguine had he known that Balfour was at the time writing:

> One of the most unlucky sides of all this business is that George Curzon's visit here, from which I had hoped so much, has largely lost its value . . . [His illness and Mary's] rendered difficult and indeed impossible, the full personal discussion of all the questions which press for solution . . . I frankly admit that I am now rather puzzled as to what ought to be done.[63]

And he would have been even more disturbed had he known that before that Christmas Balfour would be writing to Kitchener himself, in the course of a long letter, 'I have not touched on questions of Indian Army Admin, but my personal conviction is (at least as at present advised) that the existing division of attributes between the C-in-C and the Mil. Member of Council is quite indefensible.'[64]

Finally, on 1st January 1905, Balfour committed himself even more strongly to Kitchener: 'I have read with great interest and admiration your paper on the Indian Council and its relation to Indian Government . . . all my sympathies are with you.'[65]

Before returning to the battlefield in India, there is one further aspect of Curzon's leave in England which was to have a permanent effect on his mind – and that was the near-fatal illness which overcame Mary as they holidayed in Walmer Castle which Curzon called 'this ancestral doghole'. It was caused, it is believed, by defective drains outside her bedroom window – which infected her internally giving her peritonitis, complicated by phlebitis. She was in a coma for days and concern for her life was so grave that King Edward enquired about her daily. Curzon wrote to the King,

'Hope is sinking lower and lower within me, and the cloud of darkness seems to be settling down.'[66] Years later he wrote on sheets torn from a pad, 'These are the notes made by me at Walmer Castle in September 1904 when my darling lay dying, and when she gave me her last instructions and bade me farewell.' Her biographer, Nigel Nicolson, truly writes, 'seldom can so moving a document have been made and preserved.'[67] They show clearly how deeply they were in love and yet the astonishing thing is that when she recovered, but might still have had a relapse, Curzon returned to India. It is true that as he embarked on the boat on 24th November 1904, he wrote to her, 'All the way through I have thought of Kinkie only – Kinkie through all the phases of her fearful illness, Kinkie's courage, her beautiful and unparalleled devotion, her resignation, her patience, her combat with all the foes of evil and death, her serene and conquering love for poor Pappy . . . It is with a sad and miserable heart that I go, leaving all that makes life worth living behind me, and going out to toil and isolation – and often worse. But it seems to be destiny . . .'[68] But he still went off, believing that she would never return to India, yet feeling that he must, as it was 'destiny'. In the tragic sense, it was to be just that in the year ahead.

On the day before his departure for India, Curzon received a placatory letter from Brodrick saying: 'Your friendship has meant so much to me for nearly 30 years, that shadow upon it has given me intense pain. I meant from my heart what I said to you at the end of the evening [they had dined togther] and recognised the generosity of your reply. If you would let our official relations date anew from today, I do not think you would ever regret it.'[69] But they did not and they lived to regret it.

Chapter Eight

Kitchener's Deployment of Forces

When Curzon returned to India – alone – at the end of 1904, he did not for one moment expect that Mary would be well enough to rejoin him, nor did he expect to have to stay in India for more than about three months. He had come through the trial of Mary's illness at Walmer Castle, and the trial he was now to face, the battle with Kitchener, did not loom all that large in his own scheme of things. Unknown to him, the previous tenants of Walmer Castle were to play a key role in his defeat, by their unremitting support for Kitchener. It has always been a mystery why Alice, Lady Salisbury – for the Cecils were these previous Walmer tenants – should have played such a strange and unworthy part in the plot against Curzon. The explanation has to do with the price of furniture and is given by the Cecils' biographer Kenneth Rose. 'It was the custom that each incoming Lord Warden bought his predecessor's furniture at valuation. Curzon was reluctant to do so. He intended to refurnish the castle in the elaborate style to which he was accustomed. He wrote that many of the carpets were swarming with maggots and he was obliged to sleep on bare boards impregnated with Carbolic ...'[1] The Salisburys were much angered, but agreed to abide by the decision of an arbitrator. Curzon complained that their solicitor was acting in a 'malicious, malignant, vindictive and resentful manner' and caused him 'an infinitude of trouble that has gone far to embitter my brief holiday in England'.[2] Eventually he paid £1500.

Salisbury (formerly Cranborne) was cross, saying, 'How I dislike brilliant men – I mean for practical life,'[3] and his sister said, later, that Curzon was hardly sane: 'It is the Walmer furniture incident translated into politics.'[4] Also, later, Salisbury said that while Curzon was 'very able, very vigorous, and very industrious . . . he is very rough and he is very often wrong'.[5] As a result of their combined attitudes, and the attraction which Kitchener had for Alice personally, the Salisburys became convinced that they must do all they could to enable him to defeat Curzon. A further explanation may have been Cranborne's extraordinarily strong feelings of guilt when the British relief force failed to reach Gordon in Khartoum. At his own expense, he hired a professional speaker to tour the country to explain how the nation had let down their hero. It followed that Kitchener, who exculpated that guilt, in turn became Cranborne's hero, and 'his enemy (Curzon) my enemy'.

Curzon knew nothing of this, indeed it is possible that he never knew till the day he died that Alice was his enemy because we find him writing, soon after the 1918 war, a recommendation that Salisbury should be appointed ambassador in Washington, saying, 'Lady Salisbury is incomparable both as wife and hostess.'[6] His innocence about the Salisburys was paralleled by his belief that his relationships with the Home Government and with the Secretary of State, St John Brodrick, although they had been difficult at times, were characterised by respect for his opinions.

His attitude to differences with his colleagues is well summed up in a letter he had written to 'dear Willie', his old friend Selborne, a member of the Cabinet, and also married to a Cecil. The subject was Curzon's row about a taxation announcement at the Durbar:

> You are quite mistaken if you think that I was angry with my special friends in the Cabinet for differing from me on one or two very important points. I can assure you that I have no such feeling. In public life differences of opinion must occur even between the closest friends and a man would be unfit to take part in it who was not prepared to accept this situation. . . And here I think the analogy used by you and often employed by St John breaks down. I do not come to the Cabinet as the head of a department, arguing a case against that of other departments. I came as the head of the Government of India, which though a subordinate administration, is yet the greatest governing organisation in the world. I spoke on behalf of a unanimous Cabinet of my own, with a constituency of 300 million behind. There is no parallel between this situation and

that of a departmental Minister. However, I should never have alluded to the matter had you not mentioned it, and you will recollect that in no letter from me to you has a word about it hitherto escaped my pen.[7]

And later, in reply to Selborne's response Curzon wrote:

You spoke as if I had objected to being overruled about foreign politics which as you say are not Indian but Imperial. No one ever heard me protest on this point. I have often been urged and I have sometimes thought that the Home Government was mistaken; but I have never once contended their absolute right, or failed loyally to accept their decision.[8]

All through interchanges such as this, it is clear that Curzon thought that the issues he discussed with London would be settled on a constitutional – even intellectual – level, but he was wrong to do so and Brodrick saw more clearly than did Curzon that the battle with Kitchener would be fought with much more personal manoeuvrings. Brodrick not only had first-hand knowledge of Kitchener's character, when he had dealt with him in South Africa, but he was also anxious that in his new post at the India Office he should be a success, overcoming any major difficulties even if this meant unorthodox methods. Furthermore, he was on Curzon's side, at this time late in 1904, in believing that the status quo in India should be retained. Immediately after Christmas he was back in his office and telegramming Curzon about the despatch which he had recently sent, asking for the Indian Government's official views on the relations between the Commander-in-Chief and the Military Department, and the possibility of an official enquiry. In the back of Brodrick's mind was the letter he had privately received from Kitchener on 9th November 1904 saying, 'I had rather hoped you would send out a commission to inquire into the whole subject on the spot.'[9]

'Shall any enquiry from *here* be necessary?' Brodrick asked Curzon, 'would it be possible for it to have begun before the hot weather? I ask because it appears, from indications that have reached me from various quarters that Lord Kitchener is becoming increasingly restless.'[10] Curzon replied immediately that he doubted if a reply could be ready before the end of February 1905, because the papers had already been with Kitchener for a fortnight, and he had not yet submitted his views, and that the Military Member would require as long again to formulate his own views. 'The civilian members [of Council] cannot be expected to formulate views on grave constitutional change without some consideration. Then there will be further discussion in Council to follow, and the final framing of the despatch.'[11] Curzon clearly thought the whole matter was a 'constitutional question' to be dealt with with appropriate gravitas, whereas Brodrick saw much more clearly that it was a matter of personalities, and, more important, he felt that he saw how it could be resolved by his manoeuvrings in London, if only Curzon would be a little more flexible.

His telegram of 12th January 1905 to Curzon reveals quite clearly what he had in mind as the sequence of events:

> Unfortunately, if the reply only reaches me by the middle of March and is unfavourable, no enquiry could be held in India before November by any authorities from here. This involves the alternative of a decision here, without an enquiry in India, on the papers forwarded by you, or the acceptance of Lord Kitchener's resignation, which will certainly be tendered. I deprecate either course, especially as I am convinced that the evidence taken and the opinion given by an independent and expert committee would, if unfavourable to Lord Kitchener, make the actions he proposes difficult to sustain and detrimental to his future. If you can expedite the reply so that I can receive the gist of it early in February by telegraph, a despatch following, I can induce Lord George Hamilton to go out and take evidence in March. I should propose to associate two colleagues with him, one of whom would be a soldier of Indian experience [he had Lord Roberts in mind]. I venture to urge this course on you because Lord George Hamilton will carry special weight. He has an open mind, but for the last ten years has been strongly opposed to undue concentration in the C-in-C at home, and though he is desirous of retaining Lord K, he values your work and opinions immensely.[12]

If Curzon had not been so stubborn, and so strongly inclined to the view that Brodrick knew little or nothing about conditions in India, he would have seen plainly that the telegram was saying, in as many words, 'If I can send Lord Hamilton to India in charge of an enquiry, then it will come down in your favour, and Kitchener's threat of resignation will be difficult to sustain.' But Curzon did not see it, and blundered on. Furthermore he was sure, he told Brodrick, that the rumours that Kitchener was becoming impatient, were nonsense. Curzon still thought he could handle Kitchener, as is clear from his telegram to Brodrick of 14th January 1905:

> With reference to your private telegram of 12 inst. I have just had a long and friendly conversation with Lord Kitchener. He desires me to say that he is quite satisfied that the ordinary official procedure should be followed, provided there is no undue delay, and that he knows of no reason for exceptional haste unless HM Government contemplates early dissolution. We will expedite the matter as much as possible, but Lord Kitchener only handed in his proposal to the Military Dept. on 5 January. That department, whose existence is at stake, must be allowed at least equal time to state its case. It is absolutely impossible that a Council of seven members should study rival military opinions and pronounce upon a proposal to *revolutionize the Constitution of Government* [my italics] in a few hours or even days, and I could not associate myself with any such procedure. Lord Kitchener agrees that it would be unfair to expect any decision from our Government at the earliest before the middle of February. We will telegraph its nature, but it is surely not contemplated that the Government will send out a Commission before it has even seen Lord Kitchener's new proposal, which differs from any that has yet been put forward, or Sir E. Elles' reply, or the opinions of the Viceroy and his colleagues. Even if the Commission arrive in March, they could hardly complete their enquiry before the Government leaves Calcutta and would probably require to go to Simla. Neither Lord Kitchener nor I see any reason for postponing the enquiry till November. We think that in any case it would be finished in April. Of course, I did not mention Lord George Hamilton to Lord Kitchener. He seems to me to be an admirable choice, and we would all co-operate in every possible way with him.[13]

Curzon's naivety, in continuing to believe what Kitchener told him, was remarkable in the light of his discovery of the Kitchener papers in the files of the Imperial Defence Committee back in London in the previous June, which he knew Kitchener had promised him to withdraw, and yet had 'suddenly turned up again'. Behind his back, Kitchener's staff were engaged full-time

deploying their efforts in London as well as in India. Hubert
Hamilton was at this very moment writing to Marker in Whitehall,
'I am thinking what will happen if the Mil. Dept is not knocked on
the head as the result of this campaign. Kitchener will resign of
course, but it is most important that in doing so, he should receive
general support and approval, which can be assured by careful
preparation beforehand, whereas if we wait until the bomb bursts,
the press may go astray. The opening with H. A. Gwynne [Editor
of *The Standard*, a pro-Kitchener, and anti-Curzon paper] is a good
start. Think how you can enlarge on this with discretion yet
sufficiently to ensure our object.'[14] And in early February Hamilton
says:

> I cannot enter into details, but the Viceroy is being nasty and is
> evidently preparing to put K in the wrong if it comes to his
> resignation. Knowing the Viceroy's cleverness you will understand
> how very careful K has to be, and you know this is not his
> inclination. He likes to talk and to be dodgy and to play the ostrich –
> all without meaning any harm but all decidedly inconvenient
> weaknesses at a time like this . . . According to the present arrange-
> ments, the case is to be taken in Council on 10 Feb. and opinions of
> the Govt of India wired home. Curzon will go dead against change
> and will have his whole council at his back. Then I understand a
> Commission is to be appointed to report, so that on its composition
> *very* much depends. Hence the wire of 30th on receipt of Frank's
> letter giving his conversation with Brodrick. If the final decision is
> against K, the Viceroy knows he will resign – he hopes it will be and
> so is preparing to secure his position when the time comes by putting
> K in the wrong. Meanwhile the Mil. Dept. are very confident and
> almost truculent . . . What I am rather afraid of is that the Civilians
> and Politicians will range themselves against the Soldiers and defeat
> us, simply, as they think, to protect themselves. Then again, the
> Army Order published early in January on reorganisation of
> Commands at home establishes the very system of dual control that
> we are trying to abolish here – or at least a similar system . . . You
> explain how you became Ass. Sec. of State. [Actually Marker was
> Assistant Secretary to the Secretary of State] It is as we thought, and
> is really *quite* the best thing you could have done for K at this
> moment . . . All points to the probability of war before [the end of]
> 1905. As K grimly remarks, 'Here is all this wrangling while we are
> on the brink of war at any moment, and preparation for it goes to the

winds' . . . In the meantime, K is very fit and in capital spirits except for a short time this morning when he was writhing under Curzon's bullying, and thought that even to succeed Milner [at the War Office] would be better than this!!![15]

In another letter to Marker, Hamilton said:

> K foresaw the necessity of directing to some extent the formation of the Commission . . . Elles let out that the Administration case was not to be taken until the 2nd March . . . It is just over 3 weeks ago today that K saw Curzon on the subject of settling the question . . . When K realised that the case was not to be taken until 2nd March . . . he did not like it a bit and began wiring you again, because it is evident Curzon is playing a game with an end in view and we must be level with him. You have a delicate job, my dear Conk, but I am sure you will be equal to it . . . we must be most careful and discreet, e.g. I noticed your last wire came *State*; of course anything of this sort must be *private* and paid for, no matter what it costs – we will refund you. K asked me to mention that in the event of a change of Govt. and their wanting him in the Ministry or otherwise in charge of the Army, he would make it a condition that his proposals for India should first be accepted – he thought you might mention this to Edward Grey [a Liberal, not in office, but shortly to be Foreign Minister]. I think the idea possibly prevails, that K might want office at home. There is nothing that would be more distasteful to him, although he might feel it his duty to try what he could for the Army.[16]

Brodrick continued to press Curzon most tactfully: 'I am very conscious of the difficulties which you state forcibly in your telegram,' he said on 16th January 1905. 'I regret the appearance of haste, but it would seriously militate against getting anyone of weight here to go to India, if they are run into hot weather, and Lord George Hamilton will only go if he is allowed to go early. I am very glad you approve of his suggested appointment. Please let us arrange the dates to suit, if possible.'[17]

All this tact was wasted on Curzon, and he replied in his most superior and difficult tones, even though Brodrick had doubly made his position clear by saying in a telegram, 'My mind is more open than the Prime Minister's and I am therefore specially anxious that the enquiry should be held by Lord George Hamilton.'[18]

Curzon replied:

> With reference to your private telegram of the 16 inst. *all that I am concerned to defend is the constitutional position of the Government of India.* [my italics] I hardly think that our constitution should be exposed to revision and possible revolution upon a private telegram from the Viceroy informing the Secretary of State that the Commander-in-Chief and the Military Member have written notes in which they disagree, and that the Viceroy is in sympathy with one party or the other. It was in order to avoid all such difficulties that I suggested to the Prime Minister the present procedure, and the delay in its execution is solely due to the time taken by the Commander-in-Chief in formulating his scheme. I think His Majesty's Government, if they now desire to appoint a Committee without awaiting our views, should do so exclusively on their own responsibility. We will loyally obey whatever orders you may issue, and our procedure is already being expedited to the uttermost to meet your wishes. It is with regret that I do not go even further. It would, however, surely be unfair to create the impression that the Home Government were acting in consequence of our views when these had not even been formulated or received, and I should not be acting fairly by my colleagues if, as head of the Government, I accepted this position on their behalf.
>
> I think you exaggerate the discomforts of travel in May. When I returned in that month last year, I found it less hot than in London in July.[19]

And when Brodrick told him that Lord Roberts 'who defends the present position'[20] [i.e. was against Kitchener] had called at Brodrick's office to urge him most strongly, from accounts which had reached him (although he did not say so, these were Kitchener's own letters and Mullaly's report) to expedite the enquiry, then Curzon merely retreated still further into his unrealistic position that it was a matter for the Indian Government. Brodrick made it quite clear that it was not.

> His Majesty's Government will be forced to make a decision without enquiry, which I greatly deprecate. We do not want to issue orders, but surely the constitutional position could be safeguarded while meeting the difficulty of dates, which is partially caused by the unavoidable delay in your return to India. The Prime Minister's

pledge as to enquiry, and also mine, were given to Lord Kitchener in September, but in order that you might be able to deal with the despatch, it was delayed, as you know, for two months.'[21]

In his private telegram, on 19th January 1905, Curzon told Brodrick:

> I do not quite understand what is at issue. Lord Kitchener thinks that our Military System is faulty, and, on hearing this, you propose to send an official of high distinction to enquire into it. The remainder of the [Indian] Government have not yet examined the case and are not in a position to say whether they agree with Lord Kitchener or not. We cannot therefore ourselves ask for a Commission at this stage. But if the Home Government send it on their own responsibility, whether in February or March, we will expedite its labours in every way.
>
> I did not know that your Despatch was delayed for two months for me. The Prime Minister will remember my suggesting it to him on November 9th and an advance copy left on November 25th.
>
> In the concluding paragraph of the Despatch no hint was given of the present procedure, which has naturally taken me by surprise, and when they hear it, it will surprise my colleagues still more.
>
> Lord Kitchener says nothing written by him has justified the impression produced by Lord Roberts which is quite unfounded.[22]

Curzon's naivety, particularly revealed in the final sentence of the telegram, finally decided Brodrick that his old friend was beyond help, and from that moment onwards it appears that not only was he willing to let events take their course, but he positively joined the forces which included the Salisburys, Clarke, Stedman, Balfour, Derby and, of course, Kitchener's own clique. He replied to Curzon tersely and finally the following morning: 'Lord George Hamilton, in view of the telegrams which have passed, declines to go to India. I shall postpone action until the receipt of your Despatch, but no further enquiry will be possible before the hot weather (see private letter).'[23]

Curzon seemed oblivious to the harm caused to his relations with Brodrick, or to the difficulties he was creating for himself by setting up such a long and tedious investigation. At the same time, events on the Indian Frontier and the Far East ensured that he would remain in India and would not return after a few more months to take up his political career in London. At the end of January 1905, Balfour referred to the conversation they had held in November in London, and asked if he would be returning in April as they had then planned. Had Curzon decided to return, his whole future might well have been quite different, as Kitchener would have done battle with a new Viceroy. But he did not. He replied, 'I have been anxiously considering the subject named by the Prime Minister and I wrote to him about it last week. My private inclination would be to carry out the suggestion referred to. But in face of the situation at Kabul, which may before long develop into an exceedingly grave crisis, I feel that withdrawal now is out of the question, and would be a desertion of public duty. Moreover, any defence of my early resignation that would have been supplied by Lady Curzon's health has been removed by sudden intimation from the doctors that she should without delay join me in India.'[24]

This last news had indeed been sudden and surprising to Curzon, who had heard by telegram at the end of January from the doctors that they were sending her out on 18th February. He was overjoyed and went 'dancing off to the Belvedere Ball (usually the most hateful of functions) in an indecent state of glee. I told everybody and they were in a wild state of excitement. K. looked a new man.'[25] He wrote to his friend Willie Selborne, 'I had not dreamed that she could be moved before April, nor when she last wrote to me had she. This rather changes things and it leaves the future more uncertain for of course I have no idea until she comes what her health will require or demand.'[26] He also told Selborne that the Afghan impasse and 'the doubt and peril that it opens out, [makes] it of course impossible for me to talk of going away. It would be an act of desertion on my part and quite unfair on my successor.' Curzon had long ago told Selborne that he wished him to succeed as Viceroy, so he added, 'I have merely to urge and implore you to keep the Government in, so that the fair prospect of being ultimately followed by you, to which I attach so much importance, may not be shattered.'[27] Incidentally, it does not seem that Selborne shared this wish to be Viceroy because six months earlier he had himself written to Balfour urging Brodrick's claim to the Viceroyalty.

It is from these times onwards that Curzon's deepset irritation

with the India Office and with the Cabinet in London began to rise
to a crescendo. It was reciprocated by their irritation with him and
their belief that he was trying to assert some kind of independence.
His own poor physical health, his ingrained habit of overworking,
and Mary's poor health all added to the strain on his nerves. In
April 1905, there was an earthquake at Lahore and Mary had a
very narrow escape, a heavy chimney crashing into the room
immediately above her head. Curzon became even more determined that he would not be hurried by the India Office on the
matter of the Indian Government's reply to the despatch.

By contrast, Kitchener was losing no time building up support in
London, which was where the decision would be made, and not in
India, where Curzon was concentrating all his efforts. In January
1905, less than a month after Curzon arrived back in India, Sir
George Clarke was writing to Kitchener in optimistic terms about
the outcome, quite without reference to the views of the Indian
Government upon which Curzon was putting such reliance –
indeed his full reliance.

> Private
>
> Many thanks for your letter of 5th and the very powerful memoran-
> dum on the higher administration of the army in India. I will
> give the letter to the Prime Minister whom it cannot fail to impress.
> The present system is wholly indefensible. It retains, with aggrava-
> tions, all the drawbacks of the Horse Guards and the War Office,
> and the earlier muddle which all but caused national disaster in the
> Crimea . . .
>
> In the case of war, certain considerations arise which you have
> touched upon in para 19. There is, in a non-military country, a
> distinct jealousy and almost a contempt for professional soldiers. It
> would not be aroused [?], but it is the fact that military officers are
> assumed to be 'incapable of national and responsible action'. They
> are also regarded as reckless spendthrifts, although if there is
> anything in this allegation it is wholly due to their training . . . In
> India I imagine that jealousy of soldiers has been the cause of the
> dual system so long maintained. '*Divide ac impera*' has been the motto
> of the advocates of administrative muddling . . .
>
> I earnestly hope you will win all along the line . . . do not give up
> the task, unless you are convinced it is hopeless . . . There are forces
> here on your side. [He then talks about the prospect of war with

Russia saying "There has been nothing like it since the French Revolution . . ."] It is in no one's interest to intervene in Russia, even if the dynasty fell. [He concludes] We grow steadily more hysterical and more sentimental, qualities incompatible with natural greatness.[28]

And two weeks later Clarke wrote to Kitchener again:

Private
I have now received your letter of 26 ultimo. I do not know what was actually communicated to the Viceroy in regard to the change of administration; but I gathered that the general feeling was that a step of this magnitude could not be taken over the heads of the Council. If however the majority of the Council were opposed, then an independent body might examine the situation with a view to letting down the opponents easily. I thought this was the general situation and I did not know that Lord Roberts was likely to be sent out. As you know he is not in favour of the change but he has left on record some fairly strong opinions against the present system and he does not know the way it is now working. I should not think it impossible that he might become a convert to your views. [He refers to the probable change in government which might result in one "inclined to fall in with your views"] I need not say I am in the most complete sympathy with them; and that the little it is possible to do I should do . . . The opinions of the generals that you kindly sent me seem conclusive.[29]

Private
Mr Balfour has read every word of your long paper to Stedman which you sent me and is very much impressed. That paper puts the whole question most forcibly . . . The main points you have so well explained – that
1. The system is contrary to the first principles of administration.
2. It has never worked well . . .
3. To say that there have been times when it has worked without friction is irrelevant to the issue. A machine may run without friction and yet be capable of accomplishing nothing.
4. As a matter of fact there has almost been friction . . .
5. Retention of the Mil. Dept. is wholly incompatible with the exercise of the functions of a C-in-C.
6. Its tendency to promote the selection of incompetent Cs-in-C.

I have given Mr Balfour and Mr Brodrick the opinions expressed by Lord Roberts when C-in-C which I sent you.[30]

Marker was assiduously beavering away for the War Minister by day, and deciphering Kitchener's and Hamilton's private and coded telegrams by night. His pencilled transcriptions tell the story of how he carried on his treacherous work in the firm belief that the end – the triumph of the Army over the civilians – justified the means. A curious side note is that the telegrams occasionally contain items of a domestic nature, such as this from Kitchener to Marker: 'I do not like the samples [of material] from Liberty's and am getting Hampton, Maple and Gillow to suggest something.'[31]

On 31st January 1905 Kitchener sent the following telegram to Marker:

Decipher yourself and keep secret. Council decision here will be 10 February, and result telegraphed home. Commission will be at once appointed in London. I suggest Sir R. Low, Sir G. Clarke, and Sir Arthur Godley. Tell this to Frank [Maxwell] at once in answer to this letter and to Lady Salisbury too. Repeat in conversation to Stedman. You and he must work vigorously as not much time. If Commission composed as I suggest, all will be well I think.

Kitchener cabled again:

Secret, decipher yourself.
It has got out that I referred the question of dual control to some generals here, so be very careful and if possible warn those who know my views privately at home that no reference whatever be made to them, until opinion of government of India is received. Tell Frank [Maxwell] to warn Mr B [Brodrick].[32]

Hubert Hamilton explained the above telegram to Marker by saying that Gwynne of *The Standard* had 'plunged into the breach, and I fear it may do the cause no good. He was only allowed to know what he does, to provide for the contingency of resignation, and in the meantime to make no use of his knowledge. Press people are always dangerous. Curzon was away shooting, but at once wished to extract a denial from Kitchener. He did not get much change out of him, and Kitchener said he would mention the matter in Council, which he did. Please tell Gwynne discreetly that K has been obliged to disclaim him and *The Standard* altogether.'[33] And later Hamilton, referring to *The Standard* article says, 'You know how K. shudders when a Mahdi's head is about.' He went on: 'Frank Haig [later the Field Marshall of the 1914-18 war who had been in India] will be very useful, so see him and talk over matters . . . K is sending everything by mail to Stedman, so it might be well for you to see him – in fact I think you *should* do so, as no doubt he wants the stiffening you can give him. Lady S is also well posted.'[34] And from Kitchener himself, a cable saying, 'Tell Lady S of my letter [to Stedman].'[35] This was followed, probably, by an undated telegram from Kitchener to Marker which read:

Private and secret: decipher yourself.
Notwithstanding assurances that administration questions would be pushed forward and taken in Council on 10 February, I hear that Council is now postponed until 2 March. It seems to me evident that it is hoped Government will go out before deciding question . . . If Govt. wishes to keep promises of last September to me . . . [It is not clear to what this refers] the increased friction between the offices [creates] under the circumstances the serious danger of prolonging present situation and in my opinion makes early decision necessary. To bring matters to crisis, after Council of 2 March which is sure to be against me, I shall probably resign.'[36]

On 4th February 1905 Kitchener wrote to Marker: 'Give Lady S a copy of this and desire her to keep enclosure of my letter of 26 January which will reach her on February 11 quite private. Chief.'[37] [This was a copy of Kitchener's letter to Stedman]

From India, Hamilton was also busy orchestrating the campaign in London at other levels. He wrote to Marker:

You have been appointed Ass. Secretary to the S of S [at the War Office – where Arnold-Forster was the new Minister]. We can only think you know it won't be for long and you see the opportunity of peeping behind the scenes for K. You might see Wolfe-Murray who has a copy of the Minutes – he will be interested and after his success in knocking out Arnold-F's scheme (how very indiscreet this sounds to his Ass. Secy) he might be of some use in expounding K's views.

They seem to have a rather vague notion of affairs out here and of how hopelessly unprepared we are for war. The Viceroy has had two wires from the S of S urging expedition in dealing with the question and the second just received says "Lord Roberts has just been to see me [Brodrick] and urges the great necessity *from reports that have reached him* [his underlining] of acting without delay. Evidently the little man has heard rumours about K drinking more than is good for him *and believes them*." There is the mischief, and he would believe them . . . How terribly hopeless when one has to deal with people who are so dull to the facts that they will believe any idle chatter.[38]

These rumours about Kitchener's drinking greatly worried his staff. Maxwell was sent specially to London to refute them 'because of his facilities for approaching Kings and Queens'.[39]

'News of the lies that are being carried to the King about Kitchener having become lethargic and drinking more than is good for him have been occupying our attention,'[40] Hamilton told Marker. Later he wrote to congratulate Marker on 'how well you and Frank have been able to dispose of the business'. He added, 'K was of course much relieved' and 'roared with laughter over the idea of Kelly Kenny's rapid departure for the Nile to escape the King's displeasure'.[41] The latter was presumably the rumour-monger. Lord Roberts also apparently believed the stories and Hamilton recalled how 'Old Bob's took it all quite seriously when some woman in Lancashire wrote to him saying that she was K's wife . . . and that since he became distinguished, he had deserted her!'[42] [These and similar stories about Kitchener's life were a constant source of rumour]

Hamilton kept up the pressure on Marker with weekly letters, and Marker was glad to have work to keep his mind off other matters, as the problem of his love for Daisy Leiter had reopened. The Leiters had come to England again to be with Mary during her illness at Walmer. Marker took the opportunity to try to see Daisy but was rebuffed. He was told that she had decided to marry another of Curzon's ADCs, Lord Surrey (the wedding took place in America on Boxing Day 1904). Marker told his friends the facts, and so did Maxwell, and Hamilton wrote, 'I am quite disgusted at Frank's account of DL's behaviour. I could not have believed it of her. The only good point to my mind is the proof it affords of what might have been. I never cease to feel for all you have suffered, but I know you will take the right view.'[43] And later he added, 'I think that after all that has passed, and the time that has elapsed, you cannot but accept the fact that it settles matters. Whether she is influenced by her own feelings or merely by the prompting of mother and sister, a woman who gives way to worldly considerations rather than personal attractions is not worth bothering about. I am very sorry, my dear Conk, for all that you have suffered, but it is better to know the worst than to discover it when too late.'[44]

This conventional advice to the overthrown lover not only consoled him, but also renewed his dislike for the Curzon family, particularly Lady Curzon, who was 'the sister' mentioned by Hamilton as having poisoned the ear of Daisy Leiter by telling her that Marker was not good enough for her, and that Lord Surrey would be the better match. Hamilton, who had now assumed the position of Kitchener's mouthpiece, proceeded to bolster up Marker by repeating to him how valuable was his role in their current battle. Marker had already written to him complaining about Mullaly's activities, and Hamilton agreed 'he is a defective tool'. He told Marker, 'I never cease to realise the great stroke of luck for K that he has made [you his] agent. That is K's great weakness — the Morgans, the Colenbranders, Kaffir Wilsons, Gobby Armstrongs, Mallesons, Mullalys (I might mention scores of others) all appeal to him to the exclusion of that type which alone is worthy of doing his work. When I think of the risks he runs, I always shudder, but he has luck on his side and somehow manages to steer through the rocks.'[45]

Two further letters in February indicate how closely Hamilton was working with Marker in London:

We are very much in the dark here as to the course of events at home and we are naturally a bit anxious when there is too much at stake. Your message has cleared the air and K is much happier. K knows [India] is the place where the trouble will come, and where the strength of the Empire will be tried . . . he realises that whatever he might be able to effect at home will be of small avail if we are to tumble to pieces in India on a rotten Army system. The case is not yet in circulation . . . tho Baring told me this afternoon that it is ready and thinks it has started on its round, all printed up and like a novel.

I mentioned Repington [*The Times*] had written to K suggesting that he should receive a weekly letter from me or Birdie to keep him in touch . . . On the whole I thought the tone rather objectionable – to me it read rather like 'I can make or mar you; I am prepared for the former, you can choose'. I don't think K took it too badly, but what he really dislikes is the individual. He hates having anything to do with a man who has behaved as he has, and his first inclination was not to answer. He has now written quite a nice put-off, and has told Repington he has no objection to Birdwood answering any questions he may wish to put . . . Repington must make the best of this and need not expect to hear again from K. Do you think you could hint this to him if he seems inclined to write again? . . . K would like you to do so . . . K is making up his dinner for Lady C on 8 March. I wish she had stayed at home.[46]

K's letter will have given you an insight into the situation. You see we always have to consider how things will stand 3 weeks ahead. Now we reckon the Admin case cannot be taken before 17 March. . . We are confronted with two contingencies (1) a settlement here in March, (2) . . . the prospect of delay. If the former, well and good – you will only get one word from me, by wire about 18 March – *Settled* – and you can tell Lady S and General Stedman. In the latter case you will also get one word *Delayed* from which you will know that K is so satisfied that the case cannot then be settled here in March that he will send in his resignation. This, too, please communicate to Lady S and Gn. Stedman and take whatever other step your discretion and complete knowledge of the whole circumstances may suggest to you as being in the best interests of K and of the Empire. I do not need add more. You will realise how impossible it is for K to remain longer in a position, which 6 months ago he declared to be impossible, if nothing is being done, and war hanging on a thread. You will understand it is his duty to put all personal considerations aside in his efforts to end a system which he has described as "fraught with danger to the Empire in case of war".[47]

A short digression on this pre-occupation with war in India would not be out of place here. Both Kitchener and Curzon were clearly committed to it, and for the latter it had been a theme about which he had written for more than a generation. Balfour, perhaps the deepest thinker on defence matters of any statesman of his time, wrote papers for the Imperial Defence Committee on the defence of the Indian NW Frontier on 30th April and 20th May 1903 amounting to nineteen pages of print, and in November of that year he circulated 'elaborately constructed papers on Indian Defence together with Curzon's and Kitchener's criticisms on it'.[48] He was convinced that Russia was the enemy, perhaps to be allied, in a European war, with France, and at the end of 1903 he wrote for the Cabinet, 'Russia's strong point is her vast population and the unassailable character of her territories.'[49] She was the obvious menace, and the danger of war with her became imminent when ships of her Baltic fleet sank British fishing boats in the North Sea, mistaking them for Japanese torpedo boats – the Russo-Japanese war was about to commence, and tension persisted from October 1904 to April 1905. For example in November, Lord Fisher, the Admiral, wrote to his wife, 'I have been with the PM all day. It has nearly been war again. VERY NEAR INDEED – but the Russians have climbed down.'[50] The great Japanese naval victory on 28th May 1905 reduced tension, and changed the balance of power against Russia.

Yet even in 1905 when Balfour was preoccupied with the development of new field guns for the Army, these were progressively handed over to India as they were delivered, only fifty-four being retained in the United Kingdom. An important aspect of the national preoccupation with a Russian war in India is the effect it had on Kitchener's position. As Esher said, 'The Prime Minister cannot possibly allow Lord K to leave India at the moment, because he was the leading military man, and India was not the back door but the probable front line.'[51]

Meanwhile, Curzon was engaged in ploughing steadily ahead with obtaining the Indian Government's considered views on the despatch. In late February, when the council met, Kitchener said that he felt it was inadvisable to delay further their reply to London. Curzon's reply, according to Kitchener, showed him to be the 'the accomplished actor'.[52]

'Oh! Has it not reached you yet? Surely it must have? Where is the case now?' The other members of Council had all noted it, except for Hewett, who was away, and Kitchener. It was waiting for Hewett's return and the Viceroy's sanction for Kitchener to see it.

' "But surely you have seen the notes?" asked Curzon. Kitchener

said no. "Oh, that is soon put right. I will send you a copy of mine
at once. Sir Edmund, have you a spare copy of yours? Will you let
the C-in-C have one?" Sir Edmond [Elles] was heard to mumble
something which was taken for assent.'[53] When he did read it,
Kitchener agreed that the Viceroy's case was well done, but
contained 'nothing new, only the old threadbare arguments dished
up in the most palatable form'.[54]

Hamilton wrote:

> We are all surprised that with all the resources at their back, and all
> the effort they have made, they have not been able to do better, but
> we shall have to see how these papers impress others. K. will make
> quite a short note dealing with a mis-reading by the Viceroy of one
> statement of his, and he will ignore Elles altogether. Whether the
> system stands or falls, the line Elles has taken makes it impossible
> for him and K. to go on together in their present positions . . . Elles'
> case has been edited by the V so it must have been awful before. I
> hope K will be allowed another year here at least to launch his
> scheme, and then he might perhaps tackle the Home Army if there is
> any left to tackle . . . K is very fit and in the best of spirits, I have
> never seen him better . . .[55]

And on 9th March 1905, Hamilton wrote: 'We are all prepared for
the fray tomorrow, but don't expect any unforeseen development.
Whatever happens, the way is well prepared.'[56]

Indeed it was. The following plan sets out the targets, and the
'troops' Kitchener used to achieve his ends. Mortimer Menpes, the
artist, said, 'If I had to sum Kitchener up in one sentence, I should
say that he set before himself always the doctrine of essentials in
relation to success.'[57] It was an essential that K should win in
London. Meanwhile he kept his favourite card – resignation – up
his sleeve, writing with his usual guile to Lady Salisbury on 2nd
March, 'I hate always threatening to resign, but what is one to do?'

Kitchener's Deployment of Forces

Primary Target		Initial Target	First line of attack
Crown	King Edward VII	Lord Knollys	Kitchener
		Lord Esher	Maxwell
	George, Prince of Wales	Lord Knollys	Kitchener
			Marker
Cabinet	Balfour	Lady Salisbury	Kitchener
	Lord Salisbury	Lady Salisbury	Marker
	Eddie Stanley (Lord Derby)		Kitchener
	St John Brodrick	Lady Salisbury	Kitchener
War Office and Army	Arnold-Forster		Marker
	Lord Roberts		Mullaly
	Ian Hamilton		Kitchener
Imperial Defense Committee	Balfour	Clarke	Kitchener
	Lord Esher		Mullaly
			Marker
India Office	Brodrick	Stedman	Kitchener
	Godley		Marker
	Stedman		
Press	Pearson		Kitchener
	Ralli		Kitchener
	Repington		Marker
	Gwynne		Marker

Lord George Curzon in Viceregal robes
(National Portrait Gallery)

Above: Curzon with his daughters Irene and Cynthia in 1904. A third, Alexandra, was born the same year. (Curzon Collection)

Below: Curzon, Lady Curzon and the Viceroy's staff. (Curzon Collection)

Right: The studio photograph of
Mary Curzon taken for the Durbar
album.

Below: 'All the swells in India' lined up
outside Government House, Calcutta,
in January 1899 to welcome the
Curzons. (Curzon Collection)

Above: The Viceregal Lodge at Simla where the Curzons spent the greater part of the year. Neither of them liked it. (Curzon Collection)

Below: 'Snowdon', the house in Simla that Kitchener restored

Above: Kedlestone Hall, owned by Curzon's father who unexpectedly inherited the
title Lord Scarsdale. The architect was Robert Adam upon whose designs
the architect of Government House, Calcutta, modelled his building.
(Curzon Collection)

Below: Kitchener was born in this house in County Kerry in 1850

Kitchener in full regalia at the Delhi Durbar in 1902, shortly after his
arrival in India. (Curzon Collection)

Above: Kitchener seems to have enjoyed being photographed with 'The Boys'. Raymond Marker is in the centre of the back row. Hubert Hamilton, Horatio Kitchener and William Birdwood are in the front row

Right: Kitchener as a subaltern in 1873 when he was twenty-three years old

Below: The key figures in this photograph, taken in South Africa in 1902, are ringed: (left) 'Hammy' Hamilton and (right) 'Conk' Marker, both on Kitchener's staff

Arthur Balfour
(National Portrait Gallery)

The *Punch* cartoon of
St John Brodrick as
Secretary of State for War

Field-Marshal Lord Roberts

Ian Hamilton

Lord Cromer

Lord Salisbury
(Curzon Collection)

Chapter Nine

Let Battle Commence

Kitchener had a nervous habit of chewing the ends of unlighted cigarettes and this was much in evidence as he sat silently brooding at the Council meeting on 10th March 1905, making no reply to the detailed and, it seemed, indisputable answers which Elles and Curzon made to his views; he simply contented himself, so the other Members present believed, with appending a short minute to the despatch which stated, with characteristic brusqueness: 'Some attempts have been made to dispute my facts, but in my opinion without success. My assertions have been contradicted, but not, I think, disproved. My arguments remain uncontraverted and are, I believe, incontravertible.'[1] He thought nothing of Curzon's memorandum believing 'I could have made a better case myself against myself'.[2]

Kitchener's biographers are delighted with this dignified silence on the part of their hero. Magnus says, 'That silence, although premeditated, was due [to the fact that] Kitchener knew his limitations: he could lead or command but he had no gift of eloquence or argument. He had stated his views on paper, and on that paper he took his stand.'[3] Philip Warner, writing thirty years later, follows suit: 'He had made all the necessary points in the paper he had submitted . . . he was probably wary of being drawn into a public debate with such a skilled practitioner as Curzon.'[4]

'He had made all the necessary points in the paper he had submitted,' yes, but alas it was not in the papers to which his biographers allude, but in another and totally different paper composed two days before the Council meeting by this devious man, and not produced in Council at all, but sent secretly to London, in the form of a private letter, forty typed foolscap pages long, to Sir E. Stedman, the ex-general who was Secretary of the Military Department in the India Office in London.

Months later, when Curzon finally saw this letter, he said sarcastically, 'Well, Lord Kitchener *did* honour Sir Edwin Elles and me by writing a long and detailed reply to almost every paragraph of our respective minutes.'[5] Its final 'remarkable' paragraph claimed: '*I send you this privately and confidentially* [K's underlining] There is nothing in my criticisms that is not well known in India, or that would, in my opinion, have the slightest effect on the decision of the Govt. of India, which I fully saw would be against my proposals – *vide* my telegram to the Sec. of State of November 22nd last. But if, as you say, the question is likely to become a Cabinet one at home, *I hope Mr Brodrick will, should he see fit, use some of the points I have mentioned in the letter so as to ensure the Cabinet not coming to a decision without a correct appreciation of the case from all points of view.*'[6]*

Thus Kitchener's silence was not honourable but dishonourable; he knew that the battle would be fought not at the Council table in Calcutta but in the Cabinet rooms in London, and that was where he had deployed his forces. Curzon made the fatal mistake of not understanding this, believing that the enemy attack was fading before his eyes, whereas it had reformed in great force 7000 miles away. And Mr Brodrick did, indeed, see fit to use the letter. As Curzon later sarcastically noted, the letter's 'private character would appear to have vanished from the moment of its arrival in England. It was duly communicated to the Secretary of State, and was printed by his order and circulated to the Committee whom he had appointed to consider the question . . . in the India Office, and to the eminent authorities who were consulted by that Committee . . . It is within my knowledge that it passed officially into other hands. At a later date, after it had fulfilled its purpose, it was suppressed and cannot now be procured [A copy was given to Curzon on his return to England and is with the Curzon papers]. Nor was its range of circulation confined to official or semi-official

---

*Sir Beauchamp Duff attempted to justify the Stedman letter by saying quite untruthfully that 'no reasoned minute of dissent by Lord Kitchener stood any charge of transmission and that the attempt to force one through meant endless delay.' (T. H. O'Brien, *Milner*, 1979)

quarters.'[7] It was sent to *The Times* but no copy was of course sent to Curzon, or to the Council of India, at whose tables Kitchener kept silent like a soldier who has sent out his troops in the night.

This is no place to rehearse the whole of the argument used by Kitchener in his letter to Stedman, but some of the more generalised comments from its detailed critique, paragraph by paragraph, of Elles and Curzon's views, are worth noting. Kitchener wrote:

The raising of this question of Army administration has so greatly increased the friction between the two military officers as practically to bring all army work to a standstill. In the circumstances, it is to my mind of the utmost importance, for the good of the army, that this question should be settled without delay. Were I to contravert in further notes the statements made and opinions laid down by the Viceroy and Military Member on the subject, it would necessarily lead to almost endless further discussion . . .

Under the existing system of Military Administration even the four divisions . . . have never been properly equipped for mobilisation . . .

It is hardly possible to name a single requirement that has been fully supplied even as regards placing the troops in the field.

The Mil. Member is the supreme authority in military matters, and the C-in-C his direct subordinate, charged with carrying out his orders, but having no authority of his own . . . but the C-in-C is responsible to the Govt. for the efficiency of the Army. Herein lies the fatal defect.

When the case comes up for discussion in the Viceroy's Council, I am prepared to prove everything stated in my memorandum. [Curzon noted in pencil – *He did not even argue it*]

I entirely repudiate the account of these transactions given by Sir E. Elles.

The transfer of the Supply and Transport Corps (to me) has been sanctioned . . . [Curzon put two exclamation marks beside this]

It was only through the intervention of the Secy. of State that this very important reform is about to be carried into effect. [Curzon noted: 'quite untrue']

I have already dealt with the error into which the Viceroy has fallen regarding the supposed unanimity of opinion in favour of his views. But as he seems to think that there is no trace of any desire for change 'except in the immediate surroundings of the C-in-C'. I give below the opinions of General Officers whom I have consulted . . .[8]

There was another notable feature about this letter. It concluded by quoting opinions in favour of Kitchener's scheme, procured from several of the leading generals in India. These opinions were of a broad, and indeed one might say, naive nature, but they served their purpose. Some extracts are: General Hunter: 'Your arguments and conclusions unanswerable and I believe you have done a true service to the British Empire.' General Blood: 'Should convince anyone who is capable of being convinced. Unqualified admiration.' General Gaselee: 'Hope it will be the death blow to our present dual system.' General Wodehouse: 'I can honestly say that I agree with every line.' General Kitchener (Kitchener's brother): 'Your case is unanswerable.' General O'Creagh Moore (who was to succeed Kitchener as Commander-in-Chief): 'I most heartily agree.' General Henry: 'I entirely concur.' General Smith: 'Delightful reading...I have chuckled at its many delightful points.' General Richardson: 'I agree with every line.'[9]

Two or three weeks before Kitchener sent these opinions secretly to London, Curzon had heard that he was consulting his generals without the knowledge of the Government of India. As the whole question was still very much under discussion at the time, and as Lord Kitchener's minute on Military Administration had been sent to the generals, although it was a confidential document addressed to the Government, and should not have been communicated to anyone without the permission of the Viceroy, Curzon wrote a short note to Kitchener asking to see the views of the generals when they were received. Kitchener irritably replied that their opinions were private and for himself alone. As we shall see, when they went to Stedman, were printed by Brodrick, given by Marker to Repington and so reprinted in *The Times*, Kitchener once more lied to Curzon, in writing, about their origin. A comparison of the 'opinions' cited in this letter to Stedman shows they were in fact the identical words cited in the newspaper. Even as late as December 1905, Kitchener was still lying on this subject, instructing his new Military Member, Major-General Scott, to tell a native member of the Legislative Council in Calcutta, who asked if the generals had been consulted and if their opinions could be published, that they had not, 'As it is not usual for Government to consult the officers mentioned on questions of policy.'[10] Of course it was not the Government that had consulted them but Kitchener, and in secret.

To return to events in March, Hamilton described the despatch which Curzon produced as 'far from being as terrible as he threatened, but it was certainly very misleading and a carefully drawn-up document . . . the Despatch is [now] to be redrafted and goodness knows when it will go to London'.[11] In fact it went out on March 23rd.

After the meeting Kitchener telegrammed secretly to Marker. 'Taken in Council today, result as foreseen. Tell Lady S to cancel my letter of 23 Feb.'[12] This was the letter in which he had asked her to urge Brodrick to insist that matter of the Despatch be dealt with, without further delay. Kitchener had already written to her again on 9th March 1905, sending her a copy of his long letter to Stedman and once again threatening resignation. 'Those at home who would rather I stayed on should I think fully realise this as being final and not blame me if I can stand no more.'[13] Lady Salisbury copied the letter to Godley.

But Kitchener knew that if the decision of the Council in India was unfavourable to his case, it would then be put before a private committee which Brodrick would convene in London. It was vital that the members of this committee should be drawn to his side, if they were not already on it. One member would certainly be Lord Roberts, and he was against abolition of the Military Department. Kitchener secretly cabled Marker on 22 May: 'I think it is most unfair putting such a partisan as Roberts on the Commission. To my mind, case looks gloomy. Are there any later developments?'[14]

It was thought that Ian 'Johnny' Hamilton, who had been in South Africa with Kitchener and was on a visit to India, had the ear of Lord Roberts and Hubert Hamilton wrote: 'We quite understand Lord Bobs' attitude generally and . . . have no hope of changing him until he sees the Government go for K, and then Bobs will change automatically.'[15] In fact Curzon was writing to Roberts saying that Kitchener would not be satisfied until 'he makes himself Military Dictator. This will be a national danger, and I will on no account accede to it . . . I hope you will use your great influence to keep HMG straight.'[16]

Hamilton described his Chief's moods – while himself remaining steady about the objective they were all working towards. 'Your letter of 7 April was admirable,' he tells Marker, 'showing you have foreseen the whole situation eye to eye with us and are prepared to act just as K would wish . . . I don't think K writes to anyone at home except Lady S and Ralli and latterly to Stedman and Clarke, also an occasional letter to Eddie Stanley [later Lord Derby] and Pearson. K himself thinks the odds are almost even for or against him . . . Personally I think they are 3:1 on him. K had a line from Mary [Curzon] this morning saying they are *amazed* (!) at *The Standard* articles and that George's leg is still troubling him. Of course George would like to see the whole press flocking to his standard, and cannot understand anyone venturing to criticise his judgement. But by now he must be getting used to knocks.'[17] Kitchener was taking considerable pains to ensure that the press did not flock to Curzon, in particular by making a fuss of Mr Buck, the Reuter correspondent in India, and thus the channel for all the information which passed to the press in England. Kitchener was always 'delighted to receive' him at his home in Calcutta.

'Curzon has been in bed for a fortnight with his leg and looked seedy,' wrote Hamilton. 'He whined pitiably about the press, but K was ready and would take no notice of it – he never does one way or the other – Curzon wanted to extract some sort of disavowal. Last night they had a farewell dance for the Barings at Viceregal Lodge and Mary tried to pump K as to what he had heard of the progress of the case, but all he gave her was that Clarke entirely agrees with him, and she on her side supposes there will be some kind of compromise, as compromises are what appeal to Arthur B [Balfour].'[18]

In fact, although Kitchener was by now mounting a press campaign which would have gladdened the heart of a skilled public relations professional eighty years later, neither Curzon nor his staff made the slightest effort to get the press on his side. This was a major error, because while the halfpenny papers had Kitchener as a hero, the more serious journals were obtaining masses of material from the Kitchener camp while nothing whatever came from 'the other side'. The position was explained very clearly by the journalist Lovat Fraser of *The Times of India*. He had never met Curzon personally, except as one of a party of twenty press people at the Durbar Press Camp. He wrote in 1908:

The aloofness of the Viceroy from the press during Lord Curzon's Viceroyalty was almost singular, and I believe other journals rather resented it. I never did so, because I thought if there were no personal relations, one had greater freedom for criticism. I am not sure that this rigid policy of the Viceroy's was quite wise. Had he permitted his advisors to take us into their confidence, perhaps we might have made fewer mistakes. But at least it makes the outburst of feeling which followed the publication of the special *Gazette* of June 23 perhaps the most spontaneous and genuine (and comprehensive) expression of opinion ever witnessed in Indian journalism.

I used to prepare Reuter's messages from Western India. I had an urgent letter from their agent, "Our people keep on cabling for opinions on the other side." I had to reply, "There are none."[19]

To return to Kitchener's high grade intelligence system, which had Marker, picking up his mail at the Guards Club just off Berkeley Square – it was safer there than at the War Office. The Chief cabled to him [undated], 'Can you ascertain cause of delay and give me approximate date when the decision will be taken? You might think it advisable to represent to authorities from me that delay is serious matter.'[20]

He also wrote privately to Marker at his Club:

My dear Conk, I have had good letters about the case from Clarke and Esher. I primed Johnny [Hamilton] about Nick's [Nicholson] statement re Japan and I hope he will bowl him over. Nick of course wants to get my place. I never knew a more unscrupulous creature. Frank [Maxwell] writes "Eddie Stanley [later Lord Derby] thinks it is all right, whereas another equally important personage unnamed thinks it will certainly go against you." Who is the unnamed? . . . No, I will *not* be Chief of General Staff, so please don't let them ask me.[21]

May 11th: Kitchener again to Marker:

Many thanks for your last and the refreshing wires I have received. I hope all is still going well and that Johnny Hamilton has been able to upset Nick's evil influence – I had a nice letter from Esher saying that he quite agreed with me – I hope all will go well. I think Curzon will take it lying down if it comes to deciding against him. He told Hammy [Hamilton] on one occasion he could not understand why I was going to resign on the point, as he Curzon would accept any decision loyally and make the best of it . . . Lady Curzon is much better and almost quite well again [she had nearly been killed in an earthquake]. She told me they were shortly going into camp at Naldera. I very nearly said, "I hope it will be a boy, but what will you call him?" [This joke shows that Kitchener had a sense of humour. The Curzon's third child, born a year earlier had been called Naldera because she was believed to have been conceived at the camp.] I shall wait patiently the result from home – of the India case. I know everyone is doing their best and if there is delay that it is unavoidable.[22]

Clarke was keeping Kitchener closely posted. In May he wrote, 'Thank you for your letter of 4th inst. Nothing is yet settled, but I am still hopeful you will win the day. Yes, Nicholson [at the War Office – later a Field-Marshall] has of course been very active on the opposite side, but Esher has had a long talk with him lately and found him wholly accessible to reason. Whatever happens, he has not the faintest chance of succeeding you.'

By June 1905, then, the position was that Kitchener sat calmly awaiting the outcome from London. Curzon having sent off his own carefully-worded despatch to London also awaited the outcome with confidence, and neither man foresaw the remarkable outburst which would engulf both them and the politicians in London within a few weeks.

Esher, who claimed to be 'a very old friend of Lord Curzon' was working behind the scenes with the King, and with Balfour. He wrote to Kitchener:

I have had an opportunity of reading your letter to Stedman and have today been pressing it upon Mr Balfour who is – as you know – so much occupied with continuing crises that it is hard for him to find time to read anything which does not bear upon the actual work of the 24 hours before him. Still, the question is so important, and your argument so unanswerable, that he *must* bring the full force of his personality to bear on the right side . . . Your principal opponents are Lord Roberts and Lansdowne . . . Personally I am always against resignations. As old Harcourt used to say, "When a man jumps off a coach, it rolls on without him." But it is impossible to see how you can remain with dignity and efficiency after what has happened, unless your view prevails.

For the first time in my experience, the *Military* views of how the army should be administered have prevailed . . . I hope Clarke sent you the memo which Mr Balfour drew up with the assistance of a subcommittee of defence . . . Please do not answer this which is prompted by reading your argument.[23]

It is interesting to note that despite Esher's support for him, Kitchener's view (given to Lady Salisbury) was that 'Esher is an outsider who knows little or nothing about the Army'.[24]

Strangely enough, relations between Kitchener and Curzon remained reasonably unstrained at a personal level. The Viceroy did take the step of advising Kitchener not to influence matters by threatening to resign, and Kitchener, who seems to have had a rough kind of humour at times, although his contemporaries said he had none, responded that things would be evenly balanced if Curzon also threatened to resign. Kitchener passed this witticism on to Lady Salisbury. Curzon also made another practical proposal to solve the problem. 'Look here,' he told Kitchener, 'Elles' term is drawing to a close. He has told me that he would not be unwilling to go. What would you say if the government were to select as his successor a Military Member with whom you could work, and who was imbued with your own ideas? Could you work with him?' Curzon told Balfour about this conversation when he wrote to him on 30th March 1905. According to Curzon, Kitchener replied 'Oh certainly!' which, if true, meant that he had given away his whole case for abolition. He did not want to change the system – merely to get his own way. Curzon hoped Balfour would understand.[25]

Curzon wanted his letter to Balfour to be read alongside the Indian Government's despatch. He asked Balfour to believe that this was not a mere matter of departmental reforms, and he reminded the Prime Minister that he had backed Kitchener's other reorganization reforms. He quoted Ampthill: 'Even during my brief time at Simla, the Mil. Dept. saved us from several dangerous mistakes which with Lord Kitchener as the sole military advisor of the government we should neither have seen nor been able to avert, and thus I received practical proof that the Military Dept. is essential to the proper administration of the Army in India.'

Curzon went on to explain how Kitchener had used every method to destroy the Mil. Dept. and how he disliked Elles because 'K's schemes (which I can assure you are not uncommonly framed in the most startling ignorance of Indian conditions with which his subordinate officers have not the courage to acquaint him) could be criticised and their flaws sometimes exposed by a General officer of inferior prestige and rank.' He hoped the Home Government would give the Government of India an objective hearing. Should they be overruled, 'I could not accept so striking a proof of want of confidence in the Government which I have now administered for over six years.' [26] This was a clear threat that he would resign. Balfour never answered this letter, not unusual behaviour in his case, but when Curzon returned to England he found either that he never received the letter, or failed to read it, or had completely forgotten it.

Kitchener meanwhile was continuing to get support from home. His letter to Stedman had gone to Godley and to Clarke, who said it was 'absolutely unanswerable',[27] and to Esher who wrote to Kitchener, 'I do not think that when the pinch comes, the government will view calmly your departure from India.'[28] Balfour also saw it and was very much impressed.

Kitchener decided that letters to Stedman were highly productive in the best circles, and he wrote again on 23rd March 1905 attacking Curzon. 'All military power falls . . . actually into [the hands] of the Viceroy personally – and when a Viceroy believes, rightly or wrongly, that like Napoleon he combines the highest talent for military administration with genius for civil government, such a situation may appear peculiarly advantageous to him. But if this is to be the object aimed at, it could be more cheaply and directly attained by abolishing *both* the C-in-C and the Mil. Member, and making the Army over technically as well as practically to Civilian control.'[29] He knew that plenty of the readers in London would sympathise with the comparison of Curzon with Napoleon, while the military amongst them would quake at the prospect of the civilians in charge.

Alas, Curzon himself was not taking the battle into London too, and suggestions in Brodrick's memoirs that Curzon had influential people working for him at home are nonsense. During the whole period from the end of March until the end of May, he knew nothing of what was going on in London, because they told him nothing. Brodrick lied to him by saying only that he 'possessed an open mind'. Curzon wrote to Ampthill (now back governing

Madras), on 12th May 1905, 'I imagine that they are anxiously considering whether they would lose more by Kitchener's resignation or mine. Military prestige is so much greater than the Civilian, that the result may be anticipated. I have had so little backing from the present Secretary of State that I am quite ready to go, and to be relieved of a task which he has for some time been engaged in rendering distasteful to me.'[30]

Brodrick now set up a committee to discuss the matter. He was in the chair, Godley (his Permanent Secretary) and Stedman (his Military Secretary) were both secretaries, and the members were Sir G. White and Lord Roberts, both former C-in-Cs India, and Lord Salisbury whose wife was Kitchener's closest confidante and who, as Brodrick told Cromer either maliciously or naively, 'has had some special opportunities of learning the ins and outs of this particular subject'.[31] The other members were Sir J. Mackay and General Sir John Gordon who had served in the army in Bengal until 1887, and finally Sir Edward Law, a friend of Kitchener, whom Ampthill described as 'a hopeless crank and the very incarnation of cussedness, with a morbid and distorted mental outlook'[32] who particularly disliked Curzon. The committee was notable for what it failed to represent – no ex-Viceroy, no ex-Secretary of State, no ex-Military Member, although there were many varieties at large in London of all three species. Curzon said that the lack of such authorities meant no one represented the constitutional aspects of the case, to him the heart of the matter. Kitchener, as we have seen, thought it was unfair to have Roberts on the committee, simply because he believed he would vote for Curzon.

Lovat Fraser, the journalist, gave it as his opinion that much of the opposition to the Government of India, which Brodrick's committee had now under scrutiny, arose because its despatch had rejected Kitchener's criticisms *in toto* and did not offer a diplomatic olive branch (although Curzon offered a personal one to Kitchener, as we have seen, in the form of a substitute for Elles).

Lovat Fraser believed from what he had heard from military friends that there was some truth in the charge that the Military Department had been getting too big for its boots. Curzon said, 'The answer to this charge is very simple. Lord Kitchener's scheme had convinced us that no mere amendment of our system was at that moment in the field of practical politics . . . The Military Member was no longer to be tolerated even in an inferior garb, but was to be swept away altogether. We realised accordingly that we *were fighting for the very existence of our constitution.*'[33] Curzon explained that his Council was under pressure from Kitchener's threat of resignation so 'of what avail would it have been . . . to put forward proposals for amendment which would merely have evoked another threat of resignation?'[34]

Curzon commented drily that 'it was a somewhat unusual proceeding for the Secretary of State to preside over a Committee to advise himself',[35] and perhaps partly in answer to that criticism, Brodrick formed a sub-committee of his committee, consisting of Godley as chairman, Lord Roberts, Sir J. Mackay, Sir J. Gordon, Sir E. Law, and Sir E. Stedman as secretary. Curzon commented that 'neither the Committee nor the sub-Committee was a strictly impartial or judicial body, and that from neither of them could any pronouncement except one favourable to the existing system have been expected',[36] Godley had never concealed that he would support Brodrick. Curzon claimed that the committees had decided from an early date that some sort of Military Member must be retained, and acting on this, the sub-committee proceeded to draw up a scheme for the future division of labour between the two military authorities, and suggested that the head of the emasculated Military Department should be called the Military Supply Member. The report of the sub-committee was accepted by the committee, and in turn accepted by the Secretary of State and the Cabinet.

Although in his subsequent despatch, Brodrick spoke of the 'important constitutional questions',[37] these were deliberately excluded from the terms of reference of the committee and never discussed. Curzon charged, 'I have reason to believe that the one-sidedness of the committee and the issue that was expected of its labours were manifest from the start, and formed the subject of remonstrance even at its meetings.'[38] Actually, the committee did invite written evidence from an ex-Viceroy (Lord Elgin), from two ex-Finance Members (Sir D. Barbour and Lord Cromer), and ex-Military Members (Sir H. Brackenbury and Sir E. Collen). But neither in the despatch nor in the committee's report was any hint given of the nature of their replies. Any reference implied that they were in agreement with the new scheme. In reality, said Curzon, every single one of these authorities reported strongly in favour of the existing system and against change. Lord Cromer, in particular, was highly incensed that his advice was ignored and that Brodrick did not understand the facts. Lansdowne wrote a minute broadly against Kitchener, but he too was ignored.

White and Roberts, the two former Commanders-in-Chief, found themselves in the curious position of being the only members of the committee who did not favour the views of the present incumbent of that appointment. White had originally backed Kitchener, and when he changed, Brodrick tried to persuade him to recant, telling him that he was disappointed. White wrote to Roberts, 'Such an expression disposes of the "open-mind" he professes.' White also said, 'It seemed to me the forces of the India Office were arranged against Lord Curzon from the beginning.'[39] Brodrick kept Frank Maxwell, whom Kitchener had sent to London, informed about progress, and Maxwell passed the news on to Lady Salisbury, who, in turn, would have made it her business to stiffen Balfour's backbone. On 18th May 1905 Brodrick told Curzon that the report was completed and reassured him that he had till now kept an open mind, but explained that this did not mean an open mind about the merits of the case, but about the practibility or form of change.

Brodrick needed to carry the Cabinet with him, so he sent them eighty-eight foolscap sheets of printed documents on 24th May and, the following Monday, the full report of the committee with a covering note in which he advised them that one man could not fulfil the duties proposed by the Commander-in-Chief; but that because Elles was 'embarrassing to the C-in-C and destructive of rapid or effective administration' he would be replaced 'by some less distinctively military administrator'.[40] Curzon himself did not see the report until a month after he resigned, and he then wrote bitterly: 'The entire theory, according to which the Govt. of India is conducted by confidential co-operation between the Secretary of State and the Viceroy, was ignored and abrogated, and the Viceroy was treated as a suspect person, who must be kept in the dark until he receives his orders.'[41] Yet on the very morning that the papers reached most members of the Cabinet, the Kitchener propaganda machine, operated by Marker, and orchestrated by Hubert Hamilton, ensured that a long and important article appeared in *The*

Times under Repington's name, based on Kitchener's much-publicised 'private' letter to Stedman.

The Cabinet took less than twenty-four hours to consider their decision and approved the solution proposed by Brodrick's committee. The only member of the Cabinet with Indian experience, the ex-Viceroy Lansdowne, said later in the year that he would have left the government sooner than consent to Kitchener's proposals, while Lord Esher, although not on the committee, was moving influentially in the background, telling the Prime Minister Balfour that Kitchener's resignation must be avoided at all costs. He advised the King along much the same lines, producing the letter to Stedman as evidence. But the influence of Balfour appears paramount.

Kitchener's spy Marker got the news of the decision from Stedman and hurried to the Post Office to send a coded telegram to the Chief:

> Decision as follows. Mil. Member disappears, Member of Council Finance and Stores taking his place; he may be either civilian or soldier below the rank of Major Gen. . . . All Depts. now under Mil. Dept. except Finance & Stores to be handed over to C-in-C. The surviving Dept. maintain Civilian staff. C-in-C to have direct access to Viceroy and to be his sole Mil. Advisor. HQ Staff organisation to be practically as suggested by you.[42]

Kitchener was overjoyed and wrote at once to Lady Salisbury. 'I am so happy at the result, I do not know what to write . . . I hope you will tell AJB how grateful I am . . . You might tell St. J he has my very best thanks for all he has done. I know he must have worked very hard in my favour against a lot of opposition.'[43] Hamilton was also quickly on the wire to Marker:

> [The Chief] wants you to get him if possible a copy of the proceedings of the Commission or Committee which enquired into the case at home. The evidence will be very interesting. He has asked for Stedman secretly by this mail for this . . . The Mil. Dept. have turned sulky and put up their shutters. They are passing all cases involving finance to the Finance Dept. of the Govt. of India, and are removing their notes from all other unsettled files. Elles will go at once I fancy, and with him the bulk of the obstruction and

opposition that has been so much to the fore since K came out here. I have no sympathy for a soldier who has deliberately thrown his lot against soldiers. Had he been a bigger man, he would have recognised when K came here that when 2 men ride a horse one must ride behind, and that man could not be K. However, he [Elles] is not worth discussing now. Bobs has been a sad disappointment. His jealous nature has made him go against the army and the man who made him in South Africa.[44]

That night the Curzons came to dine with Kitchener at Wild-flower Hall by long-standing invitation. As they sat talking, Hamilton studied their faces and guessed quite rightly that they knew nothing of the decision taken in London. They were going to know nothing of it for nearly three weeks.

Curzon's disgust with Brodrick's despatch, when it finally arrived, may be imagined, but curiously Kitchener too was downcast. He immediately cabled Marker, 'Despatch received. Decisions not at all what you anticipated in your telegram. Tell Lady S my letter of satisfaction written under wrong impression. Thanks however stand.'[45] His attitude had been anticipated by Stedman who wrote by the same mail that the Prime Minister thoroughly understood his position, and:

I earnestly hope that the decision will, in great measure, meet your views. As I understand it, all that is vital is conceded. It will be possible now to create an Indian War Office on sound lines, and the Mil. Dept. as it had been, will cease to exist. There will probably remain some difficulties as regards finance, but if good arrangements can be made from the starting of the new system, I do not think that there would be trouble. The military budget for the year would, I assume, be settled in Council, and it should provide more latitude for the military authorities than is possible here, having regard to the H of C. I mean that within his financial limits of the Budget, the military authorities should be able to make savings on one item and apply them to another.[46]

This caused Kitchener to re-read the despatch, and Hamilton, who had a clearer mind, had long discussions that day with his Chief who gradually came round to seeing that the thing could be turned to his advantage. Hamilton was most persuasive, and by

evening the Chief decided to wire Marker again: 'After consideration I think things can be worked out and I feel happier. Take no
action on my wire of this date.'[47] Hamilton realised the significance
of the despatch quite clearly, as his letter to Marker shows:

> This decision of the Cabinet opens up a new era and puts our
> Military interests on quite a new footing. Had K been obliged to
> leave, the Army must have followed its downward path to disaster.
> Now there is hope. The decision is far more than one for the C-in-C
> against the Military Member or for K against Curzon, or for the
> Home Govt. against the present constitution of the Govt. of India.
> Whether the Cabinet realise this or not it is a decision for the Soldier
> against the Civilian – one which recognises for the first time the
> paramouncy of the Soldier in military matters and in the control of
> the Army – at least that is what it must come to, for they have
> actually recognised it here in India by giving K control. And when
> he has finished his great work here and not before, he will have to
> take up the greater task at home, but on the same lines, and what the
> politicians have given him here they will not be able to refuse him at
> home . . .[48]

Curzon was shocked by the despatch, because he had believed that
his Council's own view of the matter was being carefully studied in
London (thus he was not anxiously awaiting a reply, as Kitchener
was) and that no Cabinet in London could refute a weighty and
considered response from a Government of India's status. Brodrick
had written the despatch himself and it was full of mistakes.
Paragraph 6 gave a lengthy refutation of an argument which had
never been advanced and other paragraphs were self-contradicting.
Elles and the Military Dept. were blamed for causing friction by
allowing junior officers to criticise the Commander-in-Chief's
proposals – which practice Curzon had stopped two years earlier.
Brodrick made great play of an incident about small arms ammo,
but the document sent to London did not substantiate this.

The gist of the proposals was this. The Military Member was to
be abolished and a Military Supply Member would join the
Council. He was not to give expert opinions on military questions
(as the Military Member had done) and his functions were limited
to supply matters. His duties were more of a civil than of a military
nature; he would not be able to veto any proposal put forward by

the Commander-in-Chief. He was specially to advise on 'questions of general policy as distinct from purely military questions'. If the Commander-in-Chief were from the British Army, the Military Supply Member must be 'an officer of considerable Indian experience and of administrative capacity, and intimately acquainted with the characteristics of the Native Army'.[49] His duties would be essentially those of a civilian administrator with military knowledge and experience, and Brodrick later stated that he might be a soldier or civilian. The Military Department's secretary could be no more senior than a Colonel, whereas the Army Department (of the Commander-in-Chief) would have a Major-General as Secretary.

Barnes, a member of the India Council in London, had tried to explain to Brodrick that the Council of the Indian Government consisted mainly of civilians who were entitled to comment on proposals coming before them, so that the new Military Supply Member could not, as a member of that Council, be instructed to comment on some things (general things) and not on other (military) things. And where would he draw the line?

In the third week of June, Parliament debated the Indian Budget, and Brodrick pointedly refrained from paying the customary tribute to the Viceroy. Noticing this, Haldane, from the Liberal benches, spoke up for him.

After the debate Haldane wrote to tell Curzon that the [Liberal] opposition members had cheered his tribute to the Viceroy and, 'Unless something unforeseen happens, I doubt whether there is any one the Opposition would rather see in your great office than yourself.'[50]

Brodrick gave a potted – and misleading – version of his despatch to the House, and, as those of its Members who were briefed on the subject were previously briefed by Kitchener, no one appeared to notice its inconsistencies. In fact the military issue was not discussed or debated because a blocking motion was placed upon the Order Paper by the Government – 'so the decision was consummated behind the back and without the sanction of the House of Commons',[51]

Brodrick was careful to send no papers about the work of his committee, nor to pass on the opinions of Cromer, Lansdowne, Brackenbury and Collen. Lansdowne wrote privately to Curzon on

26th May 1905 that he had done his best to thwart the 'insensate' proposal to discard the Military Member and Roberts also explained that the Military Supply Member was the best compromise that could be achieved in face of Kitchener's desire to abolish the entire Military Department. Roberts seemed to think the new man would provide valuable local knowledge and advice.

It was evidently thought in London that Curzon would accept this compromise as satisfactory if all of those party to it wrote to him explaining that firstly it was a good compromise, secondly it did not mean that Kitchener had triumphed, and thirdly in any case everyone from the King downwards had agreed to it, so Curzon had better do so, too. Brodrick wrote on 2nd June, Godley on 30th May and Balfour on 9th June. The King himself wrote on 2nd June, explaining that Kitchener 'is a man of such importance, and especially in India just now'.[52] Brodrick also wrote to Ampthill, presumably believing he could obtain his support, but Ampthill fully understood that it was a victory not only for Kitchener, but 'for the young lions at Army HQ who used Kitchener for their own ends and especially for Mullaly, a schemer and a wire-puller of none too scrupulous a description'.[53] Brodrick was much taken aback when he heard that Ampthill did not like his wretched compromise.

Of the soothing letters aimed at calming down Curzon, the worst, because the blandest, was from Balfour, who, not at his best, implied (as Brodrick was to do in his memoirs) that the whole fuss probably arose because Curzon was out of sorts due to overwork. His letter ran:

> The relations between the C-in-C, the Mil. Member and the Indian Council, which were so often the subject of conversation between us when you were here, have, I fear, given us both a good deal more trouble than I at one time anticipated. We never *quite* saw eye-to-eye in the matter, and, though I recognised to the full the unique authority which your opinion must necessarily carry with it, I never could bring myself to believe either that the dual control in Army administration was the right system, or that what the Despatch of the Government of India describes as 'military autocracy' could be the result of its abolition – which the view that it is necessary to have, as it were, an official Opposition *within* the Indian Council to comment on, and if need be, to oppose, the suggestions of the C-in-C

though doubtless occasionally useful, must surely, on the whole, lead to endless friction.

I had very much hoped that the Commission to which you had agreed in the winter, would have been able to deal with the subject in India, and with constant reference to yourself. This plan, however, unfortunately fell through, and we have been obliged to do the best we can, with the means at our disposal, on this side of the water. I hope that we have not been unsuccessful, and that you will feel that the compromise between Lord Kitchener's views and those of the Indian Council will prove not only of great administrative importance, but will conciliate the various opinions which this controversy has elicited. We have certainly done our best to obtain the assistance of those who, either as Governors-General, or as Commanders-in-Chief, or as Military Members of Council, have had to do with the working of the existing machine.

I cannot help thinking that part of the difficulty may have arisen from the unintentional extension which, in the course of years, the Military Member has given to the duties of his office. I find it difficult to believe that, unless by the happy conjunction of two individuals specially adapted to work with each other, the Indian system could resist the sudden pressure of a great crisis. I hope the modification of that system which has now been devised will keep in it most of what was valuable and eliminate most of what was dangerous. One thing I am sure it will *not* do; it will not diminish the authority which the Governor-General has, and ought to have, over matters of Army as well as of Civilian administration.

I should be very grieved if I thought that the new scheme did not reconcile whatever there may be of opposition between your views and those of K.

I am not happy as to what I hear about your health. I know your illnesses are only due to overwork, but overwork may first become a habit, and then a second nature; and one of the arts which you must not allow India to let you forget, is the art of taking a holiday.[54]

Curzon was much incensed with all these attempts at smooth talk, and he could see from the letters from Roberts and Lansdowne that there was no question of a decision having been arrived at upon its merits, and that Kitchener's view had been accepted in London *in toto*, and 'a disembowelled Mil. Member has been left to prevent me from resigning'.[55] If he resigned now, though, it would appear that he had had a personal quarrel with Kitchener and the

Home Government. How could he resign on a question of principle when no one, except a few intimates, appeared to understand what that principle was? He was in despair at what to do and wrote to his friend Dawkins: 'I have long ceased to extract any pleasure from my task, and I yearn to hand over and be at rest. I would come at once if I thought that Milner would succeed me. But I fear some subservient member of a Cabinet whose second ablest member recently confessed publicly his "colossal ignorance of India".'[56]

On June 30th, at Brodrick's insistence, the Government published the minutes of Kitchener, Elles and Curzon, along with the two despatches of 23rd March (from the Indian Government) and 31st May (from Brodrick). This was the second time in six months that the Government had published controversial Indian papers (the first was after the Lhasa affair) and Curzon remarked that this habit was less in accord with their traditions than with those of the *Daily Mail*. Dilks wittily observes that, 'Light relief was provided only in *The Standard*'s comment that "Mr Brodrick's reputation has been more than maintained by the masterly Despatch now published." '[57] The publication made it clear to those who cared to know that Kitchener's papers had been passed to the papers like *The Times* and *The Standard*.

The Indian newspaper editors, now reading all this for the first time, were particularly incensed, not only by the content of the documents, but by the tone of Brodrick's despatch, which they considered insulting to the Viceroy, to the Indian Government and hence to the Indian nation at large. Without exception they agreed it was a victory for Kitchener. Brodrick expressed surprise on hearing this and wrote to Ampthill, 'I hope Curzon will not take up the same line.'[58] In fact, Curzon was taking an even more serious line, discussing with the other members of the Council (except Kitchener) whether he should resign, or whether they should all resign. Three members out of six were against resignation and two of them urged him not to go in deference to 'the public good'. Reluctantly agreeing to stay, Curzon went to see Kitchener on 25th June 1905 to see what could be saved from the morass Brodrick had created. It must be remembered that, whereas Curzon had had the despatch for a few days, Kitchener, Hamilton and company had been planning their campaign in detail for nearly a month, secure in all the knowledge which Curzon had only recently possessed.

Kitchener wired Marker on 22nd June 1905, 'All of you have done so well,' and Hamilton followed with more precise instructions:

We received the Despatch late on Monday night, and the Chief was disappointed to find it differed so much from your wire. At first sight it was not easy to discover exactly what was intended, but after further consideration and talking the provisions of the Despatch with Duff and Mullaly, the Chief decided that they could be worked if the Finance Dept of the Govt of India were to take over Mil. Finance, but that it could not be worked if the new Member for Mil. Supply were to take over Army Finance . . . The Viceroy has not written or sent a word of any kind to the Chief . . . We have no idea whether the Viceroy will resign or not, but I hardly think he will, though he will likely resent the wording of the Despatch which tears the old system he has championed, to pieces. His proper course would be to send for K and say "Look here, I don't like this at all but we must see what can be done". Such a line is not in him – he is carried away by personal feelings.

Now the point the Chief wishes to discover is how the difference has arisen between your information and what has actually been decided . . . This is most important for the Chief to know, as if your wire embodied a decision which was recommended but not accepted, it gives him all he has to go on when Curzon leaves and he will understand that the decisions we have got was a concession to Curzon.[59]

Kitchener had his campaign clearly set out although there was one piece of advice which he did not quite understand and which hung about in the back of his mind: 'Let Curzon down easy,' the words of his friend Eddie Stanley, in the Cabinet as Post Master General. When Curzon came to tell him that unless there were some modifications to the despatch, he believed he should resign, Kitchener's somewhat hypocritical response was that if anyone should resign it must be he himself - but in any case he did not think, he claimed, that the Military Supply Member would be a mere cipher.

Although it appears Curzon kept away from Kitchener for a few days while contemplating the awfulness of Brodrick's despatch, Mary Curzon was still seeing him and indeed writing him letters, some of which have survived. This was written about 25th June, the day after Kitchener's 55th birthday: 'My dear Lord K. The crisis seems to be abating – so we may hope to live in peace until the 5th when St John hurls his next bolt at us [the next mail was due in on the 5th]. He has a gift of rousing officers and countries to depths of indignation – and India is going through much the same wrath that the War Office went through. The War Office however had the luck of seeing him *go*, while we have the anguish of seeing him stay. . .' She adds she is giving him for his birthday three candlesticks to match his candelabra, and that there will be 'another from home for your *next* birthday, when you will be taking a new Lady Viceroy down to dinner . . . I have some nice pictures of Naldera Camp which I want to send the Brat [Maxwell] as he used to like the camp so much – I have written that we missed him here – will some of your 'family' tell me his home address?'[60] Hamilton, who supplied the information, did not mention the purpose of the Brat's visit to London – to intrigue against the Curzons.

Curzon confined himself to telling Kitchener somewhat formally in writing: 'I am consulting the colleagues who took the same view as myself [in Council] as to their thoughts about the Government's proposed schemes and when I have obtained their views, I shall be in a position to have a talk with you. Is there any chance of your being at Wildflower on Sunday, because I could be at the Retreat on that day?'[61]

The account of the famous meeting that Sunday which is given in most biographies (describing Curzon in tears) differs markedly from that which Kitchener afterwards told to Hamilton who passed it on to Marker by letter.

> The Chief has asked me to write to you fully but it is not easy. After a week's silence, the Viceroy saw the Chief last Sunday at the Retreat. There was a long discussion resulting in conditions which you know [are] being drawn up. Duff saw the Viceroy on Monday regarding them, and after going into more detail in Elles' presence, he thought the Chief – though not agreeing with them all – would accept, in deference to the Viceroy's wishes. The V sent K a message by Duff that he would telegraph *at 3 p.m. to the S of S his resignation or submit the condiitions for consideration of Govt if K accepted them* [Marker's underlining]. He felt in the circs he must do so with the result you know, *but we have not seen the telegram or been given any idea of its contents*

beyond the conditons. I am not at all happy about the whole business, and your wires yesterday and this morning are not reassuring. K has been most considerate and conciliatory throughout. He felt that an uncompromising attitude on his part such as the V has adopted would at once produce a crisis, and in his opinion the V's demands were not sufficiently divergent from the terms of the Despatch to justify this. Thus he has given breathing time and if Govt. don't mind facing Curzon's resignation they can adhere to the Despatch exactly. Personally, I am inclined to think that they want his resignation, as there is not sufficient reason for it in the actual decision. Such an object would alone to my mind account for the tone of the Despatch.

Of course K could not assume this, and he *knew nothing,* so he could not risk producing a situation which would partly *take matters out of Govt's hands.* I hope after K's telegram of yesterday, they will realise that the points to which K has agreed do not curtail "great and most serious alterations". *There is probably much more in the Viceroy's wire than we know of* – enough at least to afford the Govt ample grounds for refusing it if that is their inclination. K is upset today, and suggested my sending you the wire to explain his reason, *and asking you to do all you can to correct the impression you mention.* I hope things will work out well, but I don't like the outlook. *I know the man . . .*
[remainder missing]

What had actually happened at the meeting at the Retreat was that Kitchener had agreed broadly to these modifications:
1. The secretary in the Military Department would be a Major General (to match the Army Department) and not a Colonel.
2. Important changes of organization should be discussed in the mobilization committee or some other body in which the Military Supply Member had a seat.
3. Curzon argued there should be no duplication of work between the Military Supply Member and the Army Department, but Kitchener agreed that the Viceroy could submit any case put by one Department to the other for advice.
4. When Curzon insisted that the Military Supply Member must always be a soldier and the new department retain the old title, Kitchener replied that although he did not consider the alterations to be improvements, 'There are none that I am not willing to accept in deference to your wishes.'[62]

After this meeting – as Hamilton's letter shows – the modifications were discussed by Duff (for Kitchener) and Elles; Curzon this time held a pistol to Kitchener's head by threatening to resign if the conditions were not telegrammed to London by 3 o'clock on 26th June. Kitchener agreed to them, and Curzon, having finally realised that Brodrick was an enemy not a friend, telegrammed his proposals (which he regarded as the Government of India's ultimatum) direct to Balfour, merely advising Brodrick, 'I have sent important telegram to the PM'[63] but not copying it to him. The wire read:

Private Teleg.
I have consulted my colleagues as to Secretary of State's Despatch of 31st May. They concur with me in thinking that the scheme therein proposed, if unmodified in important particulars, will be mischievous, if not unworkable, in operation, and that it will gravely imperil essential control of Governor-General in Council. It will further impose intolerable burden upon the Viceroy while depriving him of indispensible advice. Nor could I personally accept the position in which as head of the Government in India I have been placed by the decision of His Majesty's Government, conveyed in so invidious and derogatory a form. I have discussed the matter at length with Lord Kitchener, who realising the gravity of the situation created by the despatch, offered to put his resignation in my hands. Upon my refusing to consider this alternative, he agreed to join me in submitting certain modifications which are acceptable both to the Government of India and himself, without departing from the general principles to which the approval of the cabinet has been given, and which we will do our best to carry out. These modifications are as follows:
1. The Military Department and Member should retain their present designations, and the Military Member should be invariably a Military man.
2. All important changes in Military organisation or conditions of service or in customs affecting the Native Army or its departments, should be discussed by the Mobilisation Committee of which the Commander-in-Chief and Military Member will be essential members.
3. On submission of any case to the Viceroy by either Army Department or Military Department he may refer the case to the head of the other department for advice.

The above proposals are intended to safeguard the practical efficiency and dignity as Member of the Council of the Military Member, who will thus be available for consultation by the Government, with full knowledge of all that is passing.

4. The Secretary to Govt in the Army Dept should be of the rank of Major-General.

5. A schedule of cases should be drawn up which it will be his duty to submit to the Viceroy before orders are passed upon them.

These proposals are intended to augment the authority of the Government of India and to acquaint the Viceroy and his colleagues with the policy and proceedings of the Army Dept. Lord Kitchener advocates these additions, and the remainder of Council desire to represent strongly that without them the scheme will be impracticable. We are of the opinion that they hang together and should be accepted or rejected as a whole. If they are likely to meet with the approval of His Majesty's Government, we will submit them without delay. You will understand that in the interval my position is one of considerable public difficulty, from which I should be glad of early relief.[64]

Curzon cabled an amendment two days' later:

Please refer to my telegram to the Prime Minister of 26th inst. Modification (Para 1) Lord Kitchener suggests that I should explain that by the word 'invariably' is not meant any alteration in law, but a continuation of the existing and hitherto invariable practice. This seems to be contemplated by your despatch, as it is not clear how a civilian could possess what is there described as military experience and knowledge.[65]

Brodrick obtained a copy of Curzon's telegram from the Prime Minister's secretary, and was incensed by the words 'mischievous and unworkable' and tried, without success, to persuade Curzon to withdraw them from the official record. Brodrick immediately realised that the telegram embodied serious changes and he found it hard to believe that Kitchener had agreed to them. He spoke to Marker and to Eddie Stanley, and the latter agreed to send Kitchener a telegram in War Office cypher asking whether he had truly accepted 'such great and most serious alterations'.[66] Kitchener replied:

Communicate following from me at once Private and Secret to Prime Minister, begins:

"Viceroy informed me on Sunday he intended to resign if I did not accept certain modifications which he would telegraph to His Majesty's Government. Feeling everything possible should be done to avoid this, I accepted in deference to him . . . [this is Kitchener's first reference to Stanley's instruction to let Curzon 'down easy']. I hope we may then – we ought to – get on, but as long as Elles is here we shall have difficulties. I know nothing of Viceroy's telegram beyond bare conditions."[67]

On the back of this cable is written, in Marker's hand, a message which he presumably sent to Kitchener: 'I much fear you are giving up points which your friends here consider having been gained with greatest trouble.'

There is another undated message from Kitchener deciphered by Marker, probably of the same date: 'I fear I have been rather led away by pleasure at Curzon's at last agreeing to my views about title of new department, and that I may have possibly been rash in accepting the final paragraph of his telegram today to Prime Minister. Act diplomatically and put things right for me as I feel sure you can. Explain if necessary that as there was nothing of importance in the conditions I agreed to, I felt bound to associate myself with Viceroy in order to terminate present critical and impossible situation.'[68]

At about this time Kitchener wrote to Lady Salisbury, 'I wonder whether I have done what Mr Balfour would have wished in keeping Curzon from resigning?'[69] Balfour was, in fact, in direct touch with Curzon on 29th June:

Private. Following sent by desire of Prime Minister. Begins From Balfour to Curzon. Private Version given of Kitchener's view in your telegram of 26th instant greatly surprises me, for it seems quite inconsistent with his Minute already laid before Parliament. I should be most grateful if you would ask Kitchener to send me privately full statement of his reasons for apparent change of view, especially in relation to maintenance of Mil. Dept. under present name and with a soldier necessarily at the head: the possible submission of all matters proposed by him, whether military or not, to proposed Mil. Dept., and the creation of an officer as secretary to the Govt. of India in Army Dept. with rank of Major-General. To some of your proposals there seems in any case to be no objection. Do not know what is meant by epithets "invidious" and "derogatory". No one here has taken such a view of Brodrick's Despatch. Ends.[70]

There is an interesting paper from Hamilton in Marker's files at this time which is probably typical of the messages he was being asked to pass to Brodrick and others:

Chief much upset at idea he has not sufficent[ly] maintained position obtained by his friends. He has no wish to recede from it but felt his action was the least he could do to avert certain crisis and thus give HM Govt. opportunity of considering.

'If you examine points carefully you will not find so important. Do all you can to remove impression mentioned in your telegram to Chief.[71]

Balfour also asked Kitchener to give his own private version of what had happened and Kitchener told Lady Salisbury on 30th June 1905 that although his friends thought he had given too much away 'It really is not much and we can put things right when he [Curzon] goes'.[72] It is clear that Curzon was not dealing with people who had much time for principles. On the same day Kitchener joined with Curzon in sending the following to the Prime Minister:

Your private telegram of 29th. Lord Kitchener and I are in absolute agreement and this telegram is sent and signed by both of us. He accepted proposal about retaining name of Mil. Dept and Military Member to which I attached importance because it did not in his opinion affect main scheme. But he regards proposal as undesirable and I am prepared to meet his wishes on this point. He holds that new Member should be Military Officer, in order properly to perform functions assigned to him, but thinks, as I do, that there need to be no alteration in existing law. He cordially accepted and fully approves of the remaining modifications, and does not regard them as inconsistent with his own proposals, or with Secretary of State's despatch. As regards (3) he points out that Viceroy already possesses constitutional right of consulting any officer or department. As regards (4) he prefers to see Major-General as Secretary to

Government in Army Dept. and thinks that local rank should be given to any Colonel appointed to the post. Above proposals are so cordially agree to by both of us that if His Majesty's Government are not able to accept them, Lord Kitchener desires to associate himself with any action that I may take in the matter.

signed CURZON
KITCHENER[73]

Nevertheless, Curzon made a considerable error before sending these messages in not giving copies to Kitchener, because the latter was later able to claim he had never seen them.

Brodrick was left out in the cold, and he was most annoyed about it. Curzon stopped writing his weekly letters to him, and was (it seemed) only in touch with Balfour, who made feeble attempts to mollify his colleague, writing to Curzon on 1st July:

> I am delighted that what seems to Brodrick and myself a satisfactory arrangement can now be come to.
>
> Our interchange of ideas has in form been somewhat irregular though as I have taken the S of S opinions throughout, irregularity does not extend to substance. Please ask your people to see that nothing leaks into press until we can announce completed arrangements. Newspaper rumours cause us here considerable inconvenience. It is particularly important that exchange of telegrams between you and me should be kept absolutely private.

Curzon cabled Brodrick:

> Will you kindly explain to the Prime Minister that I have only communicated with him direct because I feel it to be constitutional practice than when a Viceroy is proffering his resignation he should do so to the Head of Government.[74]

An indication of Brodrick's mood at this time is given in a letter which General Barrow wrote to Curzon on 23rd June 1905:

> From all indications at home and from a conversation I had with Mr Brodrick, I gathered that the Cabinet would endeavour to support Kitchener and that there was no question at all of right or justice, but that they were too afraid of Kitchener coming home [i.e.

resigning], they would sacrifice anyone and everything to prevent that.

The agitation has been carefully inspired by K and engineered from Simla; no one at home knows anything about Indian Administration and cares less. I was asked by Mr Brodrick to give my opinion on the question and the papers were sent to me. K. worked in a thoroughly underhand manner, for while he did not answer your minute and the Viceroy's in the official papers, he wrote long letters [to Stedman] to the India Office contesting them para by para and making the gravest mis-statements. From another source I understand that this letter was printed by India Office (although a private one) and passed around the India Council.[75]

Brodrick was convinced Curzon would never resign but he tactlessly wrote to Curzon on 30th June 1905 that while his resignation was not desired, 'Do you think that any Government could surrender a point in which they really believed, in order to secure for a few months extra, the presence of a Viceroy who disagreed with them on as many subjects as you have recently disagreed with the Government?'[76] The key phrase, related to Brodrick's botched-up compromise, was that it was 'a point in which they really believed'. Kitchener, meanwhile, was eating humble pie, writing to Eddie Stanley:

I am sorry my attitude has been misrepresented at home. I felt that after Brodrick's despatch, if Curzon left by resignation, he would have a great deal of sympathy and could do a great deal of harm to the Govt. The only tip I had was yours: to let him down easy. I also found that Curzon knew so little of the working of the Army Admin. that he might be ridden off dangerous modifications and might be made to save his face by asking for modifications which were no modifications in reality. At home I suppose that people could not believe that Curzon with all his ability was getting nothing – and they thought I was giving up principles of importance.

Well now we come to the time when I made a mistake which really is what I am writing about. You know what occurred by my wire to Marker. I admit fully I had no right to associate myself with the Viceroy. When I saw Curzon for the first time a week after the receipt of the despatch, I found that he was going to make what in my opinion was a mistake. His course appeared to me clear – either to resign or accept, but he was not going to do either, though he had a strong feeling that he ought to resign and was prepared to do so if he could not get what he wanted. I felt Curzon's resignation should be avoided if possible for the sake of the Govt. Had he gone on the Despatch, he would have had much sympathy both here and at home and might have done a good deal of harm. After his conduct in Tibet and Afghanistan, this would have been a blow and been condemned, and it would have increased the forum of discussion to a dangerous extent. He would have appeared as a martyr to the maintenance of a constitutional govt – [forced out] by Brodrick. Moreover when it came to the pinch I felt I had made a mistake before I got downstairs. I need not have done it, but has no one ever said more than they intended? I had no right to appear to attempt to force the Govt. to take my view of the non-importance of the modifications; it was their affair, and I had nothing to do with it. I admit it all, but it did not strike me in [that way] at the time. (I have never felt happy since I did it, [crossed out]) I ought to have seen clearly it was bound to give a false impression at home. The position was that Curzon had after a warm discussion given up the one point that I considered of any importance and if he got the other, the crisis over. He said the Govt. would not grant even the least modifications and that he would have to resign and was very low. I felt *sure* they would, and went too far in throwing the weight of my influence on his side. I felt it was the right thing for the Govt. to do; but I never contemplated for a moment that having got his modifications, Curzon would, or could, turn around and ask for them officially in the way he did. There was not the slightest indication of any such tone about him then, and when the Prime Minister agreed, I fully thought the whole . . . [rest of the letter lost][77]

It will be recalled that all this to-ing and fro-ing of letters and telegrams resulted from the fact that Eddie Stanley had told Kitchener 'Let Curzon down easy' so that when the two met on Sunday 25th June at the Retreat, Kitchener agreed to Curzon's proposed modifications, although he later reneged on the matter of the title Military Member/Military Supply Member. In London all Kitchener's supporters and friends were amazed at what they believed was his about-face, since the Brodrick compromise had only been cobbled together to avoid a major public confrontation. Now it appeared that Kitchener had given back to the Viceroy all that they had laboured so hard to deliver him. Somehow Kitchener had to regain their confidence and explain why he had acted as he did. His nervous worry about the matter is indicated by the fact that on 1st July he sent Marker three separate messages at 09.50, 12.50 and 13.50 hours.

Kitchener trumped up two explanations, one more dramatic than the other. The first is given in the letter he wrote Eddie Stanley sometime in July – that he gave in to Curzon, to stop his resigning and thus save the Government at home embarassment. His letter is full of lies about the incident, particularly his claim that he 'never contemplated for a moment that having got his modifications, Curzon would, or could, turn round and ask for them officially'. Hamilton's letter to Marker, already quoted, makes it clear that Kitchener sent Duff to see Curzon and Elles the following day to get the details in writing for submission to London, although perhaps Curzon pushed him harder by again threatening resignation.

This letter, Kitchener realised, was not strong enough, so he decided to expand on the point of a 'warm discussion' and pretend that Curzon had broken down at the interview, and that he, warm-hearted Kitchener, had therefore let his nature get the better of him. He told Lady Salisbury that the latest interview with Curzon had been a stormy one, the Viceroy had broken down, so Kitchener had agreed to support his 'puerile requests . . . I could have bitten my tongue out for making such a stupid remark but really I suppose I was rather excited with the discussion. I was prancing up and down his room talking to him very straight'.[78] He also told Marker the same story. Curzon makes no mention of a breakdown. All these protestations from Kitchener, and Marker's efforts, cleared the air in London and Marker cabled, '[They] have greatly cleared complicated situations. Friends were considerably relieved.'[79]

Kitchener, having told Eddie Stanley that Curzon did not understand the modifications (they were not really modifications he claimed) now told Lady Salisbury that there had not been any modifications made.[80] But Curzon was determined that there should be no misunderstanding on the matter at home or in India, and he telegraphed to London that he and Kitchener agreed that the Military Supply Member should be available for consultation by the Viceroy at the latter's discretion upon all questions, without the limitations laid down by Brodrick. This was, indeed, the crux of the matter, because Curzon had fought to prevent the Commander-in-Chief becoming an autocrat, and had insisted that there should be a member in Council with military experience who could give the Viceroy independent military advice, if necessary, contrary to the views of the Commander-in-Chief. Curzon pointed out to Balfour on 3rd July 1905 that opinion in India, both civilian and the Army, was against the new organisation, and added: 'I hope that importance of concessions will not be minimised when they are officially announced. This would only produce renewed outbreak of public feeling here.'[81]

Curzon also warned Brodrick that the Council doubted whether even the modified scheme would work because, 'Although our proposals are not inconsistent with principles of your scheme, which we had no alternative but to accept, they do to some extent challenge policy, in so far as they attempt to provide Viceroy and council with alternative military advice.'[82] His firmness annoyed Brodrick, who told Roberts on 11th July, 'My colleagues think him unreasonably violent but he has no idea of resigning.'[83] There is no evidence that Brodrick's colleagues felt anything of the sort. Nevertheless feelings were running high and Balfour told Salisbury 'K is a traitor',[84] feeling that he had been let down badly. Brodrick finally decided to swallow his pride and telegrammed that the modifications from India did not contravene the despatch of 31st May, and in some respects exactly fulfilled it. Honour was satisfied, and an agreement satisfactory to all sides had been reached. Curzon appeared to think so, telling Kitchener on 5th July 1905, 'The Home Government after one or two ineffective wriggles have given in and our proposals are all accepted.'[85]

But Curzon had been deeply hurt by the whole affair, not only by the perfidy of Brodrick and Balfour but also by the behaviour of Kitchener, whom he had once called a friend, and to whom he, Curzon, had always acted correctly. An incident at the end of May had been enough to remove whatever illusions Curzon had left: Reuter cabled out the text of a leader in *The Times* written by Repington at Kitchener's instigation, which carried the disclaimer that no part of its contents had been received from Kitchener or officers under his command. Since they had been sent by Kitchener to Marker and Stedman and thus passed to Repington, this was tantamount to a lie. Included in the article were the comments of

Kitchener's generals. Curzon was much vexed by this and taxed Kitchener about it at once. He wrote to Kitchener on 31st May: 'Earlier in the year, you assured me that "the opinion of the generals you had consulted were asked for quite privately, and were for yourself alone, and not intended for anyone else." It would appear, if *The Times* Military Correspondent has any authority for his statement, that the results I anticipated must have occurred, viz that the opinions of the Generals . . . would be used to influence public opinion and to prejudice the case at home. In the circumstances I write to ask you if *The Times* man has been correctly informed.'

Kitchener replied on 1st June: 'I really do not think I can be held responsible for what the papers publish. It was nearly five months since I asked some generals for their opinions.'[86]

Curzon responded the same day, 'But you have not answered my question.'[87]

Kitchener replied, again on the same day: 'Of course I do not know what opinions the Generals may have expressed other than in their private correspondence with me; but I can say that in those letters, none of them used the words stated in the telegram. [This was a lie] The general sense of the answers of those I consulted was that they agreed with the views I held on the subject.'[88]

Later Kitchener added, 'At the end of my last letter please add "I did not consult all the Generals holding High Commands". If *The Times* correspondent is quoting from my private letters, he is therefore in this inaccurate as well as in the statement.'[89]

At the beginning of July, although Curzon and Kitchener claimed to be in accord, and Brodrick reluctantly agreed to be satisfied, others were not entirely at peace with the march of events. For one thing, Curzon, believing that he had got his way in retaining the essential advisory nature of the Military Member (or Military Supply Member as he would now be called) had begun to promote the appointment of General Barrow to the post. As Viceroy, the appointment of the Military Member had been in his hands, and he assumed that the Military Supply Member would also be his appointment. Hamilton was amongst those who did not like this turn of events. He wrote to 'Conk' Marker:

As time goes on, I feel less and less happy about the way things are going. Last Thursday the V wrote to a line to K to say the Home Govt had accepted his modifications which he would submit officially by wire. At Council on Friday, he gave an address on Army Admin in general and then proceeded to explain how an ignorant Govt. had attempted to foist an impossible scheme on the enlightened Govt. of which he is the head, and that after a hard struggle he had forced them to accept certain modifications which entirely changed the character of the scheme which he was now prepared to accept. K said that the faces of his colleagues [on the Council] had never looked blanker than when they heard the modifications and Hewett remarked after Council, "I think it is all very satisfactory, but why ever did we sign the despatch supporting the old system?"

On Friday, Barrow arrived from Peshawar and I gathered next afternoon he was offered and accepted the new Membership and no doubt discussed the whole situation with Curzon who saw K on Sunday. Curzon was nasty and impossible. First, he told K the S of S objected to his telegram, but he didn't mean to alter it . . . Then he went on to Duff; K no doubt wanted Duff as C of S, and V quite approved, but he could hardly give him the rank of Lt. Gen. at once. [Curzon then discussed other appointments with K who] sees the advantage of postponing any actual appointments until the India Office have had time to realise Curzon's impossible attitude, and he hopes in the meantime they may interfere. Barrow says he does not think the new system can last long as by June they are doing all they can to wreck it . . . Barrow knows nothing about Stores and Supply and cares less, so that all his inclination will be to develop and magnify the *"advice"* portion of his functions. He will be greatly encouraged in this direction by the Viceroy . . . and the dual control will reappear in fact if not in name. Barrow will have the Viceroy's ear, and every suggestion of K's will be subjected to his criticism. I do not see how the show can work under such conditions.

I am afraid K has not been altogether alive to the dangers of the situation, and was carried away by pleasure at his apparent victory and the new prospects it opened up. He should at once have fixed on Barrow as his own Chief of Staff and thus denied him to the Viceroy . . . The point is for you people at home to realise what is going on, viz: *that the Viceroy is doing his best to make the scheme unworkable, and that K is to some extent playing into his hands* [Marker's underlining] – not intentionally of course, but simply in his desire to be conciliatory and to make no difficulties for those at home who have done so much for him.

I don't think K has ever realised until the last 2 or 3 days that quite possibly the [Home] Govt wanted Curzon to resign. I suggested this directly I read the Despatch, and am still of the same opinion; if it was so, it would have been as well to have given K some kind of hint, instead of which Eddie Stanley wrote by the same mail as brought the despatch "he hoped K would let Curzon down as easily as possible". *The V. is quite impossible and really India would get on much better without him in all respects.* [Marker's underlining]

I have marked this letter *private* as it might read badly to one who did not know me, but I do not intend to prevent you making any discreet use of it . . .

It seems such a pity that we always make such a mess of things, but it must be so where personality is stronger than patriotism![90]

Curzon was now seriously worried about the growing split between the Government in India and the Home Government. Throughout his Viceroyalty he had written to the Palace, first to Queen Victoria, then to Edward VII, on matters of moment and this seemed to be a proper subject for royal consideration. He did not realise that Edward VII was a Kitchener supporter. He wrote that if the Government of India's 'advice is publicly disregarded, and if they are further exposed, as they have been both in this case and in that of the Tibetan Blue Book, to open rebuke for doing what after all is only their duty, their position in India will be a difficult one, and their prestige will disappear'.[91]

Kitchener's friend Pearson now began to publish more articles in his favour in his paper *The Standard*, edited by Gwynne. They insinuated that articles in *The Times of India* were inspired by Curzon, but Lovat Fraser is on record as saying that he had had no contact with the Viceroy. Pearson, who also owned *The Evening Standard*, the *St. James's Gazette*, the *Daily Express*, and leading provincial papers, said all his papers 'advocate the same views on subjects of national importance'.[92] The *Daily Express* published a report from its Simla correspondent that, 'All the correspondents at Simla are registered and unless we send only what the Government wishes known, we are "black-listed" and if we send views that the Government does not wish known, we are practically debarred from getting any news at all.'[93] Again, Lovat Fraser has given the lie to this, and the Indian papers also derided the suggestion, but of course Brodrick believed it. To further help Kitchener's cause, Stedman had arranged for messages in cypher to reach Brodrick direct. Hamilton claimed in a letter to Lady Salisbury that he detected 'evident signs' of a press campaign 'craftily engineered from the precincts of Viceregal Lodge'.[94] This was fabrication, like the story that Curzon used an influential friend at home to further his ends. *The Standard* also published, on 29th June 1905, as fact, that Curzon's resignation had been offered to Balfour, although the source of that information can only have been Balfour or Brodrick.

Curzon's behaviour appears to have been highly honourable; at some time in June an Indian Post Office official came to see him and offered copies of Kitchener's cypher messages to Marker, but Curzon reports that he refused to look at them, his sense of honour being such that he would not even permit himself to see Kitchener's private telegrams, which would have opened his eyes to the conspiracy operated by Marker with the Cabinet and the India Office.[95]

When he heard about this, Kitchener panicked. He rushed off a letter to Lady Salisbury, saying that, as Viceroy, Curzon would have been within his rights to see these telegrams, although they were 'personally paid for and thought safe. When Minto comes out will you ask him to ascertain if Curzon has done this or not?' He told her he had heard from a friend that when he told Curzon 'it is over now' Curzon replied, 'No it is only just begun. I have revelations to make which will quite upset Kitchener and Balfour.' Kitchener was clearly upset by this and asked his confidante 'I do not know if any such actions would bring him within the pale of the law, but I think it might?' There was another line of defence 'The only other person that I know would be likely to influence him would be the King, and if Curzon is desperate it might be as well to invoke his aid in stopping him, as if I have to justify my action in public it will do no possible good . . . If only Curzon were told that he could not make use of confidential documents acquired in his position as Viceroy, I think his attack would be innocuous . . . He would no doubt be nasty, but we could take that in absolute silence. I hope everyone will realise the importance of being prepared for contingencies.'[96]

Kitchener's attitude is surely extraordinary. Had the telegrams come out, Lady Salisbury's role in the affair would have resulted in a public outcry. Furthermore, it was a problem for which he had not prepared her. For example he had written in February, 'It is very lucky having Marker in his present position [at the War Office] as through him anything can safely be transmitted to me. I pay for all telegrams and they are private and absolutely safe.'[97] Yet now, when they are unsafe he does not apologise, or even explain; he simply tells her to arrange for the King to muzzle Curzon. The King did so, but it was not necessary, because Curzon did not wish to see the private telegrams, and never saw them, much less used them to ruin the reputations of not only the Salisburys, but also of Balfour and Brodrick as well as Kitchener. Even Lord Salisbury would not have been safe, because Kitchener often used the telegrams to ask his wife to get him to supply information. In the event, although Kitchener panicked, Hamilton took a much cooler stance on the matter. He wrote to Lady Salisbury, 'Poor Lord K has realised at last that the Viceroy has all his private telegrams and is very unhappy. Personally, I do not think it matters now that things are settled . . . It is very difficult to know what to do. It is like waiting the attack of an unscrupulous (should I say savage?) enemy in a strong position . . .'[98] Hamilton also managed to persuade Kitchener to take a calmer view, and the following was soon posted off to Lady Salisbury at Hatfield. 'As regards the telegrams I mentioned in the last mail, there was not very much in them . . . Marker suggests that I should ask you to tell Brodrick that his name was never mentioned in them. One of them was [even] sent at the request of Lady Curzon to help poor George . . . They were sent to Marker as a private friend who was working with me.'[99] This last sentence shows that Kitchener was even prepared to lie to Lady Salisbury if he thought he could get away with it.

Kitchener, who could hardly remember what lies he had told to whom, was meanwhile writing to Marker, 'I felt I could not go back on what I had said to Curzon at The Retreat,' just at the moment when he was busy doing just that very thing.

Brodrick continued to believe or to claim that it was Curzon who was writing to the press, telling Ampthill, 'Any public opinion there is in India has been manufactured at Simla.' Ampthill replied that the idea was laughable. Brodrick had decided to keep a stiff upper lip about the modifications to his plan, and announced them to Parliament as if they were entirely within its original intentions, instead of being the opposite. The gist of his speech was cabled to

India by the press, and the following day, 18th July, Curzon made a speech in the Legislative Assembly, attended by Kitchener, in explanation.

Unfortunately for Curzon, Reuter telegraphed a summary of the speech in a few very misleading sentences and implied that he had criticized the Home Government. Both Brodrick and Balfour were incensed. Curzon's belief was that he had to explain to the Indian public 'why I had offered to resign, what were the flaws [in Brodrick's plan] which I had been struggling to correct [and] . . . that I felt bound to disclaim responsibility for the scheme as amended'.

Balfour wrote formally to the King that the speech was, 'deplorable in taste and temper; and that no such public exhibition of disloyalty to the Home Government has ever yet been made by an Indian Viceroy. Mr Balfour looks forward to the development of the incident with the gravest anxiety. Sir Herbert Fowler [a former Secretary of State for India] is understood to be so indignant with the Viceroy's conduct that he means to press the attack to the utmost; and how the Govt. are effectively to defend against an unanswerable charge, one who has left no means unused, legitimate or illegitimate, to defeat their policy, it is difficult to see. On personal, even more than on public grounds, Mr Balfour is deeply grieved.'

It is a pity that Balfour had not read the speech when he wrote this, as it was moderate throughout. A few days later Balfour wrote to the King, 'Neither of these eminent men can be said to emerge from the controversy with any credit whatever. But as they have come to a working agreement and as this agreement leaves untouched the essence of the proposals which, largely in consequence of Lord Kitchener's views, the Government have pressed on the Viceroy, it seemed to the Cabinet that "least said soonest mended" and they therefore resolved not to make more bad blood even by the most legitimate condemnation of the tone which the Viceroy thought fit to adopt in his recent utterances.'

Brodrick, still without seeing the text of Curzon's speech, told Lord Salisbury that if Curzon were reprimanded, his resignation would follow. The Cabinet was in any event rattled, still more so when after a debate on 20th July they were beaten in a division by four votes.

When the Cabinet met formally to decide whether to censure Curzon's speech, Brodrick told them that the content was gratuitous, that it had been concocted for public consumption in India, and that a campaign in the Indian press had been 'assiduously dictated for the Indian newspapers, which were supplied from day to day with the subject matter of confidential telegrams until the Prime Minister himself telegraphed urging the Viceroy to keep communications secret.'[100] All this was untrue, as was his statement that Curzon had been 'counting for months on the fall of His Majesty's Government and the advent of a Government who may recall Lord Kitchener for work at home. The division of last week will encourage this hope.'[101] Thus Brodrick, not satisfied with telling lies about his old friend Curzon, was now trying to stir his colleagues' resentment by suggesting that he wanted them out of office.

The Cabinet also discussed the growing discord between Curzon and Kitchener, and noted that although it was true that they had appeared to agree on the modifications, their account of their conversations was wildly divergent. But it was decided that after all, the Cabinet would not censure Curzon for his speech.

Relations between Curzon and Brodrick became still more strained when some exchanges concerning the resignation of Sir E. Elles leaked out, and Brodrick cabled Curzon to ask whether he knew the names of those responsible, and, if so, 'Whether you think it desirable to take any steps to make them amenable under the Official Secrets Act.'[102] Curzon thought – quite reasonably it seems – that the implication was that he was responsible and should apply the Act to himself. He asked Ampthill, 'Can you conceive anything in an official telegram more spiteful or yet more puerile?'[103]

Brodrick's icy language to Curzon is well-illustrated by his official telegram accepting the modifications:

The preamble and the concluding sentence of your Excellency's telegram appear to show that you have misapprehended the intention and practical effect of the orders of HMG. Your modifications do not contravene the provisions of the Despatch, and some of them are in exact fulfilment of the wishes and intentions it conveyed. HMG deem it a matter of satisfaction that, although Your

Excellency's views are averse to change, the points which you think it necessary to raise appear to have its general principles untouched, and that Lord Kitchener . . . is now in accord with the rest of your Government.

The extraordinary thing was that while all these official exchanges on matters of high moment were continuing, we find that the two men were conducting the daily business of government – for example, from Brodrick, 'Correspondence regarding dredgers. No objections to proposal.'[104]

Chapter Ten

The Resignation

The scheming Hamilton said in mid-July that he was 'afraid K has not been altogether alive to the dangers of the situation and was carried away by pleasure at his apparent victory'. The danger Hamilton foresaw only too clearly was that Curzon would place his nominee as Military Supply Member and the two of them would, as in the past, run rings around Kitchener and the Army. Hamilton's observation, already noted, was that Kitchener 'should at once have fixed on Barrow as his own Chief of Staff and denied him to the Viceroy'.

Barrow was indeed the key element in any success that might have resulted from Curzon's modifications, which attempted to salvage something from Brodrick's despatch. It will never be known if Barrow could have succeeded because he was never tried, although it is true that when, instead of a competent man being appointed Military Supply Member, a mediocre nominee of Kitchener's took on the job, the results were disastrous. Barrow's competence had been obvious to Curzon for many years. In 1901 he had described him as 'the most capable of our young generals, both in the office and in the field'[1] and in 1903 he advised the Secretary of State that Barrow was the right man – indeed the only man – to take over from Elles as Military Member should he go. Barrow was broad minded, free from bias and extremely able, said Curzon and 'I have never worked with any military officer with greater satisfaction, or parted from him with greater regret'.[2] Barrow had been in the Military Department until October 1903 when he was posted to Peshawar to command the Division there.

He was regarded as one of the more distinguished soldiers, and, perhaps wisely, Kitchener chose not to consult him when he was polling his generals on their opinions about his memorandum. Now, in early July 1905, Barrow was about to go to England on leave, and Curzon asked him to call at Simla *en route* to Bombay. Barrow was, however, intercepted by Kitchener who had been told by Curzon that he favoured Barrow for the post of Military Supply Member. This was Barrow's account of their meeting.

> K said, 'Let us impress upon you one thing. That if you accept, you urge Lord Curzon to get you put into office at once. I cannot get along with Elles and this scheme has got to be got into working order by 1st October, so there is no time to be lost . . .' I replied that I could not propose this course. Gen. Elles was a personal friend of over 20 years' standing and my host at the moment . . . K. said, 'If you will not make the suggestion, I will.'
>
> The impression I got was that Lord Kitchener was quite prepared to cooperate with me, though he knew I did not regard the new system with any satisfaction; at any rate he volunteered the opinion that we should 'get on all right together'. The general effect of the interview was that though we did not see eye to eye we might make things work. Our conversation lasted considerably over an hour. I left Simla (after another session with K) with the idea that Lord K. was quite satisfied to have me as a colleague in Council.[3]

Barrow, immediately after leaving Kitchener, went over to Vice-regal Lodge and reported the conversation to Curzon, who explained that while he could not appoint Barrow, he could recommend him to Brodrick. Barrow did not think the scheme would work for long, and reported that when he had made this observation to Kitchener, the latter had agreed. Barrow also explained how Kitchener had wanted him to give up his proposed leave in England and take over from Elles at once, but Curzon pointed out that Elles had already been asked to stay on until 1st October, so there was no reason why Barrow should not go on leave. He did so, and the scheme to make him Kitchener's Chief of Staff, (a new appointment) and thus forestall his appointment as Military Supply Member soon came to nothing, because Kitchener realised that he was a man of independent views, who would not be one of his cyphers.

Kitchener cabled Marker on 7th July: 'Please give the following to Stedman. I sincerely hope there is no idea of making Barrow Chief of Staff. I should have no confidence that there would not be a leakage in my office. I am personally too unmethodical to work satisfactorily with so inadequate a Chief of Staff.'[4] Kitchener cabled again to Marker on 9th July, rubbing in the point, 'Barrow inside my office would be too great a danger.'[5] On another occasion he told Marker, 'Best course I think would be for the S of S to ask the Viceroy to send for his consideration my opinion as to *officer most qualified* [Marker's underlining] and suitable for Military Supply Member. I will then advocate Scott.'

While all this was going on, Kitchener's 'oriental mind' allowed him to tell Curzon that he thought, 'Barrow was altogether too good a man for the billet,'[6] and he would prefer to have him as his own Chief of Staff. Indeed, according to two of Curzon's correspondents Kitchener actually offered Barrow the post of his Chief of Staff. Curzon's response was to express surprise, and suggest to Kitchener that his present military officer, General Duff, would surely expect to be Chief of Staff? And who would be Military Supply Member if Barrow was not? Kitchener suggested Egerton, which caused Curzon to laugh, as he was an elderly caricature of a general with no administrative experience. Curzon, turning the tables, said to Kitchener, 'Why not take Egerton as your Chief of Staff?' The reply was, 'Oh no, I don't want a duffer!'[7]

Curzon wrote to Balfour recommending Barrow, but at the same time, a letter from Marker also found its way to the Prime Minister, suggesting that as a former Military Department Secretary, Barrow did not believe in the new system and did not consider it would last for long. It suggested that Curzon was determined to wreck the system, and that Barrow would in practice maintain the old system. This was a crude way of saying that Curzon was trying to make Brodrick's ineffective scheme into something that would at least operate. Hamilton wrote to Lady Salisbury: 'Barrow is capable and experienced, but he has been too much in the Military Department and his sympathies lie there I think. His inclination in the new post [Military Supply Member] will be to magnify and develop the *advice* portion of his new function . . . You may think me indiscreet, but I feel it is as well to tell you what passes through my mind . . .'[8] And ten days later he added: 'Men are apt to be dazzled

by the intellect and talent of a Curzon . . . and few pause to scrape
below the surface where they might read the true character which
these very characteristics – should I say virtues – impel to certain
disaster.'[9]

The intrigues by the Kitchener camp were becoming so complex,
and potentially so dangerous if discovered, that Hamilton decided
to employ a safer code. He told Marker, 'I am sending you one of
our HQ Y cyphers. I am the *only* other person with a copy, and its
existence is not known. In any message I send you by it, I will
begin HQYHH.'[10]

The probability is that Kitchener was leading Curzon up a blind
alley, encouraging him to believe that he would agree to Barrow's
appointment, so that he could later deny having done so. Meantime, he had told Stedman that he wanted Scott, although the
former thought it unlikely that Brodrick could approve, as one of
the requirements of the appointee was that he should possess
experience of the Native Army and Scott had none.

To Curzon's surprise, he now received a private letter from
Brodrick, written on 16th July, remarking that he proposed to
nominate a Military Supply Member from England, and anticipated that Curzon would agree, as the Secretary of State had 'twice
given way' to the Viceroy over nominations to the Council. Curzon
replied on 17th July, disputing Brodrick's claim; Brodrick had
suggested four nominees for two posts, and offers had been made to
two of them, but for various reasons these had not been able to be
accepted, so that Curzon's candidates had after all been nominated. Brodrick repeated the charge (for example in his 1939
memoirs), but did not bother to publish Curzon's letter setting the
record straight. Truth had begun to matter very little to Brodrick at
this stage, desperate as he was to survive in his appointment. It is
not known what individual Brodrick had in mind for the Military
Supply Member position when he proposed a nominee from
London. Curzon for his part slipped back into the error of believing
what Kitchener told him, and cabled Brodrick that Barrow 'would
be acceptable to both Lord Kitchener and myself'.[11]

About this time, Lady Curzon wrote to Kitchener a private
letter, which is revealing in showing that, like her husband, she
naively believed that Kitchener was acting rationally and playing
by the rules. It almost seems from the letter that she is confiding in

Kitchener aspects of the matter which her husband might have preferred her to keep to herself.

> Wednesday,
> There is a new phase in this horrible question which I am going to write to you about *most privately*. It relates to Barrow's appointment about which you know I feel strongly, and about which we talked at Wildflower. Well – a wire has just arrived from Home Govt. (S of State) saying 'They have been advised' to make him Chief of Staff. This was because of G's [Curzon's] proposal to make him Supply Member.
>
> I do deplore things drifting to a personal impasse. There was a 'mauvais moment' when it appeared that a private note to Stedman had been privately circulated to the Council and Committee at the India Office. This caused a stir. I had believed that you and Duff and Barrow could have *started* this troublesome system, but I fear that it is impossible to reconcile really divergent views, and G will make a stand for Barrow and has wired to this effect. But I do not know what advice they are acting on at home.
>
> Please do not answer as I write confidentially – as a friend I believe I am.[12]

Curzon was still unsure what the Home Government's attitude would be to the speech he had made in the Legislature on 18th July. Hearing nothing, he sent a long telegram on 29th July to Brodrick which was never included in the published papers, and which stated that, had the Government felt it necessary to make one, 'Any expression of censure would have been followed by my immediate resignation . . . My view . . . is that I have been treated throughout, however unintentionally, with extreme lack of consideration, while my speech is universally regarded in India as having been characterised not by impropriety but by self-restraint.'[13] The Kitchener camp believed Curzon had, by his speech, made a fundamental error. Hamilton wrote on 20th July to Marker:

> K did not seem to think Curzon has given himself away but Reuter this morning shows quite a different impression has been given at home and I hope he may have committed himself so far as to cause his own downfall. The sooner he goes the better. He is quite unscrupulous and would wreck the Empire sooner than subject

himself to discipline or modify his own opinions and personal feelings.

Your letter to K of 30th received last mail conveyed the first impressions in all their nakedness, brought K straight into my room for consolation – poor man, I could not give him much beyond pointing to Brodrick's telegram as having quite established his position, and I was sure his friends do now understand his [Kitchener's] action. Still the *bad* impression was made and will remain to some extent.[14]

Despite the first sentence of the letter just quoted, Kitchener wrote the same day to Lady Salisbury, 'Curzon has I think given himself away by his very improper speech. I wonder what action the government will take – he is evidently at their mercy.'[15]

Hamilton's description of poor Kitchener coming to his room for consolation about 'the slip' he had made is revealing both of Kitchener's remorse at taking a false step and of Hamilton's conviction that he can manoeuvre the Chief who is full of weaknesses. He marks the letter 'Very Private!! Very!!!'. In a later letter, he tells Marker that Kitchener still expected 'the friends' in London to send more wiggings [but] both you and Lady S made it quite plain that the "association" slip was quite understood and quite forgiven. This was the greatest relief to him, for all along the consciousness of that blunder has weighed upon him. "If only I had not made that one mistake," he often repeats, and one morning, after wiring to you, he added, "I would give £500 to be out of that." So you can picture his relief. As soon as the rain stopped, he went outside and laid out a tennis lawn.'[16] And later still, he told Marker 'Your wire with Eddie's [Stanley's] message to say all is forgiven and forgotten just received and welcome.'[17]

Hamilton also wrote:

I am sorry to realise it but K is human like the rest of us and is too much influenced by his likes and dislikes – he'll run his pals to his own destruction and unfortunately his pals are seldom the right sort. Attributes which we despise are generally those which most appeal to him. K. has fought a great fight and gained a great victory and then proceeds to scatter its fruits by indulging in a boyish gratification which throws him entirely off his guard and in personal idiosyncrasies which destroy confidence and have the worst effect. I

only mention this to enable you to appreciate the situation . . . K did
not in the least object to the idea of Barrow as C of S except on Duff's
account . . . K. has of course always wanted Scott as Supply
Member.

Brodrick's wire accepting the modifications received last Friday
was excellent and put things on proper lines again. His speech in the
House last Monday was based on his wire and if K. puts his back to
the wall and stands no more nonsense he will be all right. But he will
have to fight and will have to be thoroughly alert, active and
unbending. He must adhere absolutely to the terms of the Despatch
and insist in every detail on the stricter interpretation of its spirit.
Then he will not only hold his own, but may drive Curzon, who has
had so much rope, into a nasty corner.[18]

Kitchener's desire to ditch Barrow (despite having implied they
could work together) and appoint Scott as Military Supply Member and Duff as Chief of Staff was finding a ready supporter in
Brodrick. He claimed that he had learned 'from a number of
private sources'[19] that Curzon, in order to defeat the new scheme,
had summoned Barrow, offered him the appointment of Military
Supply Member, and sent him on a short leave, all without a word
to the Secretary of State with whom the appointment rested. None
of this was true. But Kitchener had sent letters home to Brodrick
making it clear that Barrow was unsuitable to him, and on 1st
August Brodrick cabled to Curzon that 'he was advised' that
Barrow was unsatisfactory and concluded, 'This is also the view of
the Cabinet, who are not willing to appoint General Barrow. I hope
to telegraph . . . very shortly the name of the officer we propose for
the Military Supply Member.'[20]

Unfortunately for Brodrick, there was a debate looming in the
House of Lords, when Roberts was expected to speak on the
subject, and his sympathies were known to lie more with Curzon
than with Kitchener, although he had reluctantly voted for Brodrick's plan. Brodrick vainly tried to stifle him before the debate. He
begged him to say nothing that might be used to justify Curzon in
giving the new Military Supply Member the authority of his
predecessor. Roberts replied that if Kitchener had his own way 'as
the member's of [Brodrick's] sub-committee were evidently bent on
letting him have, I should have been surprised if there were not
trouble in India. As it is, I hear on good authority that there is a

good deal of dissatisfaction throughout the Indian Army.'[21]

In the debate, Roberts said quite unequivocally that the Viceroy must not be dependent on the advice of a single soldier, despite the fact that this was precisely what Brodrick was arranging, by putting a Kitchener nominee in as Military Supply Member. General Sir Edwin Collen, a former Military Member, commented that Lord Roberts' declaration in the Lords appeared as if it was a tardy profession of repentence and added, 'Of course in the meantime Nicholson [General Sir W. G. Nicholson] had spoken strongly to him.'[22] Roberts' support was however too little and too late.

Further support for Curzon came from Lord Ripon, who described Brodrick's despatch as the greatest rebuff inflicted on the Government of India since Ellenborough's about fifty years earlier. Of this earlier missive it had been said it was no doubt 'a very fine piece of writing, and may rank with many passages from our classics. But was it fitting that the Government should hurl these sarcasms at a man placed in the position of a Governor General?'[23] and Curzon commented that if he could not truthfully repeat the first sentence, he might well have re-echoed the second. Speaking in the Debate, Lord Lansdowne, the Foreign Secretary, who, it will be remembered, was pro-Curzon although he had not voted favourably in Cabinet, said that the Government had decided against Kitchener's demand for the disappearance of the Military Member, who would 'remain very much in the position which he had always occupied'.[24] This was an extraordinary statement, clearly made in all good faith, but showing a lamentable ignorance about what had been happening in India. If what had been said in the House of Lords was truly the Cabinet decision, then Brodrick was acting absurdly in trying to contest Curzon's actions – but the fact is that the Cabinet, despite Lansdowne's experience of India, did not really grasp the position and a number of them, perhaps including the Foreign Secretary, did not really understand Brodrick's proposal thoroughly.

Curzon tried to clear the air by telegraphing that the new Military Supply Member, if he were to give general military advice, as the Brodrick plan stated, must be a soldier of the highest qualifications. Unless there were strong reasons to the contrary, the Viceroy's candidate should be appointed, since the Commander-in-Chief had had full knowledge of the Viceroy's proposals, and, Curzon added, 'If any contrary advice has reached you, I cannot accept its validity.'[25]

Curzon evidently still believed that Barrow might be appointed – as is clear from this account by Hamilton of a conversation Kitchener had with Mary Curzon over tea: 'She was evidently relieved that the crisis was over, and said the V was much better. She did not enter much into detail, but said St John had been obliged to knuckle under all along the line. I wonder if she supposes anyone believes her lies! K is very pleased with himself just now.'[26]

Two days later, on 3rd August, Kitchener was writing to Marker, 'For goodness' sake don't let me have Barrow as C of S. I could not trust him a yard, and you know how openly I speak sometimes . . . I would far rather see Barrow as MSM *outside* my office than C of S *inside*. I should never be able to sleep on both ears if he were [here]. Of course Scott would make an A1 MSM but I doubt Curzon agreeing. He is as obstinate as anything you like, and will look on Scott as not having sufficient knowledge of the Native Army. [Scott] and I would agree which is of course what Curzon does not wish.'[27] Marker went to see Brodrick, and tried to make Kitchener's position clear, and Brodrick sent a message in code to Kitchener confirming that he too opposed Barrow and Kitchener should not support him. Stedman also wrote to Kitchener, probably at Brodrick's suggestion, 'I am quite sure that you do not believe in Barrow (clever man though he may be) to the extent of wishing to go out of your way to get him made MSM.'[28] On the same day Brodrick telegraphed officially to Curzon that because Barrow had worked as Secretary to the Military Department, he could not be expected to have an open mind about the new system. In the opinion of his military advisors (i.e. Stedman) the Military Supply Member should have technical experience. 'Will you consult Kitchener as to who in his opinion is the best qualified man for the post, and let me know his views? We will willingly consider any names you and he desire to put forward . . . we must avoid any appointment which would in our opinion tend to reproduce previous difficulties.'[29] What was clear from this missive was that Curzon's nominee, Barrow, could not have the post, which would go to someone nominated by Kitchener – yet Brodrick reiterated that the appointment was in the hands of the Secretary of State.

The demand 'Will you consult Kitchener?' was a great blow to Curzon and he told Lansdowne, who had cabled urging him not to resign, that he could have moulded Brodrick's proposals 'into shape consistent with what I believed to be the policy of HMG until I received the S of S telegram,' but if he was 'given a dummy as MSM. . . the task is hopeless. That is why I have asked for a man I know and can trust, and do not want a stranger and a cypher.'[30]

Curzon had lost all faith in Brodrick and the Cabinet, and felt a deep sense of persecution. He now realised that Kitchener was a liar, and would use any means at his disposal to achieve his ends. Curzon may have been told by Meyer, one of the staff at the Military Department, about an interview he had had with Kitchener of 20th July. Hamilton describes it as follows. 'Kitchener gave Meyer [the Finance expert in the Military Department] details of his own unscrupulous 'Supply' dealings with Milner in South Africa. "And did you get your bargain through?" asked the greasy little Meyer. "Of course I did, and I got my money too," replied Kitchener, while I watched Meyer's eyes. Afterwards I told K I was at a loss to understand why he gave himself away so innocently to the unscrupulous enemy. He had nothing to say. . . There is nothing so damning as self-condemnation.'[31] Presumably this refers to a 'kick-back' from a supplier which benefited Kitchener.

Kitchener's staff were keeping his dislike of the Curzons aflame with fresh fuel. For example, Duff told him on 14th July that Elles, with whom he had been discussing details of the new arrangements, 'has evidently been converted from his original reasonable views to his present impossible ones by the Viceroy.'[32] Certainly when Curzon met Kitchener, to discuss Brodrick's request for a nomination, on 5th August 1905, the atmosphere was bad. Curzon told Ampthill that this was his first disagreeable interview with Kitchener, who trembled violently with rage throughout. 'He lost all command of himself, and eventually stalked out of the room, not however, before he had mentioned as his ideal Military Supply Member a dear placid old dummy named General Scott, Director General of Ordnance.' Curzon asked what the Commander-in-Chief would do if Scott criticised his proposals. 'Criticise them!' shouted Kitchener. 'General Scott criticise me? I wish you to know that I should resign at once!' Throughout the interview, Kitchener's strange version of the facts was so surprising that Curzon told Ampthill, 'Used as I am to Kitchener's complete indifference to truth, I was somewhat shocked and surprised.'[33]

Kitchener's version of this interview is quite different. He claims that Curzon lost control, shouting that, 'I had brought all this on him, and that he would make it unpleasant for everyone including myself if he resigned.'[34] Kitchener claimed that he had not earlier made plain the unacceptability of Barrow because Barrow had already said that he did not believe the new system would work. Hamilton's account of the interview is different again:

> I met K as he came in at 1.30. He was furious (quite the right frame of mind for him when he is going to see the V) and swore he would do nothing to help the V, and would not lunch there. He got back here soon after 3 p.m. in quite a different frame of mind, gobbled up a few mouthfuls of lunch, and was gone again in 5 minutes lest he should be followed by letters from Lady C and delayed here. The V had told K that the S of S had wired that he did not think Barrow suitable and told him to consult V regarding another nomination. The V said he meant to have Barrow and would nominate no one else, so K retorted, 'Then why consult me?' The V insinuated K had already acquiesced in Barrow, but K repudiated this, and when the V saw he could get no change, he said he would show up everyone and everything (including himself, of course, which he seemed to forget for the moment) K said he must do as he liked, and left. Lady C was waiting to persuade him to stay for lunch but it was no use. . .
>
> I am only anxious and interested in K's account. I know what is good for him and what is bad, much better than he does himself. . . [Hamilton refers in this letter to the press campaign mounted by Marker in London, and adds] I think they will all help. . . and will enable Govt. to bring about Curzon's removal if he doesn't actually resign, though I expect they will wait now till Parliament rises. K lays store by his expressed opinion that the V has chosen Barrow deliberately for the purpose of wrecking the scheme, and knowing all they do at home, it will be difficult to neglect this. Certainly the Govt. position is far better now than if Curzon had resigned on receipt of the Despatch. Even Meyer declared quite openly the other day that he had missed his opportunity. It will be the greatest pity if Govt. follow his example and miss their opportunity now. . .
>
> Thursday 10th August [same letter] K is inclined to think now that C will not resign. Of course he won't, but I hope there may be enough in which to get rid of him![35]

The position was by now intolerable. The Viceroy had no longer any faith in his Commander-in-Chief, and could hardly bear to communicate with his Secretary of State. Brodrick for his part was hell-bent on humiliating Curzon, and Kitchener had been bending all his energies for over a year to removing Curzon from the scene, or rendering him powerless in military matters. To use the language of the divorce courts, the relationship between the various parties had irretrievably broken down.

An illustration of how completely Brodrick had gone over to the Kitchener camp is the way he swallowed their story about Curzon's handling of the press, whereas it was obvious to all that it was Kitchener who had mounted a public relations campaign of professional proportions. Hamilton wired Marker, 'Warn Brodrick that villainous press campaign . . . hostile to K and Brodrick, now being craftily and persistently engineered from here. Wholly artificial in character as public opinion is really neutral and opposition mainly interested and unscrupulous clique. Brodrick should discount agitation accordingly.'[36] Furthermore Brodrick's Military Secretary, Stedman, was in regular touch with Kitchener using War Office cyphers; the Marker file contains various telegrams of this type from Kitchener all headed 'Following from Stedman' Kitchener was also using these channels to issue statements to *The Times*, of course without consulting Curzon. He particularly objected to articles in *The Times of India*.

In his notes, Lovat Fraser explains: 'I wrote personally [in the *Times of India*] every single article that appeared on the subject. Lord Ampthill told me afterwards that I had made allusions which led the S of S to think I had been secretly informed of the inner history of the controversy, but I do not know to what allusions he referred. My agent in Simla was E.J. Buck, who was also Reuter's agent. It was my constant complaint against Buck at this period that he never told me what was going on . . . He was, from my point of view, inefficient throughout.' This was because Buck was in Kitchener's pocket.

Curzon now knew that there was no point in holding back his feelings, and felt that deep sense of persecution when the victim interprets every action by another party in terms of antagonism. He sent Brodrick a telegram on 5th August pulling holes in the latter's criticisms of Barrow, and concluding that the position had now reverted to that of June (before the modifications). He could only introduce the new organization with the co-operation of the best qualified Military Supply Member and with the support of the Cabinet. If that could not be given, his resignation 'should be placed before the King at once'.[37] Kitchener's cables to Brodrick continued to undermine everything Curzon said, and to make it clear to the Cabinet that, if they supported Kitchener's continuance in India, anything Curzon proposed would be unacceptable. On 6th August Kitchener cabled, 'Please ask friends not to believe anything Viceroy says regarding me or my views.'[38] And the following morning he cabled again: 'Since hearing of the unwarrantable lies that have been told about me, of which I had not the faintest conception, I do not believe in any protestations of loyalty [by Curzon]. The only one General in India who would help to wreck Secretary of State's scheme has been chosen, and, I think now, deliberately for the purpose.'[39] All these messages from Kitchener were printed by Brodrick and circulated to the Cabinet. Everyone weighed in against Curzon. Godley, for example, piously minuted Brodrick: 'To allow the Viceroy, at the critical moment, to force upon you a nominee of his own, with the hardly-concealed purpose of modifying the policy of HM Government . . . would be I submit, to act unconstitutionally and in direct contravention of the intentions of Parliament. The Viceroy has no *right* to be even consulted.'[40]

Curzon's enemies in London had to find some excuse for accepting his resignation. One came readily to hand. This was his proposal for the partition of Bengal. This province had its own Lieutenant Governor – who often did not bother to consult Curzon about his policies – and as early as 1902 the Viceroy had concluded it was 'unquestionably too large a charge for any one man'.[41] When he had visited East Bengal Curzon found that there was only one English official for four million people. Curzon's proposal made in February 1905 was to form an entirely new province uniting Eastern and Northern Bengal with Assam, with the capital at Dacca, and a population of eighteen million Muslims and twelve million Hindus. Yet in putting his proposals forward to the people of the province in speeches and addresses, Curzon seemed to ignore public opinion. This was curious as he was always telling the Home Government 'Public opinion has been growing all the while, is

articulate, is daily becoming more powerful, cannot be ignored. . .
The great change that is passing over this country, and which I
believe history will recognise myself as having done much (whether
wisely or unwisely) to accelerate viz. the lifting of India from the
level of a Dependency to a position . . . of the greatest partner
in the Empire. . .'[42] Curzon quite failed to understand the
opposition to his Bengal scheme, much of it irrational, but his
proposals were nevertheless agreed by the Home Government in
June 1905.

Brodrick now said that because of 'the storm his proposals for
partitioning Bengal have raised . . . it is possible that he may seek
relief'[43] from the Viceroyalty, and Balfour also wrote to the King
that the storm 'may induce him to grasp at any expedient for
relieving himself of a task which has now become distasteful to him
for other reasons besides those which spring from his relations to
Lord Kitchener and the Home Government.'[44] Balfour also repeated to the King his worries about Curzon's overwork and
ill-health and believed he might 'get us into quite unnecessary
trouble with the Amir of Afghanistan – a calamity the magnitude of
which it would not be easy to measure'.[45]

On the same day, 8th August Balfour joined directly in the
debate again by cabling to Curzon that his Government did not
understand Curzon's position since an (unnamed) source had
informed them that, 'General Barrow has no great liking for the
system which you wish him to administer and would prefer an
office which would not withdraw him from a distinguished career of
active service. Anxious, therefore, as we are to make your task a
light one, it does not seem that General Barrow's appointment
would be the most effectual method of attaining that end.'[46] This
cable was directly the result of Brodrick's lying to Balfour, if we are
to believe General Barrow, because his notes to Curzon state that
while on leave he had called on Brodrick in Whitehall the night
before that telegram was sent, and the latter, 'Gave me to
understand that you and he were at variance on the subject of my
appointment about which there was something like a deadlock. He
clearly wanted me to pull him out of a hole, by saying that I
personally did not agree the appointment and would be content
with Chief of Staff or any other sop. I equally clearly gave him to
understand that he was not in a position to offer me that appoint-

ment, as Lord K would insist upon nominating his own man, and further that I was not open to a bargain.'[47]

After this interview, Brodrick was in a quandary, as he had long ago realised that Curzon would torpedo his scheme if Barrow took the job of Military Supply Member, and had warned Kitchener to this effect. So he now had no alternative but to lie to the Prime Minister. Much later, Balfour was to realise what had happened, because when Curzon showed Barrow the telegrams, Barrow wrote to Balfour explaining that while he had told Brodrick he did not agree with his plan, he had stated he would loyally act by them if appointed, and Kitchener himself had said that the modified system would never work. To return to Balfour's message to Curzon, the latter replied to it, again offering his resignation.

Brodrick absurdly told Ampthill on 11th August 1905 that it was Curzon's wish to leave India before the Prince of Wales, who was due to visit at the end of the year, discovered his unpopularity over Bengal. '[He] wants to saddle us with his resignation . . . I wish I felt any real confidence in his fairness and uprightness. One must try and think then aberrations are due to ill-health.'[48] Kitchener stirred the pot by telling Stanley: 'I have never known more malicious lying statement than that concocted by Viceroy and Elles in Viceroy's telegrams of 10 August. All other misrepresentations in my estimation pale before it. I have handed Viceroy a strong detailed protest as Viceroy refuses to withdraw wire. [If] Secretary of State for India would order protest to be issued verbatim he will then understand. . .'[49]

The telegram Kitchener alludes to here was a key message from Curzon because it spelled out in considerable detail 'the source of the present difficulty' by listing 11 'modifying' proposals from Curzon and Elles, based on the conversations which had been held with Kitchener's staff, to form the basis for the future organisation of the Army. The last of these was paragraph (11): 'MSM not to criticise the opinions recorded by the C-in-C on military questions.'[50] Brodrick replied the next day attempting to force Curzon into the humiliating position of accepting Kitchener's nominee as Military Supply Member – the very point he was determined not to agree. Brodrick ignored his protests and ordered: 'We rely on you to meet our views.'[51]

Brodrick's behaviour at this crisis in his relations with Curzon was curiously desperate. How he had turned from supporting Curzon's case to rejecting it in favour of Kitchener has been described. Curzon's intellecutal arrogance and his refusal to accept Brodrick's advice about the timing of the committee had been the final straw, and Brodrick's deep inner compulsion – which he did not want to admit even to himself – was to humiliate and then destroy Curzon. He had proved to himself his superior power by his extraordinary behaviour over the Lhasa affair. Again, his wife and her family supported Kitchener. Brodrick, in whose mind his first wife and Curzon were linked, used every means in his power to ensure that his former friend would be humiliated and disgraced, thus perhaps in some way expiating the guilt he may have felt at having remarried. Those who worked closely with Brodrick, such as Sir George Clarke, described his methods as 'indefensible' and those who knew him, like the merchant banker, Sir Clinton Dawkins, said his temperament was like 'the worst kind of schoolmaster. He is always wanting to read somebody a lesson'.[52] Studying all the correspondence, it is difficult to find a redeeming feature in Brodrick's character, and his whining attempts to effect a reconciliation with Curzon five years later and his feeble efforts to rewrite history in 1939 only make matters worse.

However, in August 1905 there must have been two overwhelming practical considerations for him. He was 'abnormally sensitive' and as Curzon's biographer Dilks says, his confidence in the excellence of his own solution made him resentful when Curzon criticised it so forcefully and demanded modifications without which he said it would never work, and other Ministers criticised him for his failure to get the solution right first time. Brodrick was desperate to ensure that he should not fail again, as he had at the War Office, knowing that apart from the social disgrace, his marriage to an extremely ambitious woman also depended on his achieving political success. To have any hope of doing so, he must prevent Kitchener leaving India, and it was now clear that while Curzon had out-manoeuvred the Army by getting the Home Government to accept his modifications, Brodrick could regain control by putting a cypher in the role of Military Supply Member and thus negating the concessions.

Curzon for his part had only his principles at stake. As soon as he had read the Brodrick despatch of 31st May he had decided to resign, but had been dissuaded from doing so by the Council. Nevertheless, he had told the Government that he would resign if certain changes to the scheme were not made. Upon the modifications being accepted, he withdrew his resignation but 'was compelled to tender it again when I found that as interpreted by HMG they [the modifications] were illusory'.[53] He had discovered that in the very week in which Lansdowne was telling the House of Lords of the need for a second military advisor to the Viceroy, Brodrick was resolved that he should be 'of inferior status and attainments, the nominee and agent of the C-in-C. . .'[54] or, as the Indian newspapers wittily described it, a Director of the Indian Army and Navy Stores (Limited).

How in all these circumstances it could be claimed that Curzon was resigning out of pique or for personal reasons, is incomprehensible. Yet such claims were not only made by Kitchener's supporters at the time, but have been repeated by his biographers since, for example, by Magnus who says it was characteristic of Curzon to resign on a personal issue.

It is of the utmost importance to underline that Curzon resigned on a constitutional issue, the separation of the Army from the civilian power, and the superiority of the latter, which would not exist in India if the Commander-in-Chief nominated the Military Member in Council. Curzon believed that this change in the constitution had been ordered by the Home Government 'without reference to Parliament, in the teeth of unanimous public sentiment in India, and in opposition to an overpowering consensus of expert authority'.[55] In the paper he wrote after his resignation, Curzon complained that they had 'thrust aside as valueless the reasoned arguments and the earnest representations of the entire Government of India, and have ordered a revolutionary change in the Indian constitution in deference to the views of a single soldier who had only been in India for two years, who had never served in India before, and who was not in touch with the Native Army'. Curzon went on, 'There was an even wider aspect of the case. On every previous occasion of conflict between the Civil and Military authorities in India, where the same principle, namely that of civil supremacy, had been at stake, the Home Government had unhesitatingly sided with the Indian Government . . . It was reserved for Mr Brodrick to throw over the Viceroy and his united colleagues, and to sign a public surrender to the military power.'[56]

Curzon formally and finally resigned on 12th August in his reply to Brodrick's insulting request that he should 'meet our views'. Brodrick forwarded the telegram for action to Balfour, who was out of London, visiting friends in Gloucestershire, though promising Curzon 'meanwhile all privacy will be maintained here'.[57] Balfour seems to have been quite clear that he had no alternative now but to accept the resignation, telling Brodrick, 'If he *will* go, he *must* go.'[58] The Viceroyalty was offered to Milner, but after his experiences with Kitchener when he was High Commissioner in South Africa, it was too much to expect that he would accept, and he did not. T. H. O'Brien, his biographer, says that at this time, Milner was 'physically near breaking point'. Minto, however, who had already said that he wanted the job, readily stepped into his shoes – he had given up the Governor-Generalship of Canada the previous year. Winston Churchill told his mother, 'The appointment of Minto, poor dear thing, is another piece of Arthurism [Balfourism] *in excelsis*. For cynical disdain of public interests and contempt of public opinion, it exactly matches Brodrick's appointment to the Indian Office.'[59]

On 16th August Brodrick sent an 'official' telegram to Curzon from the India Office which piously claimed that, 'I have learnt your decision to resign with very deep regret. Throughout your administration . . . my colleagues and I have endeavoured to give you constant support. . .We have spared no pains during the last twelve months to arrive at a satisfactory settlement of difficulties which arose within your Council between Kitchener and Elles. . . We have been forced, with great reluctance, to conclude . . . that you were [not] prepared unreservedly to put our policies into effect. . .'[60]

And Balfour cabled: 'If after all that has passed you still reiterate your request to be relieved of your office, I know not how to combat further what I take to be a fixed resolve and have therefore, with the profoundest regrets, communicated your wishes to the King.'[61]

Curzon was at breakfast when the formal telegram was received from Edward VII, expressing regret that matters had to end in this way. It was not, of course, the end of the matter, but it was the high point of the tragedy, and everything to follow merely proved that tragedy's laws had operated in this drama too, the hero having fallen through his own faults, but being proved right when it was too late for restitution to be made.

When the facts behind the resignation were made public through the release of the various telegrams and letters which had passed between the Viceroy and the Government in London, particularly those written by Brodrick, the press in India was virtually universal in condemning both the Cabinet and Kitchener. This must have surprised Kitchener, who had told Marker on 24th August that he was 'waiting for Curzon to put his foot in it. It will be all the worse for him when it all comes out, as it must'.[62]

Here is a selection of Indian press comment – it ran day after day, column after closely-printed colum.

Times of India 21st August 1905: 'It seems to us that there has been a good deal of intrigue and double-dealing somewhere and that the man who emerges from the controversy with the purity and selflessness of his motives unquestioned in Lord Curzon.'

The Englishman 23rd August 1905: 'How entirely all through this lamentable and serious affair, Mr Brodrick has been in the hands of Lord Kitchener.'

The Statesman 23rd August 1905: The telegrams 'furnish a further example of Mr Brodrick's untruthfulness. . . It is more impossible than ever to regard the present Secretary of State as a fit person to sit among His Majesty's advisors.'

The Madras Mail 23rd August 1905: 'The dignity and responsibilities of a Viceroy are being lowered to a point never hitherto imaginable.'

Times of India 22nd August 1905: 'The shameful and unpardonable manner in which His Excellency's resignation was practically forced upon him . . . [by] a Prime Minister who has never been nearer to Asia than Mentone, and a Secretary of State whose predominant idea for many months has been to make Lord Curzon's position untenable. . . The worst feature of the whole correspondence is the utter brutality of Mr Brodrick's peremptory order to the Viceroy to consult Lord Kitchener. . . One wonders whether the Viceroy or the Commander-in-Chief is now the real ruler . . . The sardonic and sinister figure of Lord Kitchener bestrides India. We dislike his brutal and domineering methods.'

Times of India 25th August 1905: 'The crocodile tears shed by Mr Brodrick may delude the bucolic folk of Godalming [his Commons constituents] but they will hardly mislead those who have studied the papers. Mr Brodrick's efforts to excuse himelf become merely nauseating.'

Times of India 28th August 1905: 'Lord Kitchener must either have a bad memory, or a less profound grasp of detail than his admirers credit him with; for the way he has tied himself up into knots in this phase of the controversy verges on the ridiculous.'

Kitchener made a vain attempt to muzzle the most influential of the press, sending one of his colonels to try to make a deal with Lovat Fraser, to no avail.

Three events which followed the resignation have interested the historians. The first of these was the row which Kitchener instigated at the proposal to publish the telegrams explaining how the Viceroy's resignation had come about. On 18th August Curzon told Brodrick that Kitchener 'repudiates the description of his proposals contained in mine of 10th August', and had written a 'detailed protest' and demanded its publication. He called it a most malicious libel. Curzon himself then commented on Kitchener's notes, vindicating his precis of 10th August by quoting from Kitchener's own papers, or those written by others which he had signed. He showed that the Commander-in-Chief had contradicted his own statements, and reaffirmed that all military power would now be concentrated at Army Headquarters. Yet Curzon told Brodrick, 'On public grounds, I should deprecate anything in the nature of a public wrangle between Kitchener and myself.'[63] So Kitchener pressed for publication, while Curzon advised against it.

Second, there was the row that Kitchener thought ought to have led to a duel between the two men. This arose because Kitchener denied seeing a file minuting the number of Ordnance Officers who would come under the Commander-in-Chief. Curzon refused to accept the denial. Duff, Hamilton and the others, swung into action in defence, and their letters are marked 'The Personal Affair'. It did indeed get very personal, not only between Curzon and Kitchener but between Duff and the Military Department. What appears to have happened is that Duff gave Kitchener a verbal summary, and the file was marked as seen and returned. Kitchener's biographers of course take his side, Magnus saying, 'He had just cause to be angry,'[64] others suggesting that Curzon had called Kitchener a liar. Kitchener thought Curzon had 'surpassed himself' and wrote to Lady Salisbury, 'In the old days I suppose I should have called him out and shot him like a dog. . . All I can do now is to have nothing more to do with him. . . I am going away on tour, to be clear of the whole thing. It all seems to me so low and disgusting.'[65] Kitchener was to ensure that it got lower and more disgusting still. He insisted that when the White Paper on Curzon's resignation was published, his angry correspondence with the Viceroy should also be published too. *The Times*, however, censured both men for 'a lamentable spectacle' which 'ought to have been impossible'[66] so Curzon cabled Brodrick to ask if 'in justice to me, you will make clear publication of K's note was not proposed by me – Kitchener insisted, and you agreed'.[67] Both Balfour and Brodrick were frightened of more correspondence and Curzon decently responded, 'If you think. . . facts are already sufficiently well-known, I must defer to your judgement.'[68] The perfidious Brodrick replied, 'Whatever differences there may have been between us . . . we have an earnest desire that justice should be done to your position.'[69] Their desires were rather less than fervent, in the event.

Kitchener was worried about his messages to Stedman which he asked the latter to burn, realising how incriminating they could be. Stedman replied on 23rd November 1905, 'Mr Brodrick says that he thinks it a great pity to burn them. . . They have had a great effect in pushing business.'[70] The suggestion that it was the King who put a stop to Curzon publishing the papers is quite incorrect, although the King did ask Curzon to refrain from pursuing the controversy, and he agreed. Balfour also urged Curzon to allow the controversy to die down when he wrote him a twenty-six-page letter on 23rd August 'after the melancholy formalities giving effect to your resignation had been completed'. He tried to argue that the Cabinet had been friendly and cooperative, and, in face of Curzon's criticism of Brodrick, claimed that the last six months 'have been unquestionably wretched for him, and the unhappiness of both sides has, I repeat, not been so much due to differences of opinion, important though these have been, as to the embittering effects of written as compared with oral controversy'. He concluded, 'I have

212 The Viceroy's Fall

now no desire but to save from the political wreck all that is possible of private friendship and mutual esteem. If these priceless possessions have been threatened by the form in which either my colleagues or I have carried out what we believe to be our duty, I deeply deplore it. . . Of one thing only shall I be mindful – that for nearly seven years, in sickness and in health, you have devoted with untiring energy your splendid abilities to the service of India and of Empire – And this is enough.'[71]

While Balfour took this line in his correspondence with Curzon, privately he was complaining to his secretary, Sandars, 'it is a wretched world and I really cannot get to the bottom of the Kitchener-Curzon squabble. K. distinctly declares that GC is a liar; GC with very little circumlocution indicates that his opinion of K may be similarly expressed. . .I do not easily think ill of mankind, but upon my word these two old friends of mine are gradually compelling me to take a very dark view of our poor fallen nature.'[72] This is sad stuff from a man who by dissembling had been, in part, the cause of it.

Curzon replied to Balfour's letter and turned the other cheek, saying, 'There are many generous and affectionate sentiments in your letter of August 23rd by which I have been much touched. I thank you for these, and I should indeed be sorry if anything that has passed were to impair a friendship which has been one of my most treasured possessions.'[73] Unfortunately, Balfour's generosity was not to be sustained for long.

As soon as the resignation of the Viceroy was announced, letters and telegrams of farewell, regret and appreciation began to flow in upon him, and the stream continued until he left India. They were remarkable not only for their unprecedented number, but also because they represented every community and every class of society in the Indian continent. They came from every part of Britain and India, as well as from Native States, and they were sent by persons in the highest and in the most humble positions. The large majority were from non-official persons and bodies – which was natural since it would have been entirely contrary to practice in India for any officer of the Government, except Curzon's immediate colleagues, to give expression to his feelings. But the correspondence included letters from the heads of provinces and Members of Council expressing the sincerest regret at his departure and the strongest support of his action. Officers wrote from retirement, and Members of the Indian Civil Service from their desks. The chiefs wrote from their palaces, the commercial companies from their offices, the landowners from their estates and the native communities through channels such as Muslim associations. One member of the Bar at Dacca sent a poem of regrets, and the most famous of Indian poets, Rabinth Tagore, wrote to Curzon 'with great sorrow, we are losing the great man and our Greatest Ruler. . .'[74] In all, Curzon published 389 such letters in a commemorative book. A handful of extracts follows:

Sir H. S. Barnes, Member of Council: 'I cannot tell you how grieved . . . angry and disgusted I am. Brodrick's telegrams could not have been more calculated to irritate, to provoke and to display distrust.'
Sir Lewis Tuffer, Member of Council: 'I can hardly believe that HMG could be so blind and faithless.'
Sir Denzil Ibbotson, Member of Council: 'I feel indignant beyond words at the manner in which Your Excellency has been treated. . . It was not honest.'
The Hon. E. N. Baker, Member of Council: 'I regard the loss of your services as nothing short of a public calamity.'
The Hon. H. Erle Richards, Member of Council: 'You have sacrificed your own interests for those of the country.'
Sir A. T. Arundel, Member of Council: 'Lord Kitchener's scheme will sooner or later be modified so as to secure for the . . . Government. . .the constitutional control for which we have earnestly contended.'
Hon. J. P. Hewett, Member of Council: 'It is a calamity that you should have been forced into resignation.'
W. S. Meyer, Secretary to the Government of India, Finance Department: 'Your Excellency's resignation . . . calls forth deep concern – and, if I may say so – regretful indignation.'
Sir Clinton Dawkins, late Finance Member of Council: 'I feel Kitchener will run riot and rampant now.'
Sir J. D. LaTouche West, Governor of the United Province: 'The position had I think become intolerable when Mr Brodrick's first despatch was published, and it was proclaimed to the world that the views of the Government of India were of no account. The effect of this is visible in Bengal now. Hereafter it will be visible elsewhere, and the difficulty of governing India will have been enormously increased.'[75]

'The difficulty of governing India' was indeed an issue. Hubert Hamilton's comment on this charge that the Viceroy's prestige had suffered in the 'eyes of the Natives' was: 'It comes of trusting the dignity of that great office to unworthy hands,' and he also thought 'Lord C's subsequent utterances on the one side and K's silence on the other are gradually pointing the finger of public opinion to where the responsibility for the final debacle really lies.'[76] The problem facing Kitchener and his staff was not so much a question of reputation, but of whether the new Liberal Government which came to power in January 1906 would agree to the Brodrick system, and, if they did, when it would go into operation.

Winston Churchill, for example, then a leading Liberal, wrote to his mother on 31st August 1905: 'Of course, I am all for Curzon as against Kitchener, and for Constitutional Authority against military power. I cannot believe a Liberal Government will allow the Commander-in-Chief in India to engross to himself so much power. . . I should be greatly disconcerted if I thought the Liberal party were preapred to acquiesce in the handing over of the Indian Empire to an ambitious and indocile soldier. The Military Member in India is really in the same position as the Secretary of State for War in England. What has happened is that the Commander-in-Chief has not merely swallowed up his own War Minister, but the Viceroy as well.'[77]

Others were, of course, still working for Kitchener, Sir George Clarke, for example, writing that Curzon had behaved disloyally in trying to rally opinion against a cabinet decision which he himself had accepted. It is a military axiom that when you have won a battle, you follow up the escaping enemy troops rather than relaxing over your victory, and there was no element of relaxation in the Kitchener camp. There was, though, some redisposition of forces, with Marker returning to India, and Hamilton going to London to continue the good work. (He was succeeded as Kitchener's Military Secretary by Birdwood.) Early in January he 'dined at Hatfield' where he found 'Lady S is now quite happy about the new system'.[78] And later: 'At 4 p.m. I had a most satisfactory interview at Buckingham Palace,' he tells Marker. 'Lord Knollys and Esher were present. Lord Knollys touched on all the old stories [about K] drink, artilliary (native), discontent in native ranks amounting to simmering mutiny, Arty jackets, cavalry tunics, and enough more to reach from here to India, but none I think that I did not succeed in dissipating more or less to his satisfaction. . . At last I said to Esher, "Why not drop all these personalities and start the new scheme?" He collected himself and said. . . "When Curzon can get a seat he means to go to Parliament and re-open the question, avoiding the personal. . ." Today I have lunched with Esher, and he said, "If Morley [at the India Office under the Liberal government], Lord M [Minto] and K are together, Curzon cannot get an adverse vote – that is the crux of the situation*. I am to see [Morley] on the 22nd, and will wire my impressions. All I would ask is that unless I say definitely "Mr Morley is absolutely with you," the Chief will not take too much for granted.'[79]

Esher also told him that Kitchener 'should sit absolutely tight and be in agreement with the Viceroy. . . Then I saw Lord Milner. K may count on absolute fairness from him. I have never known anyone dispose of a delicate question more frankly and fairly.'[80] To use modern parlance, the Boys continued to be worried about Kitchener's 'image', Hamilton remarking that: 'Stories about the Chief's unreasonableness are so strong that it would be strange if the King understood his real attitude – and it is of course important that he should do so. I hope to learn his impressions, and if they are unfavourable to Lord K, to correct them. . . The general public will realise the truth in time, and in the meantime, their opinion does not so much matter.'[81]

Despite this, Hamilton was busy with the editors of all the main newspapers, but comments: 'I am very careful with these gentlemen, because I think they are – most of them – all right, and it is a pity to give any impression of manipulation.' He was unsure about Repington's power with *The Times* having been told that Chirol [a Curzon supporter] was 'the real power in the paper'.[82]

A new form of code was introduced into Hamilton's letters to Marker in India. He said on 19th January 1906: 'My dear *Raymond*, This beginning means "for your eyes only" and of course your discretion in using the contents. My "dear Conk" letters will I know be passed round "the family" and even outside it at your discretion. People like Duff, Mullaly and Haig will be interested and it is impossible for me to write to them [all]. But I hope you

---

*Clarke gave exactly the same advice and used the same phrase 'crux'.

will always *keep* my letters, as some day I might ask you to return them to me.'[83] His private letters to 'Raymond' are full of jejune [sic] comments such as that *The Times* 'are putting their money on "a cur" and if they don't want to drop it they should back *Curzon* no longer'[84] as well as machiavellian plots: 'I had hoped to get at Grey and Asquith through Lord Rosebery but it would be no good if Eddie Stanley is right that he doesn't speak to them now that they serve in Campbell-Bannerman's cabinet, and I shall try to come to it by other means. . . I have been at it hard, daily, and often far into the night.'[85] He also kept the gossip up to date. 'The account of Curzon [then back in England] cutting Mr Balfour was not quite correct. Eddie [Stanley] says Mr B. told him personally that when the ladies left the table at Ribblesdale's dinner, Mr B went round and put his hand on GNC's back and said he would like to hear the latest news from India. GNC said 'Howd'do' and then deliberately turned his back on Mr B. He knew he was to meet him at the dinner. GNC also took the trouble to inform St John that he would not speak to him.'[86]

The Liberal Party finally decided that a public row with Kitchener was to be avoided at all costs, and, despite Morley's pre-election promises, the new system in India must be installed, with minor modifications. They appear to have thought that if it didn't work, it could be dropped later saying, 'We can abandon it two years hence when K goes.'[87] Hamilton got the news well in advance, and told 'Raymond' that: 'I should love to be in the House of Lords and see Lord Bobs' face when the decision is made known, and near Curzon [when he] realises his *coup de grace*. How he will fume, but it will all vanish into thin air.' He said also that Milner's modifications were 'a sop to critics'.[88]

Looking to the future, Hamilton wrote, 'The accession of Haldane to the War Office has inspired hope, but however good he may be as S of S, things have got into too great a muddle for any Civilian to put them right, and the Army Council cannot afford him sufficient backing. There is no soldier in or out of the Council except Lord K who possesses both the confidence of the nation and the determination to push through the necessary reforms in sufficient degree to give any hope of success. Times are not yet right for him.'[89]

When, in 1914, times were ripe for Kitchener to enter the War

Office and become, as Lloyd George described him, practically the military dictator, Kitchener was by then no longer the man, if he ever had been, to wield the power given him. Hamilton had forseen the problem when he commented to Marker, 'I know Lord K would say "What d———d rot. I'm going to China or Japan to enjoy myself and nothing would induce me to put my foot inside the W.O. or be bothered with such an impossible creature as the British Army".'[90] Strangely enough, Kitchener did use almost these words in 1914, telling Edward Carson, 'I don't know Europe, I don't know England, and I don't know the British Army.' Grey of Falloden agreed. 'Kitchener knew nothing of the War Office organisation, or the Army at home.'[91]

To return to 1905, Mary Curzon made a last desperate attempt to save the personal friendship with Kitchener. She wrote a hasty note (undated but probably early September) 'Mr Nathan tells me that you are coming at 11 tomorrow to see the Viceroy – I do so hope that this last interview may be as free as possible from trouble. The discussion of a fortnight ago grieved me, as out of it arose the resignation, and all that subsequently happened. Since all is now at an end, I hope that the *horror* of personal trouble may be avoided. This is so important from every point of view. Let the vital difference be with the Secretary of State – that I think you see . . . *Please do not answer.* Indeed there is no answer, and I have only put in a *human plea* for a *peaceful Finale* to this miserable experience.'[92]

Her pleas fell on fairly flinty ground. When the Curzons left Simla on 23rd October, Kitchener told Lady Salisbury that he only joined in the final farewell to stop people talking, 'Although it was not very pleasant to shake hands with a man who has called you a liar. However I consoled myself by the consideration that it was the Viceroy to whom I was saying goodbye, not Curzon.'[93] Mary Curzon described the painful scene to her mother. Curzon shook Kitchener's hand in silence. Mary said just one word, 'Goodbye' and then walked on. 'When we had made the round, we turned and faced everyone, and I bowed right and left. George stood with his hat off. The band played God Save the King. Then we got into the postillion carriage escorted by the Body Guard and the whole crowd cheered and cheered. Lord K never moved. He raised his white helmet and stood like a sphynx as our procession moved away.'[94]

Kitchener was now left behind to pursue the break-up of the system which he had striven so hard to destroy. Of course, with the Conservative government about to fall, there was a question as to whether the incoming Liberals would reject their policies in India. In due course, as will be seen, Kitchener overcame this hurdle. As for the Indian Army itself, his biographers say that he did introduce reforms, improving training, equipment and armaments. He provided better rations, encouraging the establishment of dairy farms. He promoted sport and established regimental institutes and clubs, and he caused factories to be built in order to make his Army more self-supporting in War. If the latter was his aim, he failed, because when his Army was put to the test, the results were a disaster. In a curious way, Kitchener did not seem to have the will to introduce major reforms. In 1906 he told Roberts, 'I have had a very unpleasant time in all this, but it is a lesson I shall not forget. No more attempts at Army reform for me, either here or in England. I do not think, if one tries to do one's best for the Army, one deserves to be made to live a dog's life . . . but I suppose that is the English way.'[95]

Throughout his remaining period in India, he continued to be loyally supported by Marker, and when the latter returned to England they kept up a regular correspondence, which, on Kitchener's side at any rate, appears to have been the most active of any from his hand. Marker's loyalty was unswerving and the papers which he left with his family bear the following inscription, giving his curiously distorted view of the events in which he had played a key part.

'Lord Kitchener's Memorandum on the Administration of the Army in India – which was so vehemently combated (and with such extraordinary methods) by Lord Curzon of Kedleston.

'The latter did not hesitate to suppress the truth, to tamper with telegrams, and to make false statements in official correspondence in order to try to defeat Lord K. He failed in spite of these tactics, and resigned the Viceroyalty.'

Part Three

The Aftermath

Chapter Eleven

The Ex-Viceroy

Curzon never seems to have got over the bitterness he felt when he arrived back in England and found no official to receive him except a 'third secretary'. Even a year later, he wrote angrily across the bottom of a letter from Balfour, 'His attitude at the time of my resignation was shown by the failure of himself and indeed every member of the Cabinet – without exception – to meet me at Charing Cross.'[1] They did have an unexceptional excuse – the day of the arrival, Monday 4th December 1905, was that on which Balfour resigned as Prime Minister. Nevertheless the King had wanted him and Brodrick to be at the station to greet Curzon, but both had escaped to the country to be with 'the Souls'. Esher's original journal states that on the Monday afternoon, Balfour drove to the Palace. 'He was with the King for a quarter of an hour, and then came down into Knollys room. He seemed a little moved, which was not strange, on relinquishing his great office, but his spirits revived almost immediately.'[2] Perhaps therefore the simple explanation for his not being at Charing Cross is that he was waiting to be called to the Palace.

There was less reason why Curzon should not have been met by a group of Souls, but they – George Wyndham and Alfred Lyttleton and others – were at the Elcho's country house at Stanway, one of their favourite meeting places, arguing amongst themselves what form of words they should use in the telegram they should send Curzon, welcoming him back. A telegram was never sent. Curzon forgave the friends – if not the politicians – naming them 'Georgites' or 'St John-ites'. Amongst those who were at Charing Cross was Rennell Rodd, who correctly forecast that when a short while later Campbell-Bannerman formed his Liberal cabinet, it would include Sir Edward Grey as Foreign Secretary, Asquith as Chancellor of the Exchequer, Haldane as War Minister, Morley at the India Office, and Lloyd George at the Board of Trade.

Curzon told Rodd and the others that he was eager to continue the battle, observing, 'There is not the slightest grounds for the insinuation kindly propagated in some quarters that I am or have been suffering from shattered nerves.'[3]

Immediately upon arrival, Curzon put all his energies into obtaining what he regarded as the rightful recognition of his period as Viceroy, however undignified its ending might have been – the offer of an Earldom. He went directly to the Carlton Hotel, and that evening was visited by Lord Knollys, secretary to the King, who asked whether he was anxious to proceed at once to the House of Lords. 'I replied that I would ask to be excused from an immediate decision.'[4]

A full account, from Curzon's point of view, of what happened in the following weeks and months is given in a handwritten note, found amongst his papers, dated July 1st 1906. It reads as follows:

While I was in England at the end of my first term of office in the summer of 1904, Balfour, who was Prime Minister, anticipating that his government might fall before I returned from my second term of office to England, surprised me by saying that it would be his duty to submit my name to the King for a British Peerage before he vacated office, and upon my replying that I was not at all anxious for my political future to be prejudged in this way, since I had not made up my mind about entering the House of Commons, he went on to say that if he did not take this step, his successors [presumably the Liberal Party] would not, and I should thus be excluded from the House of Lords. I replied that the office of Viceroy was in the main a non-political position, that there were many precedents for the bestowal of a peerage or honour upon a returning Viceroy of one party, by a government representing the other, and that if I were held worthy of recognition and the King desired to bestow it, I could not conceive that a veto would be placed on such an act by a Liberal government, presuming it to be in power when I returned. We agreed to refer the matter to Lord Knollys, and his letter of September 21, 1904 . . . contains the clear and emphatic reply to the King. I could not possibly regard this letter as otherwise than a direct pledge from the Sovereign that if the circumstances arose, he would insist upon a Peerage being conferred upon me by the Liberal Govt. When I resigned the Viceroyalty . . . Balfour (as he himself admitted to me) advised the postponement of the honour on the grounds of the strained relations between the Govt and myself. I knew nothing of this at the time. On the very day that I returned to England, viz Monday, December 4th, 1905, Balfour resigned.

On the morning of December 6th, I was honoured with an audience with the King. Sir H. Campbell-Bannerman was with HM when I arrived at the Palace . . . he had just kissed hands as Prime Minister. . . In my audience with the King, HM without directly offering me a peerage or asking my views about it, intimated that in his opinion an ex-Viceroy of India ought not to re-enter the House of Commons or, at least not, immediately upon his return from India, to fight a contested election. I asked the King whether, if were offered without a contest, the representation either of the City of London or of the University of Oxford . . . his objections would apply. HM replied that if I desired on [political?] grounds to re-enter the H of C he thought that either of these seats would be most appropriate, differing as they did from all others in character and dignity; but that he hoped I would not contest an ordinary constituency.

In a later note, Curzon makes the following report about Balfour's behaviour:

I heard at a later date (October 30th, 1906) on the authority of one who had heard it direct from the King, that before Balfour finally handed over the seals of office on December 4th 1905, the King had twice pressed him to propose me for an honour in his final list, but that he had refused to do so. It is thus even more apparent to whom my exclusion from the House of Lords and from official recognition was primarily due. Of course Balfour did not have the slightest intention of keeping me out of public life. He would have been incapable of any such proceeding. But he *did* mean to refrain from offering any public recognition of my work in India, simply because it had ended in a quarrel with Brodrick and himself. [Curzon goes on to explain how he was forced to decline to stand for the two seats, because it appeared that pledges had been made to others.] With the failure of these two openings, therefore, my chance of entering the H of C at the General Election – consistent with what I had said to the King – disappeared, and I left England for the Riviera at the end of December. Upon my return in the middle of February, the matter was again revived in conversation with Lord Knollys. He said the King was very anxious that I should accept a peerage, and pressed me to accept. My own health . . . the feelings which I entertained towards leaders of my own party for the manner in which they had treated me in India, and the complete capitulation of Balfour to Chamberlain led me to think I should find service in the H of C irksome, if not impossible, and so I agreed accordingly to place myself in the hands of the King. Knollys told me that he had already conferred with the Prime Minister and Morley about the matter and that they had expressed their approval of the proposal, and that if I were willing to accept an earldom, the only remaining question was the manner in which it should be announced . . . The matter had been treated throughout as one requiring only my *own* decision.

I have no doubt in my own mind (indeed no other explanation is possible) that Morley and he were extremely apprehensive that if I were raised to the Lords I should make an attack upon the Govt. for their failure to modify the Kitchener decision, in spite of the uncompromising platform protestations (during the Election) of both. The history of that controversy, and of Morley's complete climb-down after leading me to understand that he would reverse the decision of the late Govt [is then related by Curzon* who continues] A speech from me, injurious as it would have been to the reputation of Kitchener, Balfour, Brodrick and the late Govt. would have been scarcely less damaging to the credit of the new Govt in view of what its members had said, and of Morley's letters and conversations with me. I must be kept out of the House of Lords therefore, in order to keep my lips closed, and to deprive me of a platform. That these were the apprehensions entertained, was admitted to me in one of our conversations by Lord Knollys, who even hinted that the objections entertained might be withdrawn if I would give a pledge not to raise the Military question or to attack the Govt. [Knollys then advised him to write a letter to the King] Before writing it, however, I sought an interview with [Balfour]. He expressed himself as horrified at Bannerman's misrepresentations of his attitude, and said he had always contemplated that a peerage

---

*Briefly, Morley found that the Indian Office Council in London, the Council and the Viceroy in India all supported Kitchener so he went ahead, although saying 'that the scheme is final, I do not for one moment believe.'

should be conferred at least by January 1st 1906 (he did not explain how in these circumstances he had not submitted it in his final list of December 1905).*

In Knollys' letter Curzon was told that the King had made it 'a point of honour' to press for a grant of the peerage.

After further delay Curzon was once more offered the City of London seat in the Commons as the member was to suddenly retire. He sought an interview with Campbell-Bannerman as the King and Knollys were at Windsor.

[Campbell-Bannerman] hemmed and hawed, repeated his objections on the grounds that it was impossible for him to propose an honour which had been ostentatiously withheld by the Prime Minister of my own party, but indicated his desire to consult certain of his friends before giving a final decision (about an earldom)! I in no way pleaded for an honour from him or anyone else. A few hours later, his reply reached me... I sent the correspondence to Balfour.'[5]

Balfour wrote to Curzon on 2nd July 1906:

I am afraid our interview last Saturday week was painful to both of us. It certainly was to me. As regards the past, you seem to do me less than justice: and, as regards the future, you make claims, which are not indeed beyond my wishes, but which I cannot admit to be based on rights, and which, speaking quite frankly, I do not think ought to have been accompanied even by the suggestion of menace...

Let me remind you of the facts – at least as they present themselves to me. I do not go into the merits of the two or three questions which divided you from your colleagues in the late government. It is enough to say that these differences, culminating in the dispute respecting the Military Member of Council, produced a lamentable state of tension between the India Office and yourself. For the first time, I believe, in the recent history of British-India administration, the private and confidential correspondence be-

*Brodrick wrote to Balfour 'If George is elevated . . . it will be regarded as a pretty severe snub to the Ministry, apart from myself.' 12th September 1905

tween the Viceroy and the Secretary of State was interrupted, and confidential interchange of views took place for months between the King's Representative in India and his responsible Minister at home. In August, you resigned. But for public reasons, the force of which I do not question, you stayed on in India for three months after your resignation had (perforce) been accepted. These three months saw no improvement in your relations with Brodrick; and all the information at my disposal induced me to believe, what I still suppose to be the case, that you deeply resented the action taken by the Home Government, that you profoundly disapproved of its policy in connexion with the reorganisation of the Military Dept, that you desired to retain full liberty to criticise its proceedings on your return to this country, and to persuade your countrymen to condemn it.

I do not blame you. But how, in these circumstances, could I make you an immediate offer of a peerage, and how, in these circumstances, could you accept one? That your services in India should be recognised I always held, and hold still. It was always in my opinion, not a question of *what* should be done, but *when* it should be done. . . I gather however that you are of the opinion that I ought to have offered you the Peerage though you admit that, if offered, you would not have taken it. To this I cannot agree. No man is bound to make an offer which he is confident will be refused; and no man is bound to make an offer which is capable of being interpreted as an attempt to silence a critic [here Curzon has put '!!']. Since I became a private citizen, my power to serve you in this matter of Peerage is of course insignificant, but, such as it is, I have exerted the utmost and have done my best to press your claims in the proper quarters. The Peerage, to my profound regret, but through no fault of my own, has fallen through. . . [Curzon has underlined this sentence and marked '!!']

I do not complain of your asking me to aid you to find a seat; such a request is a natural corollary of the breakdown in the Peerage negotiations. But although I do not complain of the request, I am sure you will not mind my saying that I do somewhat complain of the manner in which it was made. And I complain on two grounds. Your language seemed to me to imply, in the first place, that you demanded the seat as the least recognition that could be made for some wrong that I have inflicted upon you; and you hinted, not obscurely, that if a seat were not found by the ordinary organisation of the Party, it would none the less be found by some other means; but that, when thus found, its holder would feel himself free to take up a very different position to his Party and to his late colleagues than that which he would otherwise adopt. No I do not admit the wrong and I do not like the threat [Curzon has noted: 'I never said anything of the sort']. Surely this is not the way old friends like you and me should deal with one another. . .It ought surely to be enough if I say that I am most desirous of seeing you again in Parliament. . .

Can I say more? Ought I to say more?[6]

Curzon has written at the bottom of this letter in pencil:

I could attach no weight to the exculpation or defence contained in the above letter. But I did not care to pursue the controversy, feeling too deeply the treatment I had received at the hands of my political leader and an old friend.

The view that I always took was that no difference of political opinion or even my resignation, justified Balfour in refraining altogether from the offer of a Peerage in the interval between Aug 1905 when I resigned and December 1905 when he submitted his last list to the King. It is quite true that I should have refused it – I would have taken no honour from the Ministry that had deserted me – but Campbell-Bannerman would not then have been able to use the argument that he was disqualified from considering the honour in view of the refusal of Balfour even to offer it. Balfour's attitude at the time of my resignation was shown by the failure of himself and indeed of every member of the Cabinet – without exception, to meet me at Charing X on my arrival.

It is superfluous to comment on Curzon's explanation of events, except perhaps to say that it is entirely in character that he should believe he could have persuaded Balfour (and his Cabinet) whom he had attacked publicly while in India, to humiliate themselves still further by offering him a peerage when 'it is quite true I should have refused it'. Curzon not only humiliated others, but rather enjoyed it. A memorandum written by Curzon from Hackwood (his new home) in January 1908, says,

After July 1906 I took no further steps about admission to the House of Lords, and in sheer despondency acquiesced in my exclusion from public life. The terrible grief in which I was then plunged dulled my desire to take part in public life . . . such had been the fate of much greater and better men than myself, and when I thought of Warren Hastings in the solitude of Daylesford[?] I took heart anew. Indeed I began to take a gloomy pride in my undistinguished destruction. The only correspondence that belongs to this period is some letters from Sir S. McDonnell about the likelihood of the Duke of Rutland's vacant Garter being conferred on me in 1906. [At about this time Curzon told Selborne 'I have touched the depths of human woe, nor can I easily rise again']

In April 1907 I happened to meet Lord Rosebery and he reproached me for not entering the House of Lords. When I informed him that I had been denied the opportunity, he expressed his profound astonishment (and proposed a meeting) but the talk which he kindly offered never took place. . .

I received more than one offer of a parliamentary seat in the interim, which acting upon my doctor's orders, I declined. In July 1907 Morley who was dining with me at the Atheneum Club enquired when I was likely to return to the House of Commons. Upon my answering that I was never likely to do so, because my doctors had absolutely forbidden it, and telling him something about my poor twisted spine . . . he expressed his great surprise. Struck I think with some remorse at the part which had been played by his own leader and in a secondary degree by himself, he proposed to me at a subsequent meeting in my own house – with a magnanimity worthy of his generous nature – that he should again approach Campbell-Bannerman . . . [and] admittted that a year before CB and himself had been reluctant to provide me with a platform upon which I might possibly have assailed him on the Military Question. . .

I think this talk more than anything else brought home to me how eager had been the desire of both parties, not to give me any chance when I returned from India of raising the Military question in the only possible place in Parliament. The King had dissuaded me from entering the House of Commons and neither Govt. wanted or meant to see me just then in the House of Lords. . .

The PM again shied off and I was again to be sacrificed to his hostility and vacillation. But on this occasion the excuse given was a new one. In the discussions of the previous year, the reason given for their refusal was the impossibility of superceding the action of Balfour. . . But I now learnt that I was again to be kept out of the H of L because the Liberal whips opposed. . .

Whether CB placed the matter before the King and found the latter unfavourable (for in spite of his earlier attitude, so wonderfully kind and generous, up to the date at which I returned to England in 1905, HH had withdrawn all favours from me since the return of the Prince of Wales to England from India as a strong partisan of Lord Kitchener in 1906, and had frequently in private expressed his unfriendliness towards the Viceroy whom he once delighted to honour) – or whether the excuse of the Chief Whip was *bona fida*, I never knew.

I was thus for the second time judged unworthy of a seat in the House of Lords . . . So bitterly did I feel about this matter, and so distressed was I at the loss of the King's favour, that, having to be in Windsor in November as Chancellor of Oxford University to confer the DCL degree upon the German Emperor, I had resolved to solicit an audience and place the entire matter before him.

On the very day however on which I was to proceed to Windsor, I received a letter from Lansdowne asking me if I would allow myself to be nominated for a vacancy just caused in the Irish *Representative* peerage by the death of Lord Kilmaine. I was duly elected in January 1908.[7]

Curzon also wrote a third memorandum, presumably after 1910 when George V finally conferred on him an Earldom:

This records the third and last phase of the strange history of my elevation to the British peerage which was attended by vicissitudes no less curious than those that preceded it. . . Up to and after that date [January 1908] King Edward VII continued to have a strong prejudice against me, deliberately fomented by interested parties [Kitchener's friends]. But early in 1909 my friends at Court informed me that HM was now conscious that he had done me a serious injustice and decided to effect a reconciliation . . . The King desired to see me in February 1909. After that date I frequently met the King at parties and elsewhere.

His attitude became steadily more favourable until in Spring of 1910, when he died, he had signified his intention of honouring me with a visit at Hackwood in the autumn.

The next and concluding phase was entered upon in January 1910 when I was staying at Windsor as the guest of King George V. On this occasion I had a private conversation with Lord Knollys about my position, and he told me he thought the King would desire on his forthcoming Coronation to atone for the neglect which I had so long experienced by offering me an earldom. . . The honour was one

which I in no sense owed to the Ministry [of Liberals]. After what
had passed previously, I should not have accepted it from them. It
was the personal gift of the Sovereign alone.[8]

Curzon's notes conclude with a detailed account of the problems
of 'titles and remainders' due to the fact that he had no male
children. They end with the following reference to his abiding hope
that he would one day be Prime Minister. 'May I, if ever I am
placed in a like situation [handing out honours] give more generous
measure than I have received.'

Chapter Twelve

Mary's Death

Every man's hand has long been against me, and now God's hand has turned against me too.

After their return to England on 3rd December 1905, the Curzons only spent three weeks in England, leaving for the South of France to join their children, and remaining there until March 1906. 'During this period,' says her biographer, Nigel Nicolson, 'Mary's health fluctuated no more alarmingly than it had at frequent intervals in India. When she arrived at Cap. St Martin, she had influenza and a cough . . . and her heart was giving trouble. At the least exertion, she told her mother, such as dressing or going upstairs, she became breathless. She consulted a specialist who assured her "That I am good for many years of life with care". On 12th June Mary wrote to her brother. "I sometimes fear and feel I shall never be well again," and,' says Nicolson, 'she continued to be quite active socially throughout the early summer, though still suffering from "devlish ills" which she did not specify.'[1] She had trouble in one leg which was diagnosed as phlebitis.

She had a restless night on 17/18th July and 'her health and spirits were so low that Curzon spent the whole day at her bedside, watching her strength ebb. The doctors kept her alive with oxygen and injections of strychnine, but her breathing collapsed in the late afternoon, and her last fierce struggle was unavailing. She died just before 6 p.m. of a heart attack, the bulletin said. Curzon's arm was around her in the final moments.'[2] She was thirty-six years old.

After Mary Curzon's death, little more than six months after he had returned to England in defeat, Curzon was a broken man for a time. 'I am not fit for society,' he wrote, 'and desire only to hide my head.' He received well over one thousand letters of condolence, and replied to most of them in his own hand. He may have felt guilt at the fact that she had returned to India, and certainly that he had gone back to India without her, but it does not appear to be true that India 'killed her' or that Curzon was in any way responsible for her death by keeping her in a climate that was injurious to her health. Nicolson says that, 'She did not suffer in India any illness which so weakened her that she perished like a withered plant on her return home. . . She was in fact most animated when constantly travelling and most on show. She sturdily followed Curzon even on his hunting expeditions. . . That does not conjure up the picture of an invalid. Mary's illnesses in India usually coincided with the periods when she had nothing much to do, at Simla particularly, and she was apt to blame on the climate the lassitude induced by loneliness and depression, and on the altitude the exhaustion caused by minor social duties. She had recurrent migraine and occasional attacks of dizziness, but her life in India was never once in danger through sickness. After her near-mortal illness in 1904 (at Walmer Castle when she was already weak after a bungled miscarriage) India was actually recuperative. The doctors (who sent her back to India) and her own inclination, were proved right. . . The happiness of their family life and the dry Simla air, restored Mary to complete health. . . By the early summer [1904], in fact, she was in better condition than Curzon himself.'[3]

Brodrick had an insensitive response to tragedy. He wrote to Kitchener on 30th August 1906, 'if his wife's death has only the result of making him more sane as regards his relations to the world, at least some good will come out of evil.'[4] As shown already, once Curzon began to recover from his grief in the year following Mary's death, he bent his energies towards arranging to re-enter political life. Gradually he also took on other, non-political, duties into which he plunged with his usual zeal. He had become Chancellor of Oxford University in 1908, a Trustee of the National Gallery and President of the Royal Geographical Society. An example of his attention to detail – or his incapacity to delegate – is that in the latter office he found the Society splendid new premises for which, inter alia, he personally obtained picture frames and designed the railings at the street entrance. He fought and won election as Rector of Glasgow University and became an Honorary Fellow of the Royal Institute of British Architects, which signalled his passion for restoring and saving old buildings. In 1907 he had leased a large house near Basingstoke, Hackwood House, and later he took on the restoration of two castles, Bodiam in Sussex and Tattershall in Lincolnshire.

Hackwood was the scene of splendid house parties, and at Carlton House Terrace he contined to entertain his friends, and of course, to attend to the up-bringing of his three daughters. It was not until 1908, at a ball given by Consuelo, Duchess of Marlborough, that Curzon (now in his 50th year), saw the woman with whom he was to have a passionate affair for many years until his second marriage – Elinor Glyn. She was playing the leading role in a dramatized version of one of her own books, at the Adelphi Theatre, where she acted one emotional scene as she lay on a tiger skin. This had encouraged the circulation of the well-known verse

> *Would you like to sin*
> *With Elinor Glyn*
> *On a tiger-skin?*
> *Or would you prefer*
> *To err with her*
> *On some other fur?*

Curzon succeeded in detaching her from her current admirer, Milner, and a deeply-felt relationship ended tragically for her when, at Montacute, the house he leased for them, she opened *The Times* one day in 1916 to read the announcement of his engagement to the widowed American millionairess Grace Duggan.

To return to his political aspirations, Curzon had in 1908 through the good offices of Lansdowne taken his seat in the House of Lords as a representative Irish peer (the Irish peerage conferred when he became Viceroy had specifically not carried with it a seat in the Lords, to enable him, had he been elected, to go back to the Commons when he returned to England). He knew he must now remain in the Lords for life, as he could not relinquish his title even on the death of his father. Nevertheless, he was not to obtain Cabinet office until 1915, despite desperate manoeuvres to put himself once more back into the mainstream of events. Even then, he was not invited to join the War Cabinet until the Lloyd George Coalition Government of 1916, and the part he played in joining that administration has been seriously criticised for its deviousness by most of the historians writing of the period. It was thus for a period of ten years from 1906 that Curzon, whatever consolations he was offered or sought, felt himself to be eating ashes in the wilderness, a direct result he firmly believed, of his defeat at the hands of Kitchener.

Curiously enough, Kitchener too was to eat ashes despite his victory, the glory of which lasted all too briefly, for by 1909 he not only failed to obtain the position of Viceroy, which he had eagerly sought for three years, perhaps longer, but he also found himself for the first time in his life, unemployed. We have seen in the previous chapter how the Liberals, coming into office in 1906, had, despite their pre-election assertions, agreed to allow the re-organisation in Indian army administration to take place. Despite this, Morley, the new Secretary of State at the India Office, did not like Kitchener or his methods, and resolved to keep close control over him. At the start of the new administration, things went well enough for Kitchener – the Prince of Wales visited India and was much fêted by his old friend, and wrote to say how pleased he was 'that everything connected with the new system is working so smoothly and that you, the Viceroy and the Secretary of State are so much in accord. It must be a sad disappointment to those who prophesised every evil result'.[5] It was true that Minto and Kitchener got on well, the Viceroy saying of him 'one of the few broad-minded soldiers I have ever met, very pleasant in conversation with a taste for gardening and art'.[6] (Kitchener's 'taste for art' took the form of acute kleptomania.)

Kitchener made a radical re-organisation of the structure of the Army divisions in India. This has nothing to do with his 'victory' on Army administration because it could have been carried through equally well under the old system, and he also initiated steps towards the gradual process of commissioning Indian officers. By April 1907, when he was coming to the end of his five year term as Commander-in-Chief, the Liberals offered him a two year extension of command. Although he accepted, he had already began to feel unhappy and wrote to Lady Salisbury hinting that he would like to succeed Cromer in Egypt as a stepping stone to the

Indian appointment. Much to his disgust the job instead went to Gorst. Kitchener nevertheless found time to falsify the historical records of the Army's progress during Curzon's administration. This unpleasant incident, which involved the devious Mullaly, who did most of Kitchener's writing, is explained fully in Appendix 1. Briefly Kitchener persuaded Minto that parts of the record should be expunged for security reasons, while in fact altering them to show him rather than Curzon in the most favourable light. It also rewrote the 9th Lancers episode. However Curzon found out what he had done and arranged for the records to be corrected.

Kitchener was now losing interest in India. Sir George Arthur, his biographer or, one may say, hagiographer, explained that 'the C-in-C's office work, which he constantly said had materially lessened under the new system, in no way interfered with his tours, or even with such social avocations as devolved on him and which he manifestly enjoyed'.[7] He became an even more lavish entertainer, and the improvements to his house, Snowdon, at Simla were extravagant. Part of the cost (the equivalent of £850) he had to pay out of his own pocket, which must have been a painful experience, as he shared with Curzon an extreme reluctance when it came to parting with his own money. While he accepted Morley's offer of an extension, he decided to request a long leave on the specious grounds that he had had none after leaving South Africa. Morley refused to agree, but as a sop arranged for Kitchener to be appointed GCIE (Grand Companion of the Star of the Indian Empire) in the New Year's Honours List in January 1908. Kitchener did not exactly sulk, but he immersed himself in his hobbies; orchids became a passion and 'he acquired a poodle on which he lavished much care and attention'.[8]

He found it virtually impossible to carry out any of his grand military schemes. For one thing, Morley made it clear to him that he would be most reluctant to sanction any increase in military expenditure, and for another Morley ensured that all new projects had to be referred from Simla to the India Office in London for sanction – this in effect was a return to the old days of the Military Member, but at one further remove. What was worse, in 1907 the government in London recommended that Kitchener's reorganisation plans should be spread over ten years instead of five. Not only was the Liberal party anti-militaristic, but Japan's unexpected victory over Russia meant that the threat of Russian expansion across India's borders had receded. Morley would give no approval to a 'forward' policy on the North-West Frontier. Kitchener was riled and called Morley 'pig-headed and dangerous' and also complained to Lady Salisbury about the policies of the Liberal party. One might ask why Kitchener did not protest more strongly about these cuts and even offer, yet again, to resign?

Matters were not made any better because what Curzon had forecast was daily becoming reality – in the words of Sir Geroge Arthur, Kitchener's biographer, 'The Decline and Fall of the Military Supply Department' was taking place. Despite the fact that Brodrick had claimed that this office was specifically designed to give the Viceroy independent advice, it had been filled by the incompetent General Scott, and had withered month by month into disuse. By 1909 its redundancy was apparent to all, and it was abolished, thus producing a considerable saving in the military budget. The Commander-in-Chief who was to replace Kitchener, Sir O'Moore Creagh, would thus now be completely in charge of all aspects of military organisation, just as Curzon had forecast would happen. The ex-Viceroy could not let the event pass without comment, although it was clearly embarrassing for Brodrick, who tried to muzzle political debate. This matter is more fully described in Appendix 2, but in general the public had lost interest in the question of Indian Army Administration, which they, as well as the politicians, had never properly understood, and Curzon's protests make no great impact.

By 1909, not only was Kitchener bored with the Army but he continued to brood on the certainty of succeeding Minto. 'Nothing but the post of Viceroy of India would now suit him' says his biographer Royle. At home, the question exercising the Government's mind was what to do with Kitchener. Haldane (Secretary of State for War), came up with an ingenious solution that he should take over the new position (inaugurated by the King's brother the Duke of Connaught two years earlier, and now being vacated), of Chief of the new Mediterranean Command. As bait, he also offered Kitchener promotion to Field-Marshall, at an extra £500 a year, and a palatial residence in Malta. The Egyptian Army would also be under his command and he would have a seat on the IDC. Kitchener nevertheless detested the prospect and only agreed when the King intervened and wrote personally promising that his acceptance 'would in no way prejudice your being considered for any other higher appointment hereafter becoming vacant, which may be agreeable to you'.[9] By this, the King meant the Viceroyalty in India, which he knew Kitchener craved, and for which he and Minto both thought the soldier suitable.

As usual, when he wanted his own way, Kitchener used any means at hand to achieve his ends, and in this case he set out on a world tour which would take him everywhere but Malta. Before leaving there were farewell dinners and ceremonies in India, one on 20th August 1909 at the United Services Club in Simla when Minto claimed that Kitchener had left India with better trained, equipped and paid troops than it had ever had before. As we shall see, within five years this body of men was to suffer one of the worst defeats ever inflicted on British-led troops ever, and this against an indifferent enemy. To cap matters, Kitchener committed an unfortunate gaffe in replying to Minto's tribute by reading a speech prepared by one of his staff which plagiarised whole paragraphs from a speech made some years before by Curzon. The press, never friendly to Kitchener, spotted the error and had a joke at his expense.

His world tour took Kitchener first to the Far East at the invitation of the Japanese Government, via Shanghai and Peking – where George Morrison, the China correspondent of *The Times* was horrified to see Kitchener pocket several pieces of precious porcelain that had been laid out for his inspection, and, then to turn to his two companions, Oswald Fitzgerald and Victor Brooke and urge them to follow suit. He went on to Manchuria, Java, Tokyo, Australia, New Zealand, Tahiti, California, Chicago and New York. Incidentally he made good use of his masonic connections on these trips – he was now Grand Master of Egypt, the Sudan and the Punjab as well as Junior Warden of England. He had been introduced to Masonic activities earlier when on leave in England by a member of the Royal family.

When he arrived in England on 26th April 1910, Kitchener immediately began lobbying for the job of Viceroy. He knew that Morley might not be in favour, and in fact the Secretary of State had told friends that in his opinion there might be political unrest there if Kitchener were to return to India, and his presence might undo all the trust created by his party's India Council's Act of 1909 which aimed at giving more power to the nationalists. Esher endeavoured to assist Kitchener in his campaign, partly because he was still active in Court circles and the King was known to be in its favour. In his book on Kitchener, Esher explains how the plot went awry. At a private dinner with Morley, which Esher attended, Kitchener when he was 'supposed to be guarded and silent, was lush of talk, with copiousness of indiscreet opinion, praise and blame, that made Morley say afterwards "Never, never shall he go to India." '[10] Kitchener did not realise what a bad impression he had made, or else thought that the King would over-rule the Government, but without warning on the 6th May, Edward VII died. Kitchener was shocked and told his sister Millie 'The King's death has upset everything, and I am quite uncertain about my own future . . . it has all been very sudden. I had a long interview with the late King only a few days before he died'.[11] To his chagrin, a diplomat, Hardinge, was appointed Viceroy, and worse still on 13th June, Haldane announced in the House of Commons that Kitchener would not be taking up the Mediterranean command, which would go to Ian Hamilton. For the first time in his life, Kitchener was unemployed.

In fact he had been inactive since early 1909 and was to remain so until almost the end of 1911. In the meantime, he once more left England, first going on tour in Ireland, and then planning a safari in Africa, which would take him to Kenya, where he bought 5000 acres and where he planned to winter in the future. He had no intention of ever spending a winter in England, but he was in fact never to live in Kenya, although he did, much against his will, winter in London. Another major act was the purchase of Broome Park near Canterbury for £14,000. He planned it to become a home worthy of a man of his standing and taste. In its extensive rebuilding, he was much helped by Lady Sackville, as well as by the Royal Engineers, who, quite unofficially, did much of the work.

While travelling in Kenya, Kitchener heard that it was decided to hold the Coronation, and George V summoned him home to take charge of the troops in June 1911. Kitchener also took up various commercial appointments, particularly as a director of the London, Chatham and Dover Railway, and this was to be the object of some criticism when he eventually returned to active work. This came about unexepctedly when it ws found that Gorst, who had replaced Cromer as British Agent in Egypt, was suffering from cancer and was soon to die.

Edward Grey, now Foreign Minister, arranged a meeting with Kitchener, having first sought and obtained agreement from both the new King and Cromer, and, in 1911, offered him the position of British Agent. Kitchener reasoned that if he did well in Egypt in this essentially civilian rather than military role, it would open the way to the job which he still craved, the Viceroyalty of India. After all, Egypt presented no challenge; he had lived there fourteen years in all, since 1883, and regarded it as his spiritual home. He therefore accepted, and having taken two French chefs on his staff and shipped his gold plate to Cairo, Kitchener set off for Alexandria, arriving at the end of September. He knew that in Egypt he would find his old enemy Abbas Hilmi, the puppet ruler, the man he had publicly humiliated in 1894. Already, his ambition never far below the surface, Kitchener had plans to depose Abbas Hilmi and create in his place, 'a British Viceroyalty as grand as its Indian cousin. Kitchener of course wanted to be the first holder of such an omnipotent title, and dreamed, too, of adding to it territories discarded by the Ottoman Empire. . .He could envisage the creation of a mighty British sphere of influence extending across Mesopotamia and down the Euphrates to the Gulf.'[12] So writes Royle, the latest of Kitchener's biographers.

But it was not to be. There were no great developments, political or otherwise, and Kitchener had to content himself by designing grand uniforms for his staff and refurbishing yet another house, at Kasr-al-Dubara, which he felt should have a larger ballroom. We have a glimpse of him having dinner with Vita Sackville-West, (daughter of his collaborator at Broome Park, Lady Sackville) whom he astonished by remarking, in answer to a question about his interest in Egyptian art, that he could not really think much of a people who had painted the same cat for four thousand years.

So his life continued from 1911 until the summer of 1914, when, home on leave, he was created an Earl and was about to return to Cairo when war was declared. Asquith, the Prime Minister, at once offered him a Cabinet appointment as Secretary of State for War. It is no part of the purpose of this book to discuss Kitchener's role in the war, except for one episode which illuminates the error of his military thinking and the disastrous state to which the Army in India had been reduced due to the policies which he had insisted upon introducing in his struggle with Curzon. It was a strange turn of fate that in 1914, Kitchener's successor as Commander-in-Chief in India was Sir Beauchamp Duff, the man who had been responsible for the administration work involved in the new Army system back in 1905. Kitchener himself was directing the strategy of war, including the disposal of Indian Army troops in other theatres. The Military Secretary to the India Office in London was none other than Barrow who had been rejected by Kitchener as unsuitable for the staff in India. Watched carefully by Curzon, who was still in the political wilderness, these three men were now involved in directing a military campaign which would prove whether the new Indian Army was fit for active service.

Chapter Thirteen

The Proof of the Pudding

When Kitchener left India and his 'system' behind him in 1909, he chose as successor one of his divisional commanders, Sir O'Moore Creagh, known as 'No More K'. Kitchener had concentrated his efforts on the Council rather than the Army, preparing the way, so he thought, to succeed Minto as Viceroy. The new Commander-in-Chief, alas, 'lacked administrative ability'[1] and so army reforms proceeded at a slow pace. When he in turn left India in 1913, the succession was 'fixed' by his former Chief on a routine visit to Balmoral to see his old friend George V. It was to be none other than Kitchener's aide, Duff, the man who had designed 'the system' that never was.

Lord Roberts told Curzon: 'I was much concerned, though I cannot say I was astonished, at Duff's appointment... The report now is that Kitchener is to succeed Hardinge [the new Viceroy], in which case Duff will be at his disposal to do as he is told. It is very unfortunate for the Indian Army. Kitchener does not care for the Army, and Duff is not a soldier at heart... Later on, perhaps it may be possible to get the old system brought back. No living man, as I told Kitchener at the time, can do the work of C-in-C and Member in Council.'[2] In his view Kitchener had neglected the Army – and his successor neglected the Council.

Barrow wrote to Curzon on 23rd October 1913: 'Lord Nicholson [Field-Marshal and formerly Chief of the Imperial General Staff] told me in Simla he considers the present organisation quite unworkable, and most unsatisfactory.' He added, 'Although Duff has never commanded a Regiment, a Brigade, a Division or an

Army (like myself) his connexion with K and his pliant character would commend itself to Ministers. I *know* Nicholson had in mind a modification of the present scheme . . . which would probably have saved K's face and I am sure the self-seeking Duff would have willingly offered to work it.'[3] And Lovat Fraser, who in 1913 described the new Commander-in-Chief as 'an office clerk' told Curzon: 'I don't often venture on prophecy, but I firmly believe that the terrible mistake of appointing two unsuitable C-in-Cs in succession will have disastrous effects.'[4]

Although this account is of a tragedy brought about by great issues affecting the Constitution, the 'micro' issues of Kitchener's new system for administering the Army is of significance if only because the test of any system is whether it works, and in this case, whether it works in war. Kitchener was under the false impression in 1914 that the Indian Army would be capable of extensive participation in overseas campaigns. He therefore encouraged the despatch of Indian units to France and Mesopotamia. The Somme, Mons and Gallipoli are synonymous with the muddles of the 1914–18 war, but virtually unknown is the campaign in Mesopotamia in 1914–16, which its historian, Colonel A. J. Barker, in *The Neglected War* describes as 'probably the biggest muddle of all'[5]. The fault was Kitchener's, but he escaped criticism until after his death.

Mesopotamia, the Bible land of Adam and Eve, is now known as Iraq. The Arab proverb says that after Allah made hell he thought he could improve on it, and made Mesopotamia by adding flies. By 1914, the oil had been discovered which was to turn the land into a sort of heaven. The German plan to drive towards the East was in full swing, the Kaiser already having encouraged the Turks to start a Holy War by hinting that he had embraced the Muslim faith. Two German cruisers were at readiness in the Indian Ocean and German officers controlled the Turkish military machine as (to use the modern term) advisors. The Turks were already threatening Egypt.

At the end of September 1914, Kitchener's old protagonist Sir Edmund Barrow*, now Military Secretary at the India Office

---

* Sir E. Barrow thanked Curzon on 31st January 1914 on his appointment as Secretary, Military Department, India Office, 'It will be gall and wormwood to Duff when he knows, for he will regard it as ominous of your rising ascendancy over the spirits of darkness.' CP

(Stedman's old job) put out a paper entitled 'The Role of India in a Turkish War' proposing the occupation of Basra by Indian forces to protect the refinery at Abadan. Three quarters of the Royal Navy's oil supply came from the Middle East. Initially the Government favoured a mere demonstration of military strength, and instructions to form an expeditionary force were given to the Indian Government on 2nd October 1914. India did not want to send troops to either France or Mesopotamia, fearing a war on the North West Frontier, but was overruled. Advanced forces of about 5000 men embarked from Bombay on 16th October and the General in Command had been told to occupy Abadan. Already the inefficiencies of Indian Army administration were apparent: the result of seven years of Kitchener's reforms, which had, whatever their intentions, been effectively a run-down of the Army under the Liberal Party's policy of financial stringency. 'The budget was slashed and slashed again.'[6]

The prospect of being expected to fight a European enemy was ignored, artillery was cut, and there was no mechanical transport service (the expeditionary force included 650 mules but no carts), nor even backpacks in which the troops might carry their equipment. There were very few medium guns and no light machine guns. Indeed, no light machine guns reached them until the autumn of 1916. Centralization of facilities was almost non-existent, and regiments were expected to look after themselves, including supplying their own hospitals. There was a high proportion of cavalry regiments. So much for the elegant centralized supply scheme which Kitchener had substituted for the administration of the Military Department. 'Nor was this the end of it, for Kitchener's reorganisation had not removed many of the other weak spots in the Indian organisation,' says Colonel Barker[7]. There were only forty officers on the reserve at the outbreak of war, and no proper scheme for general mobilization existed. Training was indifferent and the system for supplying reinforcements thoroughly unsound.

In these circumstances, it was natural that when the first troops disembarked near Abadan, it took them two days to get ashore. Turkey declared war, and the troops were immediately engaged in fighting: the proposed 'demonstration of strength' had become a war. The Indian force headed for Basra, but there was no planning for a large-scale expedition up a river, and this was a major cause of the disasters to come. 'Simla [the Army Headquarters] was still thinking in terms of the Frontier.'[8] They did, however, send out General Sir John Nixon, with new orders which were much more comprehensive than those given to the original force, and which included a proposed advance to Baghdad. Communications were so bad that this information did not reach Whitehall until May 1915. 'Fresh troops were being rushed out without a proper scale of equipment, and there was no additional transport. . . This was to become a problem of crucial importance, while the lack of medical facilities was to result in a near-Crimean scandal,' says Colonel Barker. Nixon's requests for reinforcements were turned down, and Lord Crewe at the India Office in London told the Viceroy, 'No advance beyond the present theatre of operations will be sanctioned. . . A safe game must be played.'[9] On 28th May, Austen Chamberlain succeeded Crewe at the India Office and he endorsed his predecessor's cautious policy. Also at this time, a new General, Charles Townshend, defender of Chitral, was sent out to take over the 6th Division.

Townshend corresponded regularly with Curzon, writing on 4th September 1915, 'I do hope that you can put in a word for us in Mesopotamia [with the Government] – we seem left out entirely in the cold, and it is a subject for discussion right through all ranks in this expedition. . . "Just because we come under India" is the comment. . . Here we have a far more difficult task to do than Lord K had in the Nile expedition, and with good artillery [facing us] instead of the miserably-armed Dervishes. Much worse climate, and yet the War Office hardly recognise there is an expedition at all. I should like you to pass on these notes to Winston Churchill.'[10] Later, in November, he wrote: 'I feel that Lord Kitchener has abandoned me, and it was he who said I should be pushed on.'[11] Kitchener was, of course, Secretary of State for War and virtual military supremo.

Barker describes how the terrain and the climate affected the troops: 'By 5 o'clock on a Mesopotamian morning the sun was too hot for sleep . . . it was even too hot for the flies. Sun-stroke and heat-stroke were common, fever, dysentery and paratyphoid were rife, yet medical facilities were totally inadequate to deal with the heavy casualty list.'[12]

One of the sick was Townshend. When he recovered, he set about advancing to Kut, 250 miles from Baghdad, but there was confusion about the onward advance to the capital, which Townshend knew would require reinforcements, which he did not get. At the battle of Ctesiphon, half Townshend's force was killed or wounded and he wrote, 'If I live a hundred years, I shall not forget that night, amongst hundreds of wounded, who were being brought in loaded on the commissariat carts. . . their suffering in these small springless carts can be easily imagined.'[13] Barker writes, 'For all the utterly inadequate arrangements made for the transport and treatment of the wounded and for their hideous sufferings, the Indian Government must be regarded as primarily responsible.'[14]

Lovat Fraser, the journalist, who was in Mesopotamia, had written to Curzon, 'The number of sick, the shortage of rations, the continued inefficiency of the transport and so on . . . the force has entirely lost morale and completely mistrusts its present commanders.'[15]

Duff, back in Simla, knew nothing of what was happening, admitting 'the layman in Bombay knew more about what was going on in Mesopotamia than Army HQ in Simla'.[16] Townshend retreated from Ctesiphon to Kut, pursued by the Turks, and reached the town after seven and a half days, an epic retreat which Barker compares to Dunkirk, and says was one of the most arduous in the history of the British Army.

Townshend had been initially successful but was later given what he described as 'an impossible task' and there was a muddle about what his instructions really were. A lady wrote to Curzon, (he kept the letter in his papers) 'Isn't it dreadful to hear that . . . one of his generals put Nixon's telegram telling Townshend to use his discretion . . . in his pocket and forgot about it for 3 days during which time they were surrounded. . . This has been kept very dark.'[17]

The British public were shocked at the retreat from Baghdad and the politicians began to look for a scapegoat. Townshend nevertheless signalled to Nixon, 'I mean to defend Kut as I did Chitral.'[18] A relief force under Younghusband was hastily assembled in Basra in December 1915, as it was wrongly thought that Townshend's rations would run out in a month. Conditions for the relief force were however typical of those earlier in the campaign and Barker says that the troops' 'misery and suffering amounted to criminal neglect'. He adds, 'The real fault lay in the system. The Army in India had been starved for so long that its commanders had lost the habit of asking.'[19] The relief force advanced ten miles towards Kut but lost 4000 men in the attempt. In the black month of January 1916, thousands more were casualties, and the suffering was appalling.

'Since the very beginning of the campaign, the military authorities had done their best by means of a strict censorship to stifle any form of criticism or prevent any unpleasant news from leaking out,' says Barker.[20] When the story was eventually told, Nixon left Mesopotamia under a cloud and he was never employed again. By an irony, Duff's Chief of Staff in London, Lake, who had 'a large share in the responsibility for what the Mesopotamian Army lacked in the way of equipment',[21] was sent out to replace the disgraced Nixon. His arrival made confusion over supplies even worse. 'The fault lay with the Army in India's organisation and its staff,' says Barker.[22] The Viceroy realised that a scandal of immense proportions was imminent, and the India Office in Whitehall ordered the appointment of a committee of investigation. Meanwhile, further disasters struck the troops trying to reach Kut, and the commander of the force doing so was relieved of his command in March 1916.

The eventual fall of Kut, with the surrender of 9000 troops, one third of them British, was a major shock to the public, which believed there had not been such a disaster for the British Army since the American War of Independence. Kitchener read the news in his expressionless voice to a grimly silent House of Lords. The captured garrison were told by the Turkish commander that they would be 'honoured guests' but their treatment was inhuman, whether walking or travelling in open cattle trucks from the battlefields. In captivity, seventy percent of the British rank and file died, and of the Indian troops, 2500 of the 9300 captured also perished.

After the fall of Kut, the War Office in London took control and appointed a new commander, Maude, who succeeded in capturing Baghdad and bringing the campaign to a successful conclusion. In total, about 100,000 soldiers, British and Indian, were casualties of the war, of whom nearly one third were killed outright or died from wounds. The casualties of all Allied forces at Gallipoli, a more famous defeat, were 250,000.

The account of the siege of Kut in Norman E. Dixon's book *On The Psychology of Military Incompetence* is based largely on Russell Bradon's *The Siege*, and its author draws a terrifying picture of Townshend's insensitivity as well as his incompetence. As regards the war itself, Dixon calls it, 'A British military disaster so total yet unnecessary, so futile yet expensive, that its like did not occur again until the fall of Singapore in 1942.'[23] Yet he puts the blame on Duff and his generals, and not on the Duff/Kitchener system in India: perhaps he had not read the Report of the Government enquiry into the campaign. Indeed, Dixon ranks Kitchener as 'a highly competent commander' which others would question as a supportable judgement.

The Government enquiry into the disaster in Mesopotamia was conducted by a high powered committee which made an intensive investigation. It consisted of Lord George Hamilton, the Earl of Donoughmore, Lord Hugh Cecil, Sir Archibald Williamson, John Hodge, Josiah Wedgewood, Admiral Sir Cyprian Bridge and General Sir Neville Lyttleton. It took evidence from the Secretary of State (Austen Chamberlain, a future Foreign Minister), an ex-Viceroy, from two ex-Commanders-in-Chief of India (Duff and Creagh), from a former Member of the Indian Council, Hewett, and from all the generals who took part in the campaign, except Townshend who was living a life of considerable luxury as a prisoner and honoured guest of the Turks. Altogether, the committee saw over 100 witnesses and held sixty meetings. So much for the assertion made by Kitchener's biographer, Magnus, that the report was completed hastily (it took a year) by an incompetent committee. Some of the comments it made refer specifically to the Kitchener system.[24]

Minute No. 3 from the Secretary of State to the Prime Minister begins. 'In this last letter to me the Viceroy observes that in his opinion "the present Army system in India has not only broken down but has been positively mischievous". I had already come to the same conclusion.'

Paragraph 12: 'While there is centralisation at the head of the administration, a curious dualism remains below. These two Departments [Army and Military supply], though under the same individual, are kept separate and distinct, and they are separately maintained in order to give substance to the fiction that one person is two persons. . . This astounding system had only to be described to be condemned.'

Paragraph 14: 'Sir Edmund Barrow expressed the view that the C-in-C is now trying to do the work of 6 men,' and commented on the dangerous extent to which the Viceroy and his Council were entirely dependent on the views of a sole military advisor.

Paragraph 36: 'Sir O'Moore Creagh cannot entirely escape criticism for the state of the Army.'

Paragraph 38: In the opinion of a senior officer, 'The Indian system is more to blame for the breakdown of the medical arrangements than anything else.'

Finding 3: 'The attempt to control and regulate the wants of the expedition from Simla was an administrative mistake.'

Finding 5: 'The C-in-C should have visited Mesopotamia.'

Finding 27: The Indian Government is severely censured: 'Their military system of administration was cumbrous and inept. It was however within the power of the Viceroy and the C-in-C to have established a more effective procedure.' [Duff, the Commander-in-Chief had helped to design the current one.]

Recommendation 29: 'It is clear that the combination of the duties of C-in-C and Mil. Member in Council cannot adequately be performed by any one man in time of war, and that the existing organisation is at once over-centralised and cumbrous in its duality below.'

Recommendation 36: 'The system . . . receives its final condemnation at the hands of the Commission.'

When he read the report, the Secretary of State wrote, 'I agree that the Military system established in India by Lord Kitchener [and approved by the Conservatives through Brodrick and Balfour] has finally broken down.' Curzon was more direct, although, it might be said, extremely restrained, perhaps because of Kitchener's recent death*, in the Minute he supplied to the committee in August 1916:

It is admitted that the system of military administration set up in India in deference to the representations of Lord Kitchener, in 1906, has broken down irretrievably: that, followed as it was by important

*On 5th June 1916

changes with regards to the chief commands, it affords as unfortunate an instance of over-centralisation as can probably anywhere be
found; and that it has been one of the main causes of the disastrous
failure of the military authorities in India to cope with the difficulties
attendant upon the Mesopotamian Campaign. It has been stated in
the Cabinet, and has been announced by the Secretary of State in
Parliament, that this system stands condemned. . .[25]

He also wrote, 'Duff ought never to have been appointed C-in-C
India. The tragedy of his failure is not diminished by the fact that
the system which broke down irretrievably in his hands, and under
which he broke down not less fatally himself, was the system which
he had assisted Lord Kitchener to elaborate ten years earlier, and
most of the papers expounding which were written by his own
hand. Sir B. Duff is now unemployed and has lost the great position
of C-in-C. . . It wil be for the Cabinet to decide whether this is an
adequate punishment for a degree of culpability which has seldom
been exceeded in modern times.'[26] After publication of the report
Curzon wrote that Duff 'would be a ruined man in public
estimation'.[27]

Duff's reputation was denigrated by Hardinge, who was Viceroy
at the time, in his book *My Indian Years*. He wrote, 'Never was there
so great a failure, followed by a most tragic ending. Curiously
enough, he was the victim of Kitchener's misguided system of the
concentration of everything in the hands of the Commander-in-
Chief . . . an impracticable system in time of war.'[28] Birdwood on
the other hand claims that Hardinge 'appreciated Duff's great
ability and welcomed the appointment, as did all of us who knew
what splendid work he had done in the days of Kitchener'.[29]

One member of the Commission had in fact pinned the whole
blame on Hardinge and on Duff. The recommendations included a
complete reorganisation of the Indian Army. A public outcry was
inevitable with the report's publication, and Austen Chamberlain
resigned on the doctrine of ministerial responsibility, although
Hardinge's offer of resignation was declined. 'Whether the Mesopotamia Commission apportioned the blame correctly is another
matter . . . [but] the two most important factors were administrative shortcomings and the effect of the terrain. . . Even the latter
was not exploited as it might have been due to lack of equipment

and the poor quality of the cavalry. The campaign was an epic of guts and improvisation.'[30]

While the Commission was sitting there was much discussion of the subject in Parliament, most of it unfavourable to Kitchener's system. For example, addressing the House of Lords in July 1916, Cromer said, 'I claim that this change of system, this very important change which was introduced under Lord Kitchener's auspices, should be judged by its results, and while it would certainly be a great exaggeration to say that the fiasco in Mesopotamia has been entirely due to the change, I cannot help thinking that it has very largely contributed to it. What has happened in Mesopotamia affords the most complete vindication of the attitude taken up by the noble earl opposite, the then Viceroy, in opposition to this drastic reform.'[31]

Naturally enough, publication of the committee of enquiry's report further re-opened memories of the Curzon-Kitchener conflict. Austen Chamberlain wrote, '[It] makes it imperative to provide in future against the excessive centralization which was the result of the Kitchener-Brodrick and Kitchener-Minto changes.' And a correspondent wrote from Hyderabad to Curzon, 'What an irony that the failure of K's scheme should have been demonstrated by his own chief himself.'[32] Curzon began to believe that his views had at last, and at a terrible price, been vindicated. Only 1st July 1917, Milner wrote to Curzon:

> This horrible report on Mesopotamia is a very remarkable vindication of the policy which caused your resignation. . . I may tell you that I was torn between my affection to you and my devotion to poor K, and as a consequence I devoted some time to studying both sides, and came unhesitatingly to the opinion that you were in the right, and had we had a more able administrator at the time than our friend St John, I think you would have been supported. The mistake has proved a costly one. It only confirms my opinion that we never had a better man in India than yourself.[33]

Others were not so outspoken. *The Times* wrote a leading article on 6th July, but Lovat Fraser explained to Curzon that the editor 'flatly refuses to allow me to "rake up" the 1905 business, and has actually persuaded himself that it has nothing to do with this present issue. I think Sir George Arthur [Kitchener's friend and biographer] is at the bottom of this.'[34]

The House of Lords debated the Report fully on 12th July 1917 and Curzon made a statesmanlike speech which to some extent spared Brodrick, who, as Lord Midleton, was now in the Chamber. Amongst Curzon's papers on this subject is a pathetic little pencilled note which Brodrick passed to him after he had spoken: 'How fine I thought your speech, although you will not expect me to endorse every para. It was quite like old times.' Of course, when Brodrick came to write his memoirs twenty years later, he did not deem the subejct of the war in Mesopotamia, or the light it threw on his policies, or Curzon's restraint, worthy of a single mention.

A curious twist to this story of muddle at Kut arises from Kitchener's involvement in the formation of the Arab Bureau. When he was British Resident in Cairo from 1911 to 1914, Kitchener developed an 'Islamic' policy for the whole area, and appointed an Oriental Secretary, the famous Ronald Storrs. Before departing from Cairo for home leave in 1914, Kitchener held secret talks with Abdullah the son of the Sharif of Mecca. What passed between them is not known, but it is known that in the weeks after war was declared, and Kitchener was detained in London, he continued to interfere in Middle Eastern affairs, cabling Storrs: 'Send secret and carefully chosen messenger from me to Sharif Abdullah' to ascertain whether in the event of German coercion of the Turks, the Arabs 'would be with us or against us'.[35] Gertrude Bell's biographer H.V.F. Winstone, who investigates all this in some detail, says, 'This began a chain of events that was to cause interminable rivalries among the allied powers, realignment of loyalties among the Arabs, and the making and breaking of promises on a heroic scale.'[36] Kitchener's talk about 'the Arab nation', led to the formation of the Arab Bureau, a policy-making intelligence organisation whose members included Gertrude Bell, Mark Sykes, Storrs, and T. E. Lawrence. Members of the Bureau, which was heartily disliked by many influential people, were able to 'wander freely round the Middle East with inexhaustible supplies of money, in defiance of generals and in open contempt of official policies and campaign strategies, when the allied cause and the lives of millions of men hung in the balance. *The only possible explanation is to be found in Kitchener's early support*'[37] [my italics]. And one strange activity of the Bureau was that T. E. Lawrence and another member came to Kut, during the siege, 'on whose authority was never clear',[38] to bribe the Turkish Commander into letting the prisoners go. 'The sum offered was £1 million. The enemy commanders replied that they were "gentlemen" and could not be bribed. They were then offered £2 million, the balance to be paid at a later date. The answer was the same.' One account of this attempt to save the Indian Army by buying its freedom is that the action had Cabinet approval. If so, Kitchener may have initiated it.[39]

What does history have to say about the Mesopotamia disaster and Kitchener's responsibility? His first major biographer Sir George Arthur, merely notes that in that campaign 'our armies were faring badly'.[40]

Magnus is much franker:

War must always remain the ultimate test of any military system and it has to be admitted that the report of the Royal Commission on the ill-starred expedition to Mesopotamia . . . stated unequivocally (July 1917) that 'the combination of the duties of Commander-in-Chief in India and Military Member of Council cannot adequately be performed by any one man in time of war'. It may be suggested, nevertheless, that the report, which deliberately echoed past controversy [what does this mean?] was too kind to the commanders of the expedition to Mesopotamia, and too hard upon the new system which Kitchener had instituted. . . The system of military administration which Kitchener destroyed was obsolete and on the point of breaking down. It is true that while he remained in India after its reconstruction, his organisation was open to serious criticism. He refused to delegate responsibility and he centralised all power in himself to an excessive and wholly unnecessary degree. That was always his weakness, and some of his less competent successors (both of them) were confused and misled by the example they inherited.

Nevertheless, on an impartial survey and despite the report of the Royal Commission on the Campaign in Mesopotamia which was completed hastily in circumstances of peculiar difficulty Kitchener's system was greatly superior to the one which it displaced. It was better adapted to needs and conditions which, together with the highly personal machine which Kitchener devised to meet them, had passed, like a dissolving view, into history.[41]

Thanks to Colonel Barker, the disaster of Mesopotamia has not
passed into oblivion, and it is a pity that Magnus was unable to
read his book before making such a superficial judgement.

Professor Cassar, the Canadian who was 'very severe' with
Magnus in *Kitchener: Architect of Victory*, appears to rely heavily on
him in this instance, and his opening sentence is identical. 'The
ultimate test of any military organisation is its performance in war.
In 1915–16 the difficulties of the Indian Army in Mesopotamia
were compounded by a breakdown of the transport and medical
services.'[42] If he had been able to read the spine-chilling letters
from soldiers in Curzon's files, he would not have used the word
'difficulties'. He says:

> The absence of Kitchener's testimony [Kitchener was dead],
> together with the fact that Lord George Hamilton, who had
> supported Curzon in 1905, presided over the enquiry, made the
> verdict predictable. Actually the Commission was much too lenient
> on Duff and much too hard on the military organisation Kitchener
> had created. . . No system can be fully evaluated on the basis of one
> man's record. There were obvious drawbacks to over-centralisation
> but, on the whole, the arrangement was workable in the hands of a
> competent chief.[43]

This was, unfortunately, never put to the test, as elsewhere in his
book Cassar admits Moore O'Creagh lacked administrative ability
and he also claims that Kitchener was under the impression that
the Indian Army was capable of extensive participation in overseas
expeditions.

Philip Warner, a military historian, in *Kitchener: the Man behind the
Legend* makes no mention of Mesopotamia and merely claims: 'The
conflict between the Commander-in-Chief and the Military Supply
Member had been happily resolved; when a series of military
expenditure cuts were made by the Liberal Government in 1907
(sic) the post was abolished.'[44] Warner makes no further judgement about the results of Kitchener's scheme.

Kitchener's most recent biographer, Royle, is the most judicious.
He says:

> The new machine contained as many flaws as the old. . . 60,000 men
> of the Indian Army put Kitchener's methods to the test during the

Mesopotamian campaign which ended in disaster and carnage . . .
as much due to bad leadership, cabinet indecision and the superior
Turkish forces as it was to the system created by Lord Kitchener.[45]

Lord Esher wrote in December 1905, 'The fact is that K and K only
caused the downfall of Curzon. That K himself will have to fall
hereafter is certain. That type of man always does.'[46] Kitchener's
system fell down at Mesopotamia, but the man himself was not
there to fall with it. The case against Kitchener can therefore be
summerised as follows:

1.   He determined to change the existing Army organisation in
India, although he had never served there, without waiting to find
out the facts for himself.
2.   On arrival in India, and for the next eighteen months until
Curzon went on leave, he continued intriguing to destroy the
system.
3.   As soon as Curzon was back in England, he tried to persuade
the acting Viceroy to change the system. When this failed, he sent a
secret memo urging the Government in London to take action.
4.   After Curzon's return, he secretly mounted a full-scale campaign in London to win the Government's support.
5.   Although a member of the Indian Government Council, he
deceived it about his intentions. He lied to Curzon consistently,
intrigued behind his back and used every means of deception to win
his case.
6.   Having won, he failed to reorganise the Army adequately in
his remaining period as Commander-in-Chief, 1906–9.
7.   He ordered the official Army papers to be forged, so that
Curzon's record in India would be expunged.
8.   On leaving India, he appointed an inadequate successor who
also failed to reform Army organisation during his term of office,
1909–13.
9.   In 1913, he 'fixed' the appointment of another inadequate
Commander-in-Chief who also failed to organise the Army for war
service – and who then mounted a disastrous campaign in Mesopotamia with the loss of tens of thousands of lives.

Chapter Fourteen

Epitaph and Conclusion

Kitchener did not write his own epitaph, but one might follow up a hint from Esher, who wrote, 'He was admirably equipped with a few simple precepts and with illimitable patience, not untinged by methods which the Israelites inherited from Jacob and the statesmen of the Renaissance from Machiavelli.'[1] What precepts of Machiavelli did Esher have in mind? Perhaps, 'It is necessary for a prince wishing to hold his own, to know how to do wrong. . . Those princes who have done great things have held good faith of little account, and have known how to circumvent the intellect of men by craft. . . But it is necessary to know how to disguise this characteristic, and to be a great pretender and dissembler. . . Every one sees what you appear to be, few really know what you are.'[2]

As regards Curzon, Esher said he was 'one of the greatest of Viceroys if not altogether the greatest'[3] and possibly no other Englishman possessed his qualities of statesmanship. Curiously however, when Curzon came to write his own epitaph, during the course of a boring Cabinet meeting, in 10 Downing Street, it referred only obliquely to the Viceroyalty:

> *In diverse offices and in many lands*
> *as explorer, writer, administrator*
> *and ruler of men*
> *he sought to serve his country,*
> *and add honour to an ancient name.*

The intention of this book has been to focus on the period up to

1905–6, rather than to go on to describe how the characters lived unhappily ever afterwards. Suffice it to say that Balfour and Curzon were again active in political life when in 1916 Kitchener finally passed out of their lives. Asquith, Prime Minister in 1914, had invited Balfour to become a full member of the Imperial Defence Committee which he had been instrumental in forming, and then of the War Council into which it evolved. Kitchener, prevented from returning to Egypt and hustled into the War Office, which he had fought so hard to avoid entering, was an immediate disappointment, Balfour noting that he was 'hopelessly incapable of facing the greatness of the crisis'.[4] Lloyd George described Kitchener as, 'One of those revolving lighthouses which radiate momentary gleams of revolving light far out into the surrounding gloom, and then, suddenly relapse into complete darkness. There were no intermediate stages.'[5]

Davidson, the unpaid secretary to Bonar Law, who later became chairman of the Conservative Party, said of him at this time, 'He was a symbol, and I have never really made up my mind whether he was a great man or not. Of course he was very impressive, but I was a very young man, and my impression was that he was rather a figure from a chapter in history, and I could not believe that he really understood modern warfare. He was a symbol, the man who had never suffered defeat.'[6]

Another more personal view of him is given by Osbert Sitwell who saw him in 1914 sitting 'as if he were a god, slightly gone to seed perhaps, but waiting confidently for his earthly dominion to disclose itself. . . He plainly belonged to some different order of creation from those around him. His appearance, his blue eyes and the cut of his features, unusual as it was, proclaimed him to be English; not an English leader of patrician type, such as Wellington, but from a class that had, since the Reform Bill, monopolised power.'[7]

It was Kitchener, who together with Balfour and Lloyd George 'governed the country' in 1915 according to Haldane who added, 'And Balfour is the real Prime Minister.'[8] In fact, Balfour was First Lord of the Admiralty, so how ironic that the ineptitude of that organisation should have played a major part in ensuring that Kitchener drowned in the North Sea. The Admiralty did not take adequate steps to ensure that, when Kitchener embarked for a visit to Russia, the sea was clear of German mines, Kitchener had long planned to visit Russia and he finally accepted an invitation from the Emperor to discuss joint military questions in May 1916. He did not want to leave London – his position there was precarious – but he was enthusiastic about the prospect of visiting Russia for the first time. In his last few days in England he addressed an informal meeting of MP's with great success, lunched with the King, and put the finishing touches to a rose garden at Broome Park. He boarded *HMS Hampshire* at tea time at Orkney on 5th June. Off the Orkneys, three hours later, it struck a mine and sunk almost immediately.

When Lloyd George formed his second administration at the end of 1916, Balfour, now Foreign Minister, was instrumental in negotiating the entry of the USA into the war, as well as being one of the architects of the peace. Curzon, who had held the minor post of Lord President of the Council since 1915, became with Balfour a member of the War Cabinet. 'Slowly the clouds began to lift. His amazing powers of work, the vast range of his experience, the sheer force of his lucidity, overcame the prejudice felt against him.'[9] He took over the running of the Foreign Office when Balfour went to Versailles. In October 1918 they changed Cabinet roles, and Curzon for the first time sat at the desk he had always coveted at the Foreign Office.

Balfour and Curzon had resumed something of the warmth of their earlier relationship, but they could be cutting in debate when opportunity arose. For Curzon this was an inevitable reaction when his opinions were challenged. Harold Nicolson, who wrote the most revealing study of his character, says 'never did his energy become more dynamic than when it was seasoned by competition' and 'even in small matters, subordination or surrender were tortures of the soul'.[10] But he lacked the cool ruthlessness of Balfour who, as Churchill said, 'Would have consigned a colleague to the guillotine with much complacency – although he would do it in a thoroughly polite manner.'[11]

The well-known ending of the drama of their political lives came in the summer of 1923 when the King asked the sick Balfour (now an Earl and a Viscount) to visit Sandringham to advise whether Curzon or Baldwin should be Prime Minister. Balfour, on a golfing holiday, returned to his friends after seeing the King, and when they asked, 'And will dear George be chosen?' his answer was, 'No, dear George will not!'[12] In the last year of his life, when Balfour was dictating his autobiography to Mrs Dugdale, his cousin, he recalled that Lord Salisbury (the younger) had expressed the view that, 'George was a very able, ambitious man, but always conscious that he was second-rate. I rather think he was,' said Balfour, 'but I'm not sure it wasn't second-ratedness that amounts to first rated-ness. In all things in which George was second-rate, I was even more second-rate. . . I hadn't George's ambitions any more than his capacities – and his powers of speech were extraordinary. He told me that he was never at a loss for a word. . . I daresay my powers of speech were of a more original kind. My arguments were perhaps of a less commonplace kind.'[13]

As for Curzon's view of Balfour, there is to be found amongst his papers one marked 'for use by my biographer'. It is a bitter memorandum of 9000 words composed in four weeks at the turn of the year 1922, and dealing with his relationship with his old friend and colleague. The harshest passages are as follows:

> I regard him as the worst and most dangerous of the British Foreign Ministers with whom I have been brought into contact in my public life. His charm of manner . . . blinded all but those who knew him from the inside, to the lamentable ignorance, indifference and levity of his regime. He never studied his papers; never knew the facts; at the Cabinet, he had seldom read the morning's FO telegrams; he never got up a case; he never looked ahead. . . In reality the characteristics that made him a failure as Prime Minister. . . It was sheer intellectual indolence, a never-knowing his case, an instinctive love for compromise. . .
>
> The truth is that Balfour with his scintillating intellectual exterior had no depth of feeling, no profound convictions, and strange to say (in spite of his fascination of manner) no real affection. We all knew this; when the emergency came, he would drop or desert or sacrifice any one of us without a pang. . . Were any one of us to die suddenly, he would dine out that night with undisturbed complacency, and in the intervals of conversation or bridge, would be heard to murmur, 'Poor Old George.'[14]

Remember that was written in January 1923, six months before Balfour as he thought, finally put the knife in, murmuring, 'Poor old George.' And two years later, as Curzon lay dying, he could not forbear to say that it was Arthur Balfour who had brought the tragedy to its consummation.

English biography is a lamentable failure, according to A. J. A. Symonds, because it adopts the panegyric mode, and attempts to record rather than reveal. This book has been critical of Kitchener first and foremost, of Brodrick, of Balfour, even of Hubert Hamilton, who seemed to believe that he should manipulate the Chief in the interests of some higher good, which his class and his fellow soldiers had a divine right to protect.

Lest it be thought that this has been a panegyric of Curzon, it must be said again that while the aim has been to reveal the motivation of the principal actors who brought about the Viceroy's fall, it has never been far from mind that Curzon himself was fatally flawed. Hence the tragedy. If then weaknesses have been inadequately delineated, let the record restate a selection from Harold Nicolson's index entries for Curzon: 'Administrator rather than politician; Historian rather than man of action; lack of demographic gift; lack of acute sense of proportion; occasional inconsistency and weakness; the egoistic angle of approach; the competitive and controversial instinct; his inability to delegate; his pompousness; his exaggerated belief in accuracy; his self-pity; his irritability; his childishness.'[15]

These are not mortal sins, and on the other scale we place his view that the principles of constitutional government were above the lies, the intrigue, the deceit and even the forgeries of those of the soldiery who believed that such methods were justified in saving the Army from the civilians.

It is easy to be filled with moral indignation, and perhaps it is more useful for the biographer to explain how, if the tragedians had acted differently, the outcome might have been a better one. Did Balfour have any alternative, if he believed that war in the Far East was probable, and that his government would fall if he accepted the resignation of the popular hero of the day? Could he have done other than make it plain to Brodrick that Curzon must be ditched? He could. The first alternative would have been to bring Curzon home to England, leaving his successor to parley with Kitchener, but Balfour had failed to adopt that course, always saying that one of the mistakes of his career was to let Curzon return for his second term to India. Having failed, had he then a second alternative? He did, which would have been to have fulfilled his pledge to Curzon that the Viceroy should have independent military advice. To have done so would have required telling Kitchener that, while he would allow him to reform the Military Department, nevertheless Barrow must be appointed. The *quid pro quo* was that the Home Government would reacall Curzon before his second term was complete, leaving Barrow, Kitchener and the new Viceroy to fight it out.

Balfour's time was short, but he did have the time to ensure that all these things happened before his government fell, and even if the speedy recall of Curzon would have presented difficulties, Balfour could have agreed this policy with the King, who, as an ardent supporter of Kitchener, would have ensured that the Liberals carried it through when they came to power. Why did Balfour not follow this course? Not because he let Brodrick's unpleasant nature become dominant; not because he wanted to destroy or punish Curzon; not because he thought his government would fall if he did not support Kitchener. It was none of these things – it was simply that his nature let langour take over from inaction, and though he could be capable of action, it was not his norm. Balfour could have stopped Brodrick from destroying his friend, but in the end he could not be bothered. It was easier, as Curzon had seen, merely to say 'Poor Old George'. With hindsight Balfour did not admit to himself that he might have acted differently, though he would have preferred to have found some way of avoiding the issue, which many believe was Balfour's unfailing posture whenever faced with one.

As for Curzon, what might he have done to avoid his downfall? Clearly he should have grasped some of the realities of political life. The position was put quite clearly by Harold Nicolson: 'The tragedy of his life was that he imagined that a man could attain the highest office in the State by the sheer worth of industry, integrity, intelligence and efficient public service. . . No man in modern England can become a great statesman unless for many years he serves as a politician. That service was the only one that Curzon had been unable to perform.'

Appendix One

Kitchener Falsifies the Records

Twelve weeks after Kitchener had drowned in the grey waters of the North Sea, Curzon sat at his desk at Hackwood (his home near Basingstoke) and wrote what his better feelings had prevented him from putting on paper during Kitchener's lifetime:

If ever the true history of Lord Kitchener's treatment of myself in India is made public, it is desirable that this very characteristic page should not be omitted from the record.

Following the invariable practice when a Viceroy leaves India, the departmental records of my administration were prepared by offices selected for the purpose in each dept. The records are of a private nature: they are the property of the retiring Viceroy who takes them away with him, a limited number of copies being left in the Private Secretary's office at Simla, and in the Departments concerned. The officer selected (not by me but in the Dept) to write the Military Record was a Major W. A. Liddell, who was barely known to me, but was a writer of some ability. I saw and very cursorily ran through his compilation and proof, just before or about the time that I left India – passed it, and thought no more about the matter.

Nearly two yeas had elapsed when I received a letter from the Govt. of India dated June 19, 1907 which explained that under the Orders of Lord Minto [the Viceroy], certain passages had been omitted from Major Liddell's Summary because of their highly confidential nature. Considering that the entire Summaries are intended to be confidential, and that no Viceroy within my knowledge had ever thought of tampering with the records of his predecessor, I was somewhat surprised at this intimation, but waited for the revised compilation to appear. Upon its arrival I had no means of comparing it with Major Liddell's original draft (which had been in printed proof 2 years earlier) but even without this text, it was clear to me that considerable had taken place. I therefore at once protested to the Secretary of State, Mr Morley, and Lord Minto replied to him, "All I know about it is that some little time ago General Bayley told me that certain very confidential matters had by a misunderstanding on the part of the officer who compiled the record, been included in it, and that it was of such a confidential nature that it should not leave the Dept. There was no suggestion whatever of bowdlerising – simply the ommission of secret matter which could not justifiably be included – and I authorised the omission *on the understanding that Curzon was to be informed* [Curzon's underlining]. Lord K has never mentioned the matter to me in any way." Minto then examined all the papers and wrote again to Morley saying he had found that "my approval to withhold secret documents was understood to include alteration of the text of the Summary which was entirely contrary to my intention. . . Am very sorry mistake occurred. Original summary will be sent to him at once."[1]

Curzon pointed out that Minto's statement that it was all a mistake, and, by implication, done without K's knowledge, must be compared with what Minto's private secretary, Colonel Dunlop Smith, told Curzon on July 16th 1908 during a visit to 1 Carlton House Terrace. Dunlop Smith explained that what had really happened was that, 'Lord Minto's consent to tampering with the record having been obtained on the bogus plea that it contained secret documents, Col. Mullaly, who was Kitchener's right-hand man, and wrote his Minutes and Memoranda for him, had, acting under Lord Kitchener's orders, written "a long and insulting note", of an "absolutely disgraceful" character laying down the lines on which the Summary was to be bowdlerised in the Army Dept. in order to deprive me of all credit, to misrepresent the Govt of my administration, and to exonerate his chief.'[2]

Curzon's record of his meeting with Dunlop Smith, written at the time, quotes him as saying it was 'shameful' and that Kitchener had been responsible for it, and that no one had been angrier about the matter than Lord Minto. 'The orders for revision were issued with the knowledge and under the instructions of Lord

Kitchener. . . whose official denial sent to me through the S of S thus stood out in its true colours.

'Under these instructions, the Summary had been cut and rewritten in the manner which I was presently to expose.'[3]

On March 8th, after working for some weeks on the two reports, Liddell's original and Kitchener's expurgated copy, Curzon described in a letter of the Govt. of India, 'The precise manner in which the re-editing had been carried out, reducing the 232 pages of the original to 184 pages under the kindly hand of Col. Mullaly and his Myrmidions, omitting anything that might reflect credit on my colleagues or myself. I venture to say that the Govt. of India had never before received such a letter from one who had been its Official head and that a transaction provoking such a letter had never before taken place in the annals of Indian Administration. I concluded by demanding that the entire bowdlerised edition in India should be destroyed, and that it should be replaced by Major Liddell's original version. I further asked that I should be presented with a copy of the accompanying explanatory [secret] documents which Lord Minto in his letter to the S of S had sought to refuse.'[4]

Curzon sent a copy of his letter to Morley, who did not reply, and to Ampthill, acting Viceroy in 1904, who wrote that, 'I trust that, for the sake of public decency, no need of exposing this contemptible scandal will ever arise.'[5] As is clearly Curzon's wish in 1916 that it should one day be exposed, it is here described for the first time. Curzon also showed his letter to Sir Edwin Collen, the Military Member in the early part of his administration, who wrote, 'I hope I may live long enough to see K exposed. . . I trust that I shall see it, for it is a disgrace to humanity that a creature so devoid of any sense of honour should be permitted to impose on the English people.'[6] Lovat Fraser, who also saw the papers, wrote to Curzon, 'I cannot conceive anything more vindictive, and – I think one may say – dishonourable.'[7]

Curzon then points out that when the Government of India sent its offical reply to his indictment, 'the author of this letter, General Hagley, Secretary of the Army Department, was the very officer who had originally entrapped the Viceroy [Minto] in the matter. He was still the subordinate and mouthpiece of Lord Kitchener who was still C-in-C.' In this letter, 'No mention was made of the charges I had brought. No defence of the wholesale expurgation was attempted: compliance with my request for the destruction of the Kitchener edition was evaded by the statement that some time before the receipt of my letter, all copies of the revised Summary had been returned to the Army Dept. No notice was taken of my demand that it should be replaced by the Liddell Summary, and I should not be surprised if a search in the archives showed that all copies of the latter had unaccountably disappeared!

'Finally, the Govt of India in their reply informed me that on the authority of the Viceroy, that Lord Kitchener had nothing to do with the matter and had prepared no orders regarding it. The value of this *dementi* was subsequently shown when the Viceroy's private secretary, Col. Dunlop Smith, called upon me of his own accord 3 months later, and gave me an exact and truthful history of the transaction.

'A year later Lord Ampthill informed me that he had for the second time been requested by the Govt. of India to give up his Kitchener copy. This he declined to do, and if my copies ever disappear, which I shall take steps to see shall not be the case, his at any rate will survive as a sufficient demonstration.

'I hope that if a true account of my administration in India, and more especially its concluding phases is ever written, my biographer may not omit this very significant passage.'[8]

It is impossible to precis here Curzon's indictment, which ran to thirteen typewritten pages and listed in detail those passages in Liddell's Summary which (1) assigned credit to Curzon or his administration, (2) were complimentary to Elles or Collen, (3) argued views not acceptable to Kitchener, (4) showed differences between Kitchener's scheme of Military Administration as at first introduced, and its revised form in 1907. Suffice it to say that Curzon maintains an objectivity about Kitchener's attempt to rewrite history, and it is to his credit that he kept the papers uncollated until after Kitchener's death in 1916, where, curiously enough, they have remained unseen, or unpublished, until now. Not one of Kitchener's biographers has seen fit to mention his attempt to distort history. Curiously many others who knew the facts were dead within ten years – including virtually all 'the Boys' – Hubert Hamilton, Raymond Marker, Frank Maxwell and Victor Brooke (who was Minto's Military Secretary).

Appendix Two

Curzon Returns to the Attack

We have seen how Curzon was effectively silenced and prevented from reopening the affair in Parliament, first by Balfour, aided by the latter's defeat by his constituents, and then by Morley and the Liberals. Morley's defection was galling to Curzon, because at the 1906 election he had told his constitutents at Arbroath: 'Lord Curzon has been chased out of power by the Military, and the Secretary of State has sanctioned that operation. If there is one principle more than another that has been accepted in this country since the day when Charles I lost his head, it is this – that the civil power shall be supreme over the military power... The India Office had been guilty of this great dereliction, this great departure from those standard maxims of public administration which have been practically sacred in this island.'[1] In the paper which Curzon had privately printed for circulation, Curzon asked, 'If these are his views, shared by all those of his colleagues who have spoken publicly on the matter, may we not now call confidently upon him, as Secretary of State [for India] to give them practical effect?'[2] But Morley did not.

Still, Curzon's silence, which he told Balfour he had faithfully kept, 'though I have often been tempted to indulge in it . . . because I thought it would be unpatriotic to embarrass the Government',[3] did not prevent him from maintaining very close touch with Indian affairs throughout 1907 and 1908. His correspondents also kept him informed. For example, one writing on 29th December 1907 told him, 'There are rumours that Lord K intends to resign in April as now that he has finished rebuilding and beautifying Snowdon, he is sick of Simla. He has given up his china mania and now has a craze for old arms. That is said to be the chief motive for his trip to Southern India. Wherever he goes someone presents him with an antique weapon which makes him quite happy.'[4]

In the following March, Curzon wrote to Sir W. G. Nicholson at the War Office asking 'Who is to replace K?'[5] and the reply was that the Government would 'not be inclined to reopen the question on the appointment of a new Commander-in-Chief'.[6] Lansdowne also wrote to him about a rumour that the Supply Member was to be abolished. On April 6, 1909, he wrote to Curzon about Sir O'Moore Creagh's appointment: 'I find it impossible to convince myself that this gallant Irishman is fit to discharge, by himself, the duties which in the old days took the whole time of such men as Roberts *plus* Chesney or Brackenbury. I agree with you in believing that it will be necessary, in one form or another, to reinstate the MM.'[7] He enclosed a letter from Minto (lost) which seems to support this.

Barrow also wrote to Curzon at length on 9th April 1909 about the shortcomings of the system, from his position as Officer Commanding the Southern Division in India.

The position of the new Military Supply Member became weaker and weaker, and this, combined with financial considerations, caused the Government in 1909 to formally declare it was to abolish the post. This gave Curzon the opportunity he was seeking to debate the matter in the House of Lords of which both he and Brodrick were now members.

But Brodrick, who was worried about what should be said, succeeded in having the debate postponed. Curzon had already written to Roberts in Egypt, asking him to speak in support, because he knew that Roberts was regretting the fact that he had turned about in 1905 and backed Kitchener. Roberts replied as follows on 21st June 1910.

While I am entirely in accord with your view that the destruction of the Mil. Dept was a grievous mistake – as I have alredy stated in the House of Lords – and that no man, however capable and industrious, can discharge the duties of C-in-C and Member of Council, I am most reluctant to take any public action in the matter just as Kitchener is vacating his appointment and leaving India. I am under great obligation to Kitchener for the help he gave me during the war in 'South Africa. His loyalty to me was great, and his self-effacement could not have been more complete, and I do not like the idea of attacking him when he will be placed at a great disadvantage and unable to reply. But in addition to the personal side of the question, it seems to me that it would be wiser politically to defer further action until the whole system has had a trial. It will assuredly break down under K's successor, and we shall then have something to go upon.[8]

Curzon protested at this *volte face* and Roberts relented and telegrammed Curzon that he would now speak for him. Curzon sent to Roberts letters from Elles and Barrow which illustrated the problems that had ensued from Kitchener's triumph. He had also sent a report to Balfour, who called it 'profoundly interesting' and 'depressing'[9]. Another supporter of Curzon at this time was Lovat Fraser, formerly of *The Times of India* and now living in England and writing for *The Times*. Indeed, in 1908 Curzon had requested Lovat Fraser to write an account of the affair, and the journalist had replied that he was 'greatly honoured' and would do his best 'to write an absolutely impartial account'[10]. In this account, he bent over backwards to do so, saying that: 'K *began* honestly enough (in the first month or so) as far as a man of his peculiarly perverted sense of political morality is capable of honesty at all. What I mean is that originally he cannot have intended to stoop to the depths to which he afterwards descended.'[11]

His support took the practical form of a long article in *The Times* supporting Curzon, for publication on the morning the debate finally took place, 28th June 1910. Lord Nathan, who watched the debate from the Strangers' Gallery, said, 'Lord Midleton [formerly Brodrick] was as inept in debate as in correspondence, and I could not but witness his discomfiture with a feeling of elation.'[12] Three or four days after the debate, Curzon received a letter from St John, asking for the return of a paper he had used in the debate, and adding:

You told me, in reply to my question, that some day you wold not be adverse to seeing me. While you were speaking [in the debate] I could not help thinking how many mists have gathered round this difference between us, and how large an element of misunderstand-

ing there has been. I do not mean that I think I could ever remove
from your mind the sense of injury under which you have laboured,
any more than you could recall what have seemed to me cruel
thrusts now continued for four years.

But somehow lately I have looked back more than ever to old
days. Only a week ago, I turned up in one envelope your affectionate
letters (and Alfred's) on Laura's [Lyttleton's] death in 1886, words
never forgettable, seeing that we have all three undergone the same
affliction [loss of wife] and I ask myself whether anything justifies
life passing away in bitterness and neglect after 30 years of unstinted
friendship.

It has been your edict and you must decide. But the necessity of
meeting in public, which is no longer a question of choice, empha-
sises the regrettable position of our private relations.[13]

Curzon's reply was short:

Since our few words the other day, I have thought over what was
said, and I appreciate fully all that you have written. At the same
time, I would sooner leave things as they are and not rake up the
past. Too much is involved in it that touches the innermost springs
of my being. I have been too deeply scarred to wish to reopen the
wounds.

I am unconscious of my thrusts continued for 4 years. My attitude
may have been negative and I have even with great difficulty
preserved silence. I think it will be better to continue in this way.[14]

Friends made various attempts to bring the two men together. The
Aga Khan had them to lunch at the Ritz Hotel. 'It was a failure.
They confined their converstion to polite exchanges about the
weather in Calcutta at different times of the year.'[15]

Nearly ten years later, in 1918, Curzon did ask Brodrick, then
Lord Midleton, to his house, to a strange dinner party to which
some twelve ladies were invited with their husbands, but about
thirty other men, who were married, were invited alone. One of
these was Brodrick. He went into a 'towering rage' and threatened
to leave.[16] It appears that in 1924, Curzon relented and persuaded
Brodrick to resume his seat on the Opposition front bench.

As for Kitchener, there is a description of a meeting with Curzon
in 1911 at a luncheon in London which is described 'as a
momentary concurrence of two icebergs'.

Kitchener and the Military Member

In Curzon's printed pamphlet on the Military Administration system, which he wrote when staying at Cannes in early 1906, he describes how in the two-and-a-half years from end 1902 to mid-1905, Kitchener never once exercised his right, when he disagreed with the Military Member, of appealing either to the Viceroy or to the Governor-General in Council. Curzon gives a number of concrete cases to illustrate the 'necessity of maintaining a safeguard to protect the Government of India from the danger of rash or ill-considered proposals'. Two may be quoted to make the point.[1]

1. Ever since the Mutiny it had been an established policy that the regular artillery of the Indian Army should be retained in the hands of British troops. The only exceptions were a small native force with inferior guns at Hyderabad, and a number of native mountain batteries. It was decided to disband the Hyderabad batteries after an agreement with the local Nizam, but Kitchener, who had been in India less than a month, asked that the proposal should be suspended, and then, two months later, recommended converting the force into three native batteries of six guns each to be built up, if successful, to a force of ten or twelve native batteries, and that a telegram should be sent to London requesting immediate approval. The Military Department pointed out that not only would this run counter to the long-accepted policy of both the British and Indian governments, but it would entirely upset the established proportion between British and native troops. Kitchener accordingly withdrew his proposal.

2. For some time it had been the practice for the native soldiers to make bricks for the construction of their own barracks, and this was much resented by the soldiers as using men of their standing as 'coolie labour'. In 1901 the Commander-in-Chief, Sir Power Palmer, who had a long experience of the native army, recommended its abolition and the Secretary of State agreed. Then in 1904 Kitchener renewed the proposals, with the further plan to instruct native soldiers as blacksmiths, carpenters and masons. The Military Department pointed out their political inexpediency and the Government vetoed them.

In all, between December 1902 and June 1905, Kitchener sent 1559 proposals to the Military Department. Of these 1260 had been accepted, 177 were still under consideration, and 122 or 7½ per cent, mostly of a trivial nature, had been refused not by the Military Department exclusively, but often on financial grounds, and sometimes by the Governor-General in Council. In considering this 7½ per cent of refusals, it must be said that in India at that time, few military cases could be decided by exclusively military considerations. 'A large number of them raise issues of an administrative and political character which may touch vast sections of the population, and produce consequences in the last result affecting the stability of British rule, in the defendent continent.'[2] Curzon warned, 'It can never be forgotten that it was from errors in the treatment of the Native Army – errors partially unsuspected, and, where suspected denied – that the Mutiny arose.'[3]

It is surely absurd in these circumstances to suggest that the Military Department 'was able to make policy suggestions to the Viceroy which were then presented to the Commander-in-Chief as virtual directives'.[4] Or that, 'The Viceroy, with his background of Eton, Balliol and Parliament, knew nothing of military matters.'[5] Or, 'Kitchener found it impossible any longer even to attempt to make the best of a system which required the Military Member to digest and criticise every plan which the Commander-in-Chief prepared and every suggestion which he made.'[6] The absurdity would not be so gross if Kitchener or his staff had made the suggestions, but it is alas his biographers who do so, against all the evidence available.

Bibliography

Unpublished Papers

India Office Library
Curzon papers
Ampthill papers
Birdwood papers
Godley papers
George Hamilton papers
India Office papers

Bodleian Library
Selborne papers

Hatfield House
Lady Salisbury papers
  Letters from Kitchener,
  Hubert Hamiliton and
  Mullalay

British Library
Arnold-Forster papers
Midleton papers
Balfour papers
Marker papers

Royal Engineers' Museum
Kitchener papers

Public Record Office
Kitchener papers
Cabinet papers
Mesopotamia Commission
  papers
Cromer papers
Foreign Office, Defence
  Committee, and Cabinet
  papers

National Army Museum
Frank Maxwell papers
Marker papers
Roberts papers

Selected Bibliography – Curzon

Bradley, J., *Lady Curzon's India* (1985)
Churchill, Rt Hon. W.S., *Mr Brodrick's Army* (1903), *Great Contemporaries* (1947) [also for Balfour]

Cromer, Earl of, *Political and Literary Essays, Third Series* (1916)
Dilks, David, *Curzon in India*, (1970)
Edwardes, E., *High Noon of Empire* (1965), *British India* (1976)
Fleming, P., *Bayonets to Lhasa* (1961)
Fraser, Lovat, *India under Curzon and After* (1911)
Fraser, Peter, *Lord Esher* (1973)
Hamilton, Rt Hon. Lord George, *Parliamentary Reminiscences and Reflections* (1922)
Lawrence, Sir W., *The India We Served* (1928)
Maclean, Fitzroy, *A Person From England* (1959)
Midleton, Lord (Brodrick), *Records and Reactions* (1939)
Mosley, L., *Curzon, The End of an Epoch* (1960)
Nicholson, Hon. Sir Harold, *Curzon, the Last Phase* (1934)
Nicolson, Nigel, *Mary Curzon* (1977)
Raleigh, Sir T., (ed) *Lord Curzon in India* (Speeches) (1906)
Ronaldshay, Lord, *The Life of Lord Curzon*, 3 vols. (1928–9)
Rose, Kenneth, *Superior Person* (1969)

The forty-seven-page document which Curzon wrote at Cannes in 1906 and had privately printed bears no title in my copy, so I have called it Indian Administrative Systems or IAS for short. The cover is marked *Private and Confidential*

Selected Bibliography – Kitchener

Arthur, Sir G., *Life of Lord Kitchener, Vol. 2* (1920)
Ballard, C.R., *Kitchener* (1930)
Barker, A. J., *The Neglected War* (1967)
Birdwood, Field Marshal Lord, *Khaki and Gown* (1942)
Cassar, G.H., *Kitchener, Architect of Victory* (1977)
Churchill, Randolph S., *Lord Derby* (1959)
Churchill, Rt Hon. W.S., *My Early Life* (1930)
Daniel, Hawthorne, *For Want of a Nail: The Influence of Logistics on War* (1948) New York
Esher, Lord, *The Tragedy of Lord Kitchener* (1921)
Grew, E.S., *Field-Marshal Lord Kitchener* (1917)
Grey of Falloden, *Twenty-Five Years, Vol. 2* (1925)
Hamilton, Gen. Sir Ian, *Listening for the Drums* (1944)
Hardinge, Rt Hon. Lord, *My Indian Years* (1948)
Hunan and Rousseau, *Methods of Barbarism* (1977) Cape Town

James, Robert Rhodes, *Gallipoli* (1965) and *Memoirs of a Conservative* (1969)
MacLaren, Roy, *Canadians on the Nile* (1978)
Magnus, Sir Philip, *Kitchener, Portrait of an Imperialist* (1958)
Mortimer, Menpes, *The Durbar* (1903)
Moseley, Sidney A., *With Kitchener in Cairo* (1971)
O'Brien, T.H., *Milner* (1979)
Portland, Duke of, *Men, Women and Things* (1937)
Protheroe, Ernest, *Lord Kitchener* (1916)
Royle, Trevor, *The Kitchener Enigma* (1985)
Repington, C à Court, *Vestigia* (1919)
Richardson, Frank, *Mars Without Venus: A Study of Some Homosexual Generals* (1981)
Steevens, G.W., *With Kitchener to Khartoum* (1898)
Smith-Dorrien, H., *Memories of Forty-Eight Years Service* (1925)
Warner, Philip, *Kitchener, The Man Behind the Legend* (1985)
Winstone, H.V.F., *Gertrude Bell* (1978)

Balfour, the Cecils and Friends

Asquith, Margot, *Autobiography, Vol. 1* (1920)
Balfour, Rt Hon. Lord, *Chapters of Autobiography* (1930)
Cecil, Lady Gwendolin, *Life of Robert Marquis of Salisbury 1921–1935*
Dugdale, B.E.C., *Arthur James Balfour* (1936)
Egremont, Max, *Balfour* (1980), *The Cousins* (1977)
Esher, Lord, *Journals and Letters of Reginald, Viscount Esher* (ed M.V. Brett) (1934–38)
Lambert, Angela, *Unquiet Souls* (1984)
Mackay, F. Ruddock, *Balfour, Intellectual Statesman* (1985)
Rose, Kenneth, *The Later Cecils* (1975)
Young, K., *Balfour* (1963)

Dramatis Personae

These brief biographical notes, grouped in sections, are intended to enable the reader to quickly check the basic facts about the main characters primarily *during the period* covered by the book.

In India

Lord Ampthill, 1869-1935.
He succeeded his father, first Baron Ampthill, in 1884. He was secretary to Joseph Chamberlain, and in 1900 became governor of Madras. After being acting Viceroy in 1904, he returned to England, and was active in Indian Affairs.

George Curzon, 1859-1925 (*The Rt Hon. later Marquess*)
Son of Rev. Afred Curzon, 4th Baron. He was made Viceroy 1898 after being the Marquis of Salisbury's Undersecretary of State for Foreign Affairs. He returned to England in December 1905 and was in the political wilderness for many years. He returned to senior government office in the coalition of 1914–1918.

Mary Curzon, 1870–1906.
Daughter of Chicago tycoon, Levi Leiter. She married Curzon in 1895. She had three daughters, She died in England.

Sir Walter Lawrence, 1857–1940.
He became Secretary to Curzon 1898, when he was known as the velvet glove on the Viceroy's iron hand. He returned to England in 1903. Later a member of the Council of India in London.

'Daisy' Leiter, 1879–1968.
Mary's sister. She went to India twice during the Curzons' Viceregality. She was in love with Marker (see below) but in 1903 married Henry, 19th Earl of Suffolk and Berkshire, 1877–1917.

Lord Minto, 1845–1914.
A popular Governor General of Canada 1898–1904 who succeeded Curzon as Viceroy in 1905. His great-grandfather had been Governor-General of India. A noted gentleman jockey, he rode several times in the Grand National. He appointed the first Indian to his Council.

At Home – Government Circles

Rt Hon. Hugh Arnold-Forster, 1855–1909.
Grandson of Arnold of Rugby and nephew of Matthew Arnold. He entered Parliament in 1892. Parliamentary Secretary of the Admiralty from 1900 and Secretary of State for War from 1903–5 during which period Raymond Marker was his secretary. His period at the War Office was clouded by the machinations of Esher and Clarke at the Imperial Defence Committee.

Arthur Balfour, 1848–1930. (*Rt Hon. later Earl*)
He was nephew of Marquess of Salisbury (see below) because his mother was a Cecil. His grandfather made a fortune in India and married into the aristocracy. He joined the Cabinet in 1886, became First Lord of the Treasury twice between 1891 and 1902, when he succeeded his uncle as Prime Minister. His party, the Conservative and Unionist, split over Free Trade and Balfour resigned in 1905. He served Curzon in coalition governments between 1914–18.

St John Brodrick (*later Lord Middleton*)
See under India Office.

Sir Henry Campbell-Bannerman, 1836–1908.
His family were in business and after attending both Glasgow and Cambridge Universities, he joined their firm. He entered Parlia-

ment as a Liberal in 1868. In 1871 he was Financial Secretary to the War Office, in 1882 Chief Secretary, Ireland and in 1886 he became Secretary of State for War in Gladstone's Cabinet. From 1888–9 he sat on a Royal Commission to assert civilian control of the Army. He became Prime Minister when Balfour resigned in 1905. He died in 1908 and was succeeded by Asquith.

Lord Edward Cecil, 1867–1918
Brother of James (the Marquess, see Salisbury, below) had five sons. After Eton, he served in the Grenadier Guards in Egypt, the Sudan and the Boer War, part of which time he spent on Kitchener's staff. In 1903 he became Agent General of the Sudan Government and then moved to India where he remained until 1918 when he died of TB. His widow married Milner.

Austen Chamberlain, 1863–1937.
Son of Joseph Chamberlain. He was one of the leading members of the Conservative Party although he had fundamental differences with both Balfour and Bonar Law. He was Secretary of State for India from 1915–7 when he resigned after the Mesopotamia enquiry. In April 1918 he became Member of the War Cabinet and in 1921 was Leader of the Conservative Party. Later knighted.

Col. Sir George Clarke, 1848–1933. (*Later Baron Sydenham*)
Like Kitchener, he was an Engineer who served in Egypt and Sudan, but saw little active service. He was secretary to the Royal Commission on Army and Navy administration from 1888–90, and on the Committee on War Office Reform (Esher Committee) in 1900. In 1901 he became Governor of Victoria, Australia, returning to England at Esher's request to become Secretary to the Imperial Defence Committee where he remained until he was ousted by those who resented his interference in politics. He aspired to become Viceroy but was mere Governor of Bengal from 1907–13, although he was created Baron Sydenham on his retirement.

Lord Cromer, 1841–1917.
A soldier trained at Woolwich who gave up his army career to go to India with his cousin, Lord Northbrook, the Viceroy in 1872. He became one of the great administrators of the Empire when he was

unexpectedly chosen – as mere Captain Baring RA – to go to Egypt as the first British Commissioner. He returned briefly to India as Financial Member of the Viceroy's Council but was recalled to Egypt as British Agent and Consul General in 1883. He remained until 1907, nicknamed Over-Bearing, and was said to be one of the few men of whom Kitchener was afraid.

Sir Clinton Dawkins, 1859–1905.
At Balliol with Curzon. In 1899 he was Financial Secretary to the Military Department of Government of India, then went to Egypt to serve in a similar capacity but returned to London to become a merchant banker. He was a close friend of Milner.

Lord Esher, 1852–1930.
He was created Baron in 1885, and Viscount in 1897. He became MP in 1880 and held a number of government positions until 1902. His wife, the daughter of the Belgian Minister, was a close friend of Queen Victoria. He became a member of the Queen's private circle and had a house at Windsor. Later he became an intimate of Edward VII and moved easily in Court, Cabinet and civil service circles. He was life-long friend of Balfour, and of Clarke (see above) with whom he worked at the Imperial Defence Committee. He was Chairman of the War Office Reconstruction Committee 1903–4 which abolished the position of C-in-C.

Lord (Francis) Knollys, 1837–1924.
He was Private Secretary to Prince of Wales from 1870 and continued to serve him when he became King Edward VII. He received a peerage in 1902. He retired from royal service in 1913.

Lord Lansdowne, 1845–1927.
Talleyrand's grandson, Balfour had been his fag at Eton. Fifth Marquess. He was Governor General of Canada, then Viceroy of India 1888-94. He was Secretary of State for War under Salisbury from 1895–1900, and Foreign Secretary under Salisbury and Balfour from 1900–1905. Salisbury's son, Cranborne was his undersecretary.

Sir Schomberg Macdonnell, 1861–1915.
Son of Earl of Antrim. He was at Eton and Oxford with Curzon
with whom he remained on very friendly terms. Between 1888–
1902 he was Private Secretary to Marquess of Salisbury. He then
became Secretary to Office of Works which brought him into
contact with Royal Family. Despite his age, he insisted on going to
France where he was killed in 1915.

Lord Milner, 1854–1925.
He was created a peer in 1901 and a Viscount 1902. The second
greatest administrator of his time, he went to South Africa in 1897
as High Commissioner, returning in 1905. He served as Secretary
of State for War under Campbell-Bannerman. He married a Cecil
shortly before he died.

Lord Morley, 1838–1923.
He began his career as a journalist on the *Fortnightly Review*. He
became a friend of Joseph Chamberlain and in 1883 was elected to
Parliament. He was Chief Secretary for Ireland under Gladstone,
whose life he wrote. He was Secretary for India from 1905–8, when
he was transferred to the Lords, but remained in the Cabinet. He
resigned in 1914 as he opposed entry into the war.

Sir Rennel Rodd, 1858–1941.
At Balliol with Curzon. He was a member of 'the Souls' and a
diplomat who, like George Wyndham, was a scholar, writer and
poet.

Lord Rosebery, 1847–1929.
He was Liberal Secretary of State for Foreign Affairs and, briefly,
Prime Minister from 1894–5. After 1900 he increasingly withdrew
from politics as he lost sympathy with Liberal policies.

Marquess Salisbury, 1830–1903.
Robert Cecil, the famous Lord Salisbury, called here Marquess to
distinguish him from his son (see below). From 1866–7 and 1874–8
he was Secretary of State for India. From 1878 he was more than
once Foreign Secretary, and from 1885 more than once Prime
Minister until 1902 when he was succeeded by Balfour (see above).

Like Curzon later, he was Warden of the Cinque Ports and Chancellor of Oxford University.

Lord Salisbury, 1861–1947.
Eldest son of above. Known as James or Jem, and Viscount Cranborne until succeeding his father. From 1900–3 he was Under Secretary of State for Foreign Affairs; and from 1903–5 Lord Privy Seal. He became a Privy Counsellor in 1903.

Lady Salisbury, 1867–1955.
Alice, wife of above, whom she maried in 1887. She was descended from the famous Whig family of the Melbournes, and was daughter of the Earl of Arran.

Earl of Selborne, 1859–1942.
The only son of the first Earl, he succeeded 1895. He was at Oxford with Lord Salisbury (above), and married the eldest child of the Cecil family, Maud. He became a Liberal MP in 1885. From 1895–1900 he was Undersecretary of State for the Colonies and from 1900 was First Lord of the Admiralty. Curzon wanted him to succeed as Viceroy but instead he was appointed to follow Milner in South Africa. One of his sons was killed in the Mesopotamia Campaign in 1916.

Eddie Stanley, 1865–1948.
Eldest son of Lord Derby, he succeeded his father in 1908 and became the most popular of all those bearing that name because of his sporting activities. He became a Conservative MP 1892, was made a junior Lord of the Treasury in 1895, became Private Secretary to Lord Roberts in 1900, Financial Secretary to the War Office in 1903, and Postmaster General with a seat in the Cabinet in 1903. In 1917 he succeeded Kitchener as Secretary of State for War under Lloyd George. In 1922 he refused the India Office.

George Wyndham, 1863–1913.
One of Curzon's friends at Eton, he then went to Sandhurst. He married Sibell, a Soul also courted by Curzon and the widow of Earl Grosvenor. In 1887 he was appointed Private Secretary to Balfour and became an MP two years later. In 1894 he became

Undersecretary of State, War Office. He was Chief Secretary for Ireland from 1900–5. He took to drink, and left active politics in 1911 to look after the family estates.

The India Office

St John Brodrick, 1856–1942.
Christened William but known to fellow Souls and others as St John (pronounced Sinjun). He was eldest son of the 8th Viscount Midleton to whose title he succeeded in 1907. From 1886–92 Financial Secretary to the War Office. In 1895 he became Undersecretary of State for War, in 1898 Undersecretary of State for Foreign Affairs, in 1900 he was again Secretary of State for War, and from 1903–5 Secretary of State for India. In 1880 he married a daughter of Lord Elcho, but she died in 1903. He lost his seat in the Commons in 1906 but the death of his father gave him a seat in the Lords.

Sir Arthur Godley, 1847–1932.
He was a brilliant classical scholar who had been a private secretary to Gladstone before going to the India Office as Undersecretary from 1883–1909. It has been said the India Office was largely his creation.

Lord George Hamilton, 1845–1927.
Third son of 1st Duke of Abercorn. He became an MP in 1868, and First Lord of the Admiralty in 1885. In 1886–92 he was Undersecretary of State for India, and then from 1895–1903 was Secretary of State. He retired from the Commons in 1905 but continued in public life and served on the Mesopotamia Commission.

Sir George Stedman, 1842–1914.
A general who served in India until 1889 when he went to the India Office as Military Secretary, remaining until 1907.

The Press

Lovat Fraser, 1871–1926.
He was editor of *The Times of India* until 1907 when he returned to

London and worked on *The Times* until 1922. He wrote a book on Curzon in 1911.

Arthur Pearson, 1866–1921.
In 1900 he founded the *Daily Express* which sold for a halfpenny, and in 1904 purchased *The Standard* which had fallen on evil days. Described by Chamberlain as 'the greatest hustler I have ever known' and by the Dictionary of National Biography as 'intellectually unfitted to guide, much less form, public opinion'.

Pandeli Ralli, 1845–1928.
He was an MP from 1875–85, and one of Kitchener's closest friends after 1878. A successful businessman, he had a house in Belgrave Square where Kitchener often lived when in London. Through his sister he had connections with the Court, and also with the press.

Charles à Court Repington, 1858–1925.
He came from a military family, was educated Eton and was the most brilliant man of his year at Sandhurst. But his army career came to an abrupt end when, after a liaison in Egypt, he was involved in a divorce case. He joined *The Times* in 1904 where he stayed until removed by Northcliffe in 1918.

The Army – London

Sir George Arthur, 1860–1946.
He was in the Coldstream Guards and served in Egypt and South Africa, where he was on Kitchener's staff. He was Kitchener's Private Secretary from 1914–16 and was his first major biographer.

Sir Ian Hamilton, 1853–1947.
General. He served for nearly twenty-five years in India, then went to South Africa where, after Roberts had left, he became Kitchener's Chief of Staff, although he actually operated as his Field Commander. He returned to the War Office in 1903 as Quartermaster General. The following year he went to Japan to head the Military Mission in the Russo-Japanese war. He returned 1905 to take over Southern Command. Unlike most soldiers, he had 'no

financial cares'. Kitchener sent him, ill-equipped, to Gallipoli and after being relieved of his command there he was offered no further active duties.

Lord Roberts, 1832–1914.

The Field-Marshal was the greatest soldier of his day, who, after Eton and Sandhurst, spent forty-one years in India, thirteen of them as Commander-in-Chief. He returned to England in 1893 and later went out to take charge of the army in the Boer War. He returned and from 1901–4 was Commander-in-Chief, British Army. He was known as 'Lord Bobs'.

The Army – India

Sir Edmund Barrow, 1852–1952.

Military Secretary to the Military Department of the Government of India from 1901–3 and Curzon's nominee for the new position of Military Supply Member. Later he commanded the Southern Division of the Indian Army and was at the India Office from 1914–17.

Col. W. R. Birdwood, 1865–1951. (Later Field-Marshall Lord)

Field-Marshal. Born in India, he served in the Army there from 1885. He fought in South Africa where he was on Kitchener's staff. He was Assistant Military Secretary to Kitchener from 1902–4 and Military Secretary from 1905–9. In 1912 he became Secretary to the Army Department, India, where he was responsible for organising the Army which went to Mesopotamia. He was one of the few British Commanders to leave Gallipoli with a reputation.

Sir Bindon Blood, 1842–1940.

General. Like Kitchener, he was a Royal Engineer. He spent thirty-five years in India from 1871. He retired in 1907 after serving under Kitchener in both South Africa and India.

Sir Beauchamp-Duff, 1855–1918.

General, Royal Artillery. He trained at Woolwich. In 1879 he went to India; in 1899 was Assistant Military Secretary for Indian

Affairs, War Office. Later the same year he went to South Africa on Roberts' staff, returning to India in 1901. In 1903 he was Adjutant General on Kitchener's staff where he worked out the proposals for reorganisation. In 1906 he was appointed to the new position of Chief of Staff. In 1909 he became Secretary of the Military Department, India Office. From 1914 he was Commander-in-Chief of the Indian Army, until recalled to England to give evidence to Mesopotamian Royal Commission in 1916.

Sir Edmund Elles, 1848–1934.
Lieutenant General. Royal Artillery, trained at Woolwich, and saw active service in India in 1871, and Egypt in 1882. He was Commander India Army Peshawar District from 1895–1900. Then he was Adjutant General until 1901. From 1901–5, he was Military Member on the Indian Government Council. He retured in 1908, and was Chairman of Territorial Forces Association from 1907–27.

Herbert [Hubert] Hamilton, 1861–1914.
Colonel. He was commissioned Queens Regiment in 1880. He fought in the Egyptian Campaign 1897 and awarded DSO. He joined Kitchener's staff and was his Military Secretary in India from 1902 until 1906, when he returned to London. He was killed two days after Maxwell (below) in France in 1914, then a Major-General.

Lord Kitchener, 1850–1916. (*Later Earl*)
Field-Marshal, hero of the British nation after 1898 when he avenged the killing of Gordon. He served as Roberts' Commander-in-Chief in the Boer War, and then went to India in late 1902 as Commander-in-Chief, a post he held until 1909. Following this he became British Agent in Egypt (the post held formerly by Cromer) and returned to England in 1914 as Secretary of State for War. He went into a decline but was drowned in 1916 before the public had lost confidence in him.

Raymond Marker, 1867–1915.
Major 'Conk' was ADC to Curzon from 1899–1900, then saw action in the Boer War before he joined Kitchener's staff. Following his rejection by Curzon's sister-in-law Daisy in 1903, he went to

London to work for Kitchener, although he also was officially secretary to the Secretary of State for War. Wounded in France at the same time as Maxwell and Hamilton, he died in July 1915.

Francis (Frank) Maxwell, 1871–1914.
'The Brat' joined Kitchener's staff in South Africa after winning both the DSO and VC there. Previously he had been in India with the Bengal Lancers. From 1902–6 he was a Captain on Kitchener's staff in India and also in London where his high-class connections were useful. He was killed on the 12th October 1914 in France.

Herbert Mullaly, 1860–1932.
Major General. He trained at RMA Woolwich, and like Kitchener, was a Royal Engineer. He became Assistant Secretary, Military Department in India in 1895. He went to South Africa where was wounded, then returned to India on the staff of Kitchener who sent him to London as his representative at the War Office. Despite criticisms of his personality from both the Kitchener and Curzon camps, he rose to command a division in 1914 and was a Divisional Commander, probably not on active service, in England in the 1914–18 war.

William Nicholson, 1845–1910.
Field-Marshal, Royal Engineer, trained at Woolwich. In 1871 he went to India and in 1880 was Secretary of the Defence Committee and from 1890–3 Military Secretary to Lord Roberts. In 1898 he became Adjutant General, India. In 1900 he was Director of Transport, South Africa, in 1901 at the War Office as Director of Military Operations, and in 1906 Quartermaster General. 1908 Chief of the Imperial General Staff. In 1911 he became a Field-Marshal, and in 1916 served on the Royal Commission enquiring into Dardanelles.

Notes

The first part of this book, which is concerned with events leading up to Kitchener's arrival in India, has been extensively written about in recent years and in the main I have contented myself with references to the work of the principal authors rather than their sources. From 1902 onwards, it seemed advisable to refer mainly to original material which may broadly be summarised as:

1. Curzon's correspondence, both sent and received, which is in the India Office. Lady Metcalfe's collection of her mother's correspondence contains Kitchener letters, as do the Balfour papers at the British Library. Others are in the Birdwood papers at the India Office.
2. Kitchener's correspondence in the Public Record Office and at Hatfield.
3. Marker's correspondence in both the National Army Museum and the Public Record Office. Alas Marker's letters to Hubert Hamilton have not, as far as we know, been preserved.

As there are three Hamiltons in this story, Lord George is referred to in Notes as Hamilton, Hubert Hamilton is referred to here as HH, and the General is called Ian Hamilton. Lady Salisbury goes by that name, although part of the time she was in fact Lady Cranborne. I have quoted extensively from Curzon's privately-printed papers on Indian Army Administration which for brevity are called IAS.

I have not referred to a thesis entitled *Curzon and Kitchener and the Problem of Indian Army Administration 1899–1909*, which is available in the library of London University. It was written by John E. Lydgate in 1965 and is a useful study.

Introduction – Two Superior Persons
1. Ronaldshay Vol. II p.4
2. Mosley p.25
3. Episode recounted by Mr Malcolm Lyell
4. Richardson p.124
5. Richardson p.123
6. Wearne, Reuter's correspondent in Peking, is quoted in Pearl's *Morrison of Peking* p.103 and p.200
7. Midleton p.216
8. Nicolson p.199

9. Nicolson p.199
10. Clarke to Kitchener 31 March 1904

Chapter One – Up the Ladder of Power
1. Royle p.13
2. ibid
3. Rose p.20
4. Magnus p.6
5. ibid
6. Mrs Sharpe to Sir George Arthur KP
7. Magnus p.6
8. Royle p.10
9. Rose p.25
10. Rose p.24
11. Rose p.20
12. Mosley p.10
13. Rose p.36
14. Rose p.28
15. Rose p.29
16. Mosley p.15
17. Repington p.159
18. Mosley p.24
19. Rose p.56
20. Mosley p.24
21. ibid
22. Ronaldshay Vol. I p.133
23. Rose p.46
24. ibid
25. Royle p.24, Esher p.192
26. Cassar p.82
27. Royle p.31
28. Quoted by Esher p.7 from Gordon's Journals
29. Magnus p.10
30. Royle p.230
31. Grosvenor papers
32. Rose p.130
33. Salisbury to Baring
34. Magnus p.95
35. Salisbury Papers
36. Royle p.85
37. Maxwell papers NAM
38. Magnus p.81
39. Kitchener to Lady Salisbury 16 March 1900 to 5 November 1900
40. Kitchener to Lady Salisbury 1 January 1902 and 2 August 1901
41. Kitchener to Lady Salisbury October 1901

Chapter Two – Viceroy and Sirdar
1. Rose p.291
2. Rose p.199
3. References to the Conservative Party are to the Conservative and Unionist Parties.

4. Rose p.322/3
5. Rose p.325
6. Rose p.326
7. ibid
8. Ronaldshay Vol. I p.294
   Another reference to his Johnsonian diction compares him to Peel. Rose p.245
9. Rose p.327
10. Mary Curzon to her father 16 April 1903
11. Rose p.326
12. Nicolson p.93
13. Nicolson p.105
14. Nicolson p.172
15. *The Times* 11 August 1898
16. Scarsdale to Curzon 11 August 1898
17. Alfred Lyttleton to Curzon 11 August 1898
18. Balfour p.230
19. Ronaldshay refers to the *The Times* 15 November 1898
20. Royle p.113
21. Cromer to Salisbury
22. Repington p.159 et seq
23. Royle p.121
24. Maclaren *Canadians on the Nile* describes Girouard's role
25. Haig to General Sir Evelyn Wood
26. Curzon to Kitchener 28 October 1898 ES 42 Royal Engineers
27. Cassar p.485
28. The Soul was Brodrick. The date 1898. The place Panshanger.
29. Kitchener's letter book is in the PRO
30. Curzon to Hamilton 8 November 1900

Chapter Three – The Curzons and Macher
1. Nicolson p.114
2. Nicolson p.122
3. Nicolson p.122
4. Nicolson p.124
5. Nicolson p.129
6. Nicolson p.158
7. ibid
8. Nicolson p.143 and p.146
9. Nicolson p.152
10. Nicolson p.145
11. Nicolson p.155
12. Sir T Raleigh (ed) *Lord Curzon in India* Vol. II
13. Ronaldshay Vol. II p.3
14. Ronaldshay Vol. II p.65
15. Ronaldshay p.96
16. Curzon to Hamilton 15 August 1900
17. See p.203
18. Curzon to Selborne 9 November 1900
19. Balfour to Lady Elcho

20. Winstone p.180
21. Edwardes p.187 et seq
22. Marker papers, NAM Archives 6803 19 December 1898
23. Nicolson p.127
24. Marker 3 March 1901
25. Marker 17 April 1901
26. Curzon to Lady Curzon January 1901
27. Curzon to Hamilton
28. Curzon to Hamilton
29. Nicolson p.118
30. Ronaldshay Vol. II p.88
31. Ronaldshay Vol. II p.89
32. Ronaldshay Vol. II p.92
33. ibid
34. Nicolson p.143
35. Mosley p.79
36. Dilks Vol. I p.84
37. Ronaldshay Vol. II p.363

Chapter Four – Curzon and the Army
1. Curzon to Hamilton 16 October 1901
2. Magnus p.148 Curzon to Hamilton 25 October 1901
3. Gore *King George V* p.264 and Dilks Vol. I p.112
4. Curzon to Kitchener 21 August 1900
5. Ronaldshay Vol. II p.71
6. Ronaldshay Vol. II p.72
7. ibid
8. Ronaldshay Vol. II p.73
9. Curzon to Godley 30 July 1902
10. Cassar p.138
11. Dilke Chapter The Army, Vol. II p.196 et seq describes this
12. Curzon wrote regularly to Queen Victoria 1899 to 1901
13. Rodd to Curzon 12 December 1899
14. Esher Journal Vol. I p.238
15. Rawlinson *Life* p.34
16. Dilke Vol. I p.206
17. Curzon to Hamilton 15 August 1900
18. Menpes p.8 et seq
19. Menpes p.17 et seq
20. Cromer to Kitchener. Warner p.105
21. Milner to Lady Edward Cecil 27 December 1900
22. Milner to Chamberlain, Hunan p.92
23. Hunan p.182
24. Buchan to Lady Mary Murray January 1902
25. Chamberlain papers JC/13/1/191 1 November 1901
26. Kitchener to Roberts PRO 20/57/21
27. Curzon to Hamilton 22 October 1901
28. Hamilton to Curzon 20 July 1900
29. Curzon to Hamilton 21 July 1900
30. Salisbury to Lansdowne 28 September 1900
31. Hamilton to Curzon 17 November 1900

32. Hamilton to Curzon 11 February 1901
33. Hamilton to Curzon 5 March 1901
34. Hamilton to Curzon 6 March 1901
35. Hamilton to Curzon
36. Curzon to Midleton 21 August 1900
37. Curzon to Kitchener 21 August 1900
38. Midleton p.201
39. Curzon to Kitchener 16 December 1901
40. Curzon to Kitchener 20 March 1902
41. Curzon to Kitchener 13 August 1902
42. Kitchener to Marker 28 October 1902
43. Curzon to Kitchener 14 December 1902
44. Curzon to Kitchener 14 December 1902
45. Ronaldshay Vol. II p.247
46. Curzon to Hamilton 13 November 1902

Chapter Five – Curzon and Brodrick
1. Curzon to Balfour 16 July 1902
2. Balfour to Curzon 12 December 1902
3. Curzon to Balfour 29 December 1902
4. Balfour to Curzon 12 March 1903
5. Balfour to Curzon 18 June 1903
6. Curzon to Balfour 8 July 1903
7. Young p.73. One of the females captivated by Balfour was Mary Curzon. In the summer months of 1901, while on leave in England, she wrote to Curzon to tell him about their mutual attraction. Curzon replied 'You have fairly bowled over Master Arthur. However, he is a tepid though delightful love' Nicolson p.149
8. McDonnell to Curzon 26 October 1901. Brodrick was also pompous. One of the most unmemorable lines in his memoirs reads 'I was I believe the last Minister to whom Queen Victoria gave a personal audience'.
9. Curzon to Hamilton 19 February 1903
10. Hamilton to Curzon 13 February 1903
11. Hamilton to Curzon 27 February 1903
12. Curzon to Hamilton 12 March 1903
13. Hamilton to Curzon 27 March 1903
14. Hobhouse quoted Hunan p.221
15. DNB
16. McDonnell to Curzon 29 April 1903
17. McDonnell to Curzon 4 October 1903
18. Young p.229
19. Balfour to Lady Elcho 3 February 1903
20. Midleton p.186
21. ibid
22. Midleton p.187
23. ibid
24. Midleton p.188
25. Midleton also claims that Curzon returned from India with a 400 page document ready for publication. There is no evidence that this is true, and it is unlikely as Curzon threw nothing away.
26. Midleton p.188

27. Midleton p.189 quoting *Great Contemporaries*
28. Midleton p.190. A study of Brodrick by L.J. Satre in 1976 describes him as 'basically insecure, politically and perhaps emotionally.'
29. Midleton p.190
30. Midleton p.191
31. ibid
32. Midleton p.192
33. Hamilton to Curzon 31 August 1905
34. Hamilton p.193 ·
35. ibid
36. Curzon to Mary Curzon quoted Harrod p.356
37. Midleton p.196
38. ibid
39. Fleming p.281
40. A full account of the Tibet expedition is also given by Dilks in Vol. II p.74 et seq.
41. Fleming p.216
42. ibid
43. Fleming p.93
44. Fleming p.95
45. ibid
46. Fleming p.271
47. Fleming p.272
48. ibid
49. Fleming p.279. The 'shabby' decoration was the KCIE
50. Fleming p.285
51. Fleming p.287
52. Fleming p.288. Balfour commented to George Wyndham 'St. John is really very odd just now. I cannot imagine why he has washed all our dirty linen in public, by giving the whole correspondence to the world' 31 January 1905
53. Fleming p.288 Curzon obtained a copy of Brodrick's letter to the press, and wrote asking for an explanation. 'Your conduct has had the result of fixing a public slur upon the Viceroy' he wrote 21 February 1905
54. Midleton p.200
55. Curzon to Brodrick 27 November 1903
56. Brodrick to Curzon 7 January 1904
57. Curzon to Brodrick 7 January 1904
58. Curzon to Brodrick 4 February 1904
59. ibid
60. Curzon to Balfour. Another example of Curzon's complacency.
61. Curzon to Brodrick 5 April 1904 to 20 April 1904
62. Churchill *My Early Life* p.165
63. Midleton p.201
64. ibid
65. Midleton p.202
66. Mary Curzon to Curzon in April 1901
    Metcalfe MSS

Chapter Six – Kitchener Arrives in India
1. Kitchener's fame is preserved in statuesque form in some strange manifestations. For example, a carved roundabout figure, clutching his army orders,

made in about 1900 and still to be seen in the Fairground of the Night exhibition at Wookey Hole Caves, Somerset. In the Swinging Sixties he appeared in Carnaby Street through his connection with Lord Kitchener's Valet.

2. Royle p.144. The looting of the South African statues came to the attention of the King (MP6801–33)
3. Ian Hamilton p.114
4. Ian Hamilton p.108
5. ibid
6. Ian Hamilton p.99
7. . Ian Hamilton p.111
8. Magnus p.380 (my italics)
9. Ian Hamilton p.100
10. Royle p.198
11. Dilks Vol. II p.19
12. H H to Lady Salisbury 5 August 1903
13. This privately-printed booklet (IAS) is in Curzon Collection.
14. IAS p.3
15. IAS p.4
16. ibid
17. ibid
18. IAS p.5
19. ibid
20. IAS p.7
21. ibid
22. IAS p.8
23. Sir Power Palmer also used this expression
24. Curzon to Cromer, 'Kitchener's language and his indifference to public opinion still retain their pristine frankness and charm' 19 March 1903
25. Curzon to Hamilton 21 May 1903
26. Curzon to Hamilton 14 May 1903
27. Curzon to Schomberg McDonell, quoted Ronaldshay Vol. II p.251. Curzon also told him 'Kitchener comes and pours out all sorts of schemes to which he asks my consent. It is all so frank and honest and good-tempered that one cannot meet these advances with a rebuff . . . But of course as yet he does not know the ropes' 13 January 1903
28. Curzon to Kitchener 15 December 1902
29. Menpes p.44
30. Marker to HH 1 January 1903
31. Mosley p.101
32. Mosley p.102
33. Kitchener to Lady Salisbury 30 December 1902
34. Kitchener to Lady Salisbury 16 July 1903
35. Curzon also told Kitchener that his frontier form would attract too much attention from those across the borders.
36. Kitchener to Lady Salisbury 25 January 1906
37. It is not certain whether Kitchener showed this to Curzon. See Curzon to Hamilton 26 February 1903
38. Kitchener Memo in Salisbury papers p.42
39. ibid p.13
40. ibid

41. ibid
42. Nicolson p.168
43. Nicolson p.169
44. ibid
45. Marker to HH 15 January 1903
46. Bradley p.38 quoting Mary to her mother 12 April 1899
47. Bradley p.39 and p.40
48. Bradley p.42. There is a fuller account of the 'little cloud' incident in Frank Harris's 4th Series of *Contemporary Portraits* p.316
49. HH to Lady Salisbury 28 January 1904
50. ibid
51. ibid
52. ibid. The choice of Suffolk must have been particularly galling to Marker as they had been ADC's to the Curzons at the same time (1899) when we read touching stories of their playing with the Curzon children in the garden at Simla etc.
53. HH to Lady Salisbury 28 January 1904
54. Kitchener to Lady Salisbury 25 January 1904
55. Kitchener to Marker 16 March 1904
56. Kitchener to Marker. Also HH to Marker 9 February 1905
57. Kitchener to Stanley 25 October 1903
58. Balfour to Kitchener December 1903
59. Balfour to Lady Salisbury 4 October 1904
60. Kitchener to Lady Salisbury 10 December 1902
61. ibid
62. ibid
63. Kitchener to Lady Salisbury 13 May 1903. See also p.104
64. Kitchener to Lady Salisbury 21 May 1903
65. Kitchener to Lady Salisbury 10 June 1903
66. Kitchener to Lady Salisbury 23 July 1903
67. There is a copy of the X-ray picture in the Royal Engineer's Kitchener papers. This shows how serious a break it was. He was in great pain after this riding accident, and the operation left him with a permanent problem, as the leg was not set properly. Indeed Mary Curzon, trying to explain Kitchener's appalling behaviour towards her husband in 1905, wrote that 'he was never the same after his accident' Metcalfe MSS
68. HH to Lady Salisbury 24 December 1903
69. Curzon to Kitchener 12 May 1903
70. This followed a night of the long knives in the Cabinet when Balfour rid himself of colleagues who supported Free Trade while cunningly appearing not to weaken his own position.

Chapter Seven – Kitchener's First Feint
1.   Mary Curzon to Curzon. Nicolson p.170 Kitchener also missed Mary Curzon. He wrote to Mrs Leiter (her mother) 'Until she left I never quite realised how much she did to make life out here agreeable' 21 January 1904
2.   Brodrick to Curzon 9 September 1900
3.   Curzon to Brodrick 11 February 1903
4.   Brodrick to Curzon 3 March 1904
5.   Godley to Curzon March 1904
6.   Godley to Curzon November 1903

7. Curzon to Clinton Dawkins 9 March 1904
8. Ampthill to Godley 5 May 1904
9. Curzon 26 April 1904
10. Godley to Curzon 19 February 1904
11. Godley to Curzon 12 February 1904
12. Brodrick to Curzon 26 February 1904
13. Curzon to Godley 10 March 1904
14. Ampthill to Godley 5 May 1904
15. Curzon had known for some time that Kitchener was planning more confrontations with Elles. He had told Hamilton in 1903 'If only Kitchener would show a little grace and tact . . . I am told, too, that all sorts of fresh confrontations are ahead'
16. Curzon to Brodrick 6 March 1904
17. Brodrick to Curzon 7 March 1904
18. Curzon to Mary Curzon. Metcalfe MSS
19. Godley to Curzon December 1903
20. Godley to Curzon 19 February 1904
21. Curzon to Godley 4 January 1904
22. Godley to Curzon 22 November 1904
23. Harrod p.123
24. Curzon 10 June 1904
25. Godley to Ampthill 29 March 1904 and 29 April 1904
26. Brodrick to Balfour 8 August 1904 and 5 September 1904
27. Brodrick to Curzon 3 September 1904
28. Curzon to Brodrick 1 April 1904
29. Kitchener to Lady Salisbury 6 August 1903
30. Kitchener to Roberts 17 December 1902
31. Kitchener to Roberts 5 February 1902
32. This must have been the memo he sent to Lady Salisbury – see p.96
33. Kitchener's criticism of Elles and the Military Department on the grounds of their inexperience was particularly absurd. His own staff had on it only one officer with Indian experience who had ever commanded a regiment, much less a division. In contrast, the Military Department's five senior officers all had more than 13 years' regimental experience, and two of them nearly double that.
34. Kitchener to Roberts 9 June 1904. The following week he wrote 'You might care to discuss with Duff the question of my successor . . . It is better to be ready.' The Esher Commission was reorganising the Army at home in exactly the opposite sense to that desired by Kitchener in India – i.e. they were further strengthening 'Civilian' controls while Kitchener wanted to abolish them.
35. Kitchener to Roberts 7 July 1904
36. Kitchener to Roberts 27 November 1904. After January 1905, when he sent Roberts a copy of his organisation paper, Kitchener wrote rarely to Roberts
37. Mary Curzon to Kitchener 9 December 1902
38. Kitchener to Marker 14 July 1904. The issue on which Kitchener offered to resign in September 1904 was different. He had proposed to dismiss an officer outside his jurisdiction. Balfour wired 'must beg you in the public interest to take no hasty action'
39. Clarke is described by Esher's biographer as 'a bouncing crude fellow' and Curzon said he was a man 'whom I profoundly mistrust'.

40.   Curzon to Balfour 15 June 1904.
41.   Balfour to Curzon 23 June 1904. Dilks says that the Kitchener memoran-
      dum was originally given to Balfour by Colonel Mullaly and that Roberts
      also had a copy.
42.   Ampthill to Brodrick 9 June 1904
43.   Ampthill to Brodrick 16 June 1904
44.   Ampthill to Brodrick 7 July 1904. At about this time Kitchener told Lady
      Salisbury that Ampthill 'is distinctly feeble'
45.   HH to Marker 31 October 1904. Balfour, in panic had cabled Kitchener
      (see Note 38 above) following conversations with Mullaly. The latter had
      also written to Lady Salisbury on 25 August 1904
46.   Brodrick to Kitchener 29 April 1904
47.   Kitchener to Brodrick 15 July 1904
48.   Stedman to Kitchener 31 March 1904
49.   Clarke to Kitchener 31 March 1904
50.   HH to Marker 20 October 1904
51.   HH to Marker mid August 1904
52.   HH to Marker September 1904
53.   HH to Marker 15 September 1904
54.   HH to Marker 22 September 1904
55.   Kitchener to Marker 15 September 1904
56.   HH to Marker 12 October 1904
57.   Marker got on well with Repington and the latter gave him a list of
      'contacts' remarking 'You can manufacture a public opinion if you go the
      right way to work' 23 October 1904
58.   HH to Marker 20 October 1904
59.   HH to Marker 27 October 1904
60.   HH to Marker 14 December 1904
61.   Balfour to Curzon 3 November 1904
62.   Balfour to Curzon 16 November 1904. They had dined on the 9th.
63.   Dugdale Vol I. p.406. In November, Curzon had written to Balfour offering
      to resign 'if you find it easier to carry out the views of the government about
      India with a new Viceroy' so Balfour can have been under no illusion that
      Curzon would oppose the abolition of the Military Department. Balfour told
      Lady Salisbury he hoped Curzon would return in April 1905 leaving a new
      Viceroy to make the reforms.
64.   Balfour to Kitchener December 1904
65.   Balfour to Kitchener 1 January 1905
66.   Curzon to Edward VII
67.   Nicolson p.176
68.   Nicolson p.182
69.   Brodrick to Curzon 22 November 1904

Chapter Eight – Kitchener's Deployment of Forces
 1.   Rose *The Later Cecils* p.83
 2.   Rose p.83
 3.   Rose p.83
 4.   Rose p.84
 5.   Rose p.90
 6.   Rose p.90
 7.   Curzon to Selborne 21 May 1903

8. Curzon to Selborne 9 July 1903
9. Kitchener also thought he might get Curzon to agree to his scheme, writing to Lady Salisbury 'My case is an extremely strong one, and George N does not much like to be on the losing side' 22 December 1904
10. Brodrick to Curzon 28 December 1904
11. Curzon to Brodrick 29 December 1904
12. Brodrick to Curzon 12 January 1905
13. Curzon to Brodrick 14 January 1905
14. HH to Marker 14 January 1905
15. HH to Marker 14 January 1905
16. HH to Marker 2 February 1905
17. Brodrick to Curzon 16 February 1905
18. ibid
19. Curzon to Brodrick (my italics) 17 January 1905
20. Brodrick to Curzon 28 December 1904
21. Brodrick to Curzon 18 January 1905
22. Curzon to Brodrick 19 January 1905
23. Brodrick to Curzon 20 January 1905
24. Curzon to Brodrick 21 January 1905
25. Nicolson p.183
26. Curzon to Selborne 26 January 1905
27. ibid
28. Clarke to Kitchener January 1905
29. Clarke to Kitchener
30. Clarke to Kitchener. Balfour cabled Kitchener about this paper. 'I am unable to see what answer can be made to it' 14 February 1905 Birdwood papers.
31. Kitchener to Marker
32. Kitchener to Marker February 1905. Kitchener had even sent his general's opinions to Lady Salisbury in early February, while refusing them to Curzon – see p.154
33. HH to Marker 16 March 1905
34. ibid
35. Kitchener to Marker 4 February 1905
36. Kitchener to Marker undated
37. Kitchener to Marker 4 February 1905
38. HH to Marker 18 January 1905
39. HH to Marker 25 January 1905
40. ibid
41. HH to Marker 1 March 1905
42. ibid
43. HH to Marker 14 December 1905
44. HH to Marker 25 January 1905
45. HH to Marker 1 March 1905
46. HH to Marker 21 February 1905
47. HH to Marker 28 February 1905
48. Mackay p.213
49. Mackay p.214
50. Fisher to Lady Fisher 1 November 1904 Mandar Vol. II p.47
51. Esher *Journals* 4 May 1905
52. HH to Marker undated

53. ibid
54. Kitchener to Marker 2 March 1905
55. HH to Marker 2 March 1905
56. HH to Marker 9 March 1905
57. Menpes p.31

Chapter Nine – Let Battle Commence
  1. Dilks Vol. II p.90. Kitchener told Lady Salisbury that when Curzon defended Kitchener at the meeting of Council 'he made us all see a sort of halo appear round Elles's head through which his few remaining hairs protruded'. 14 March 1905
  2. Kitchener to Marker 14 March 1905
  3. Magnus p.216
  4. Warner p.150
  5. IAS p.20
  6. Kitchener to Stedman 8 March 1905
  7. Note in the Curzon papers
  8. Copy in Curzon papers is dated 8 March 1905
  9. The Kitchener papers include the fuller texts, but they are mostly obsequious in tone, and the extracts give a fair impression.
10. See p.143 above
11. HH to Marker 10 March 1905
12. Kitchener to Marker 10 March 1905
13. Kitchener to Lady Salisbury 9 March 1905
14. Kitchener to Marker 22 May 1905
15. HH to Marker 11 April 1905
16. Curzon to Roberts 22 March 1905
17. HH to Marker 28 April 1905
18. HH to Marker 3 May 1905
19. Notes in the Curzon papers
20. Undated
21. HH to Marker 24 April 1905. Another well-connected member of Kitchener's 'Boys' Victor Brooke, also went to London at this time.
22. ibid
23. Esher to Kitchener 1 April 1905
24. Kitchener to Lady Salisbury. He also called him 'a born intriguer'. 14 May 1906
25. Curzon to Balfour 30 March 1905
26. Curzon to Balfour 30 March 1905
27. Clarke to Kitchener 31 March 1905 and 4 April 1905
28. Esher to Kitchener 1 April 1905
29. Kitchener to Stedman 23 March 1905
30. Curzon to Ampthill 12 May 1905
31. Brodrick to Cromer 12 May 1905
32. Ampthill to Brodrick 23 May 1905
33. IAS p.19 (my italics)
34. Curzon note on Lovat Fraser's paper
35. IAS p.22
36. IAS p.22
37. Brodrick to Curzon 31 May 1905
38. IAS p.23

39.   White to Curzon
       Kitchener appears to have realised that a compromise solution of some kind would be acceptable, and told Lady Salisbury to tell Brodrick that he would agree to a Military Member 'who would have nothing to do' once a strong HQ was established. 23 March 1905
40.   Brodrick 26 May 1905 Cab 37/77/96
41.   IAS p.23
42.   Marker to HH 31 May 1905
43.   Kitchener to Lady Salisbury 1 June 1905
44.   HH to Marker 1 June 1905
45.   Kitchener to Marker 1 June 1905
46.   Stedman to Kitchener 2 June 1905
47.   Kitchener to Marker
48.   HH to Marker 6 June 1905
49.   Brodrick to Curzon 31 May 1905
50.   Haldane to Curzon 22 June 1905
51.   IAS p.31
52.   Edward VII to Curzon 2 June 1905
53.   Ampthill to Godley 4 July 1905
54.   Balfour to Curzon 9 June 1905
55.   Dilks Vol. II p.216
56.   Curzon to Dawkins 21 June 1905
57.   Dilks Vol. II p.217
58.   Brodrick to Ampthill 23 June 1905
59.   HH to Marker 22 June 1905
60.   Kitchener papers letter 30
61.   Curzon to Kitchener 22 June 1905
62.   Kitchener to Stedman 26 June 1905
63.   Curzon to Brodrick 26 June 1905
64.   Curzon to Balfour 26 June 1905 and 6 July 1905
65.   Curzon to Brodrick 28 June 1905
66.   Brodrick to Curzon 6 July, 8 July 1905 and Curzon's reply 10 July 1905
67.   Kitchener to Stanley 28 June 1905
68.   Marker undated
69.   Kitchener to Marker 28 June 1905
70.   Brodrick to Curzon 29 June 1905
71.   Undated
72.   Kitchener to Lady Salisbury 30 June 1905
73.   Curzon to Brodrick 30 June 1905
74.   Curzon to Brodrick 4 July 1905
75.   Barrow to Curzon 23 June 1905
76.   Barrow to Curzon 30 June 1905
77.   Kitchener to Stanley in July 1905
78.   Kitchener to Lady Salisbury 6 July 1905 and to Marker same date.
79.   Marker to HH in July 1905
80.   Kitchener to Lady Salisbury 27 July 1905
81.   Curzon to Balfour 3 July 1905
82.   Curzon to Brodrick 10 July 1905
83.   Brodrick to Roberts 11 July 1905
84.   Balfour to Salisbury 11 July 1905
85.   Curzon to Kitchener 5 July 1905

86. Kitchener to Curzon 1 June 1905
87. Curzon to Kitchener 1 June 1905
88. Kitchener to Curzon 1 June 1905
89. Kitchener to Curzon undated
90. HH to Marker 12 July 1905
91. Curzon to Edward VII 6 July 1905
92. DNB
93. Dilks Vol. II p.221.
94. HH to Lady Salisbury 16 June 1905
95. Curzon to Morley 28 December 1905. The Curzons appear to have thought it was Mullaly who orchestrated the campaign. Mary Curzon wrote 'He laid the wires for the campaign for Lord K and on his return conducted the whole of the slanderous campaign from here.' Metcalfe MSS 24 August 1905
96. Kitchener to Lady Salisbury 2 November 1905
97. Kitchener to Lady Salisbury February 1905
98. HH to Lady Salisbury 2 November 1905
99. Kitchener to Lady Salisbury 2 November 1905
100. Dilks Vol II. p.224
101. ibid
102. Brodrick to Curzon 20 July 1905
103. Curzon to Ampthill 23 July 1905
104. Brodrick to Curzon 20 July 1905

Chapter Ten – The Resignation
1. Curzon to Hamilton 14 March 1901
2. Curzon to Godley 5 October 1903
3. Curzon papers dated 29 October 1905
4. Kitchener to Marker 7 July 1905
5. Kitchener to Marker 9 July 1905
6. Curzon to Ampthill 12 August 1905
7. ibid
8. HH to Lady Salisbury 13 July 1905
9. HH to Lady Salisbury 23 July 1905
10. HH to Marker 6 July 1905
11. Curzon to Brodrick 17 July 1905
12. Kitchener papers dated only Wednesday
13. Curzon to Brodrick 29 July 1905
14. HH to Marker 20 July 1905
15. Kitchener to Lady Salisbury 20 July 1905
16. HH to Marker 14 July 1905
17. ibid
18. HH to Marker 20 July 1905
19. Memorandum by Brodrick 31 July 1905
20. Brodrick to Curzon 1 August 1905
21. Roberts to Brodrick 31 July 1905
22. Collen to Curzon. In Curzon's collection of letters on his resignation.
23. IAS p.29
24. Lansdowne, speaking in House of Lords
25. Curzon to Brodrick 2 August 1905

26. HH to Marker 2 August 1905
27. Kitchener to Marker 3 August 1905
28. Stedman to Kitchener 4 August 1905
29. Brodrick to Curzon 4 August 1905
30. Curzon estimated the MSM would have 2 hours work a day.
31. Hamilton to Marker 20 July 1905
32. Duff to Kitchener 14 July 1905
33. Curzon to Ampthill 12 August 1905
34. Kitchener to Birdwood. Birdwood papers 5 August 1905
35. HH to Marker 10 August 1905
36. HH to Marker
    Buck wrote sadly to Curzon on his resignation saying 'many strings have recently been pulled from the opposite direction' He was one of them.
37. Curzon to Brodrick 5 August 1905
38. Kitchener to Marker 6 August 1905
39. Kitchener to Stanley 7 August 1905
40. Godley to Brodrick 7 August 1905
41. Ronaldshay Vol. II p.321
42. Curzon to Godley 27 January 1904
43. Brodrick to Knollys 5 August 1905
44. Balfour to Edward VII 8 August 1905
45. ibid
46. Balfour to Curzon 8 August 1905
47. Barrow to Curzon 8 August 1905
48. Brodrick to Ampthill 11 August 1905
49. Kitchener also wrote a Minute on the subject dated 17 August 1905
50. Curzon to Brodrick 10 August 1905
51. Brodrick to Curzon 11 August 1905
52. Dawkins to Curzon 20 February 1903
53. IAS p.45
54. IAS p.45
55. IAS p.29
56. IAS p.30
57. Brodrick to Curzon 13 August 1905
58. Balfour to Brodrick 14 August 1905
59. Churchill, *Letters* 31 August 1905
60. Brodrick to Curzon 16 August 1905
61. Balfour to Curzon 16 August 1905
62. Kitchener also wrote to Lady Salisbury 'It is very unpleasant to have to deal with such a man, who evidently does not know what it is to be a gentleman. I hope you will let any of his friends know what a creature he is' 30 August 1905
63. Dilks Vol. II p.239
64. Magnus p.223
65. Kitchener to Lady Salisbury 30 August 1905
66. *The Times* 29 August 1905
67. Curzon to Brodrick 29 August 1905
68. Curzon to Brodrick 1 September 1905
69. Brodrick to Curzon 2 September 1905
70. Stedman to Kitchener 23 November 1905
71. Balfour to Curzon 23 August 1905

72. Balfour to Sandars September 1905
73. Curzon to Balfour 21 September 1905
74. A copy is in the Bodlean Library, Indian Institute
75. ditto
76. HH to Lady Salisbury 22 August 1905
77. Churchill, *Letters* 31 August 1905
78. HH to Marker 10 January 1906
79. HH to Marker 12 January 1906
80. ibid
81. HH to Marker 18 January 1906
82. ibid
83. HH to Marker 19 January 1906
84. HH to Marker 26 January 1906
85. HH to Marker 1 February 1905
86. ibid
87. HH to Marker 9 February 1905
88. ibid
89. HH to Marker 1 February 1905
90. HH to Marker 9 February 1905
91. Colvin Vol. III p.79
92. Mary Curzon to Kitchener KP No.63
93. Kitchener to Lady Salisbury 23 October 1905
94. Mary Curzon to Mrs Leiter. Bradley p.165. Mary also wrote to her mother 'England thinks him a hero. I know him to be a liar'. Curzon, too, was accused of coolness, for not giving his successor, Minto, an official reception. He had the excuse, and perhaps the reason, that Minto's ship was delayed by strong currents.
95. Kitchener to Roberts 22 March 1906.

Chapter Eleven – The Ex-Viceroy
1. Curzon papers
2. Esher *Journals*
3. Curzon to Lord George Hamilton December 1905
4. Curzon's notes. Knollys was in fact hostile to Curzon.
5. Curzon's notes
6. Balfour's original letter is in the Curzon papers
7. During his tour of India, the Prince of Wales had gossiped indiscreetly about Curzon, and in London used 'a most unmeasured language' about him according to Mosley. He adored Kitchener and sadly mourned his death.
8. This part of Curzon's Notes is dated 5 August 1912.

Chapter Twelve – Mary's Death
1. Nicolson p.207 et. seq
2. Nicolson p.209
3. Nicolson p.188
4. This letter written on RMS Carisbroke Castle, shows Brodrick in his true colours. He congratulates Kitchener on his victory, and says 'our best assistant has been Curzon' adding 'The pamphlet he wrote against you has been suppressed and the type broken up.' It is not known to what this refers.

5. George, Prince of Wales, to Kitchener 30 August 1906. According to Dilks, the re-organisation was a failure, resulting in over-centralisation. Dilks Vol. II p.252
6. Arthur p.223
7. Arthur p.247. Malcolm Lyell recounts an anecdote of a dinner party of those days. Kitchener's hostess had heard stories of alleged homosexuality and decided to investigate.

   She: Lord Kitchener, they tell me you don't like ladies
   K: But I do.
   She: Although you have never married, I think.
   K: That is true. But it is because I admire your sex so much that I have never thought I should marry. It seemed to me that familiarity might breed contempt.
   She: (after a pause) Let me advise you, Lord Kitchener, that without a little familiarity it is not possible to breed at all.
8. Arthur p.221
9. PRO 30/57/104
10. Esher p.26. Kitchener would have been annoyed to know that Asquith offered Esher the Viceregality in 1908
11. Royle p.233
12. Royle p.245

Chapter Thirteen – The Proof of the Pudding
1. Lovat Fraser Notes. Actually Creagh's Chief-of-Staff was Haigh 1909-12.
2. Roberts to Curzon 2 November 1913
3. Barrow to Curzon 23 October 1913
4. Curzon Papers 23 October 1913
5. Barker p.471
6. Barker p.30
7. Barker p.31
8. Barker p.78
9. Barker p.80
10. Curzon papers 4 September 1915
11. Curzon papers 26 November 1915
12. Barker p.103
13. Barker p.133
14. Barker p.136
15. Lovat Fraser Notes 10 August 1916
16. Barker p.146
17. Curzon papers 16 April 1916
18. Curzon papers 3 December 1916
19. Barker p.198
20. Barker p.219
21. Barker p.225
22. Barker p.225
23. Dixon p.16
24. Magnus p.226
25. Curzon papers MSS WR 112/163
26. Curzon papers
27. Curzon papers
28. Hardinge p.86

29. Birdwood p.225
30. Barker p.10
31. Cromer, House of Lords, July 1916.
32. Curzon papers 14 July 1916
33. Milner to Curzon 1 July 1917
34. Lovat Fraser notes
35. Winstone p.142
36. Winstone p.142
37. Winstone Chapters 16 and 17
38. Winstone
39. Moberley. *The Campaign in Mesopotamia*
40. Arthur Vol. III p.302
41. Magnus p.226
42. Cassar p.116
43. Cassar p.117
44. Warner p.152
45. Royle p.214
46. Esher to Brodrick 6 February 1905

Chapter Fourteen – Epitaph and Conclusion
1. Esher p.11
2. *The Prince* p.111
3. Esher *Journals* 2 December 1901
4. Young p.362
5. Quoted by Esher
6. Rhodes James p.39
7. Sitwell *Great Morning* p.262–4
8. Haldane, although Liberal secretary of state for War, did not hold office in the 1914-18 war.
9. Harold Nicolson *Curzon* p.30
10. ibid
11. Churchill *Great Contemporaries* p.188
12. Rose p.283
13. Dugdale ed, Balfour, *Chapters of Autobiography*
14. Curzon papers. Curzon had forgotten an incident in 1901 when Balfour told Mary – 'I never write (to him) but love George' Nicolson p.142
15. Harold Nicolson *Curzon* – index. Ironically, the index to Magnus's book on Kitchener lists amongst 'his dislikes' the practice of 'political intrigue'

Appendix One
1. Curzon papers
2. Notes on their interview in Curzon papers
3. Curzon papers
4. ibid
5. ibid
6. Collen to Curzon. Curzon papers.
7. Lovat Fraser notes in Curzon papers
8. Curzon papers

Appendix Two
1. IAS p.47

2. IAS p.47
3. Curzon to Balfour 11 December 1908
4. Curzon papers
5. Curzon to Nicholson 25 March 1909
6. Nicholson to Curzon March 1909
7. Lansdowne to Curzon 6 April 1909
8. Roberts to Curzon 21 June 1909
9. Balfour gradually came to dislike the extent of Kitchener's underhand methods, although he had been party to them at the time
10. Lovat Fraser notes in Curzon papers
11. Lovat Fraser to Curzon 30 January 1908
12. Kitchener warned Marker that Brodrick intended to back Curzon in the debate 'I can hardly believe what I hear, . . . it would be too stupid . . . but just like him' 10 June 1909
13. Brodrick to Curzon 2 July 1908
14. Curzon to Brodrick 4 July 1908
15. Rose p.377
16. Rose p.378

Appendix Three
1. The original section in the Curzon pamphlet run to about 1200 words. The pamphlet, in fact, makes six points of this kind.
2. IAS p.8
3. IAS p.11
4. Warner p.144
5. ibid
6. Magnus p.211

Index